Reading Zone

one

1

Start-up

박지성

고려대학교 언어학과 및 영어영문학과 졸업

[현] 해커스 편입
[현] 대치동/목동 중고등 내신강사

■ 세계유명 여성리더들의 명연설문 베스트 30 (반석출판사)
■ 바로바로 하루 10분 일상 영어 (반석출판사)
■ 고등영어 서술형 기본편 (오스틴 북스)
■ 고등영어 서술형 실전편 (오스틴 북스)
■ chatGPT를 활용한 영어문제 창작하기 (오스틴 북스)
■ 리딩 이노베이터 기본편/실전편 (JH Press)

검수 **구은서**

외고전문 (현) 별별아카데미 원장

Reading A one ❶ Start-up

저 자 박지성
발행인 고본화
발 행 반석출판사
2024년 8월 10일 초판 1쇄 인쇄
2024년 8월 15일 초판 1쇄 발행
홈페이지 www.bansok.co.kr
이메일 bansok@bansok.co.kr
블로그 blog.naver.com/bansokbooks

07547 서울시 강서구 양천로 583. B동 1007호
      (서울시 강서구 염창동 240-21번지 우림블루나인 비즈니스센터 B동 1007호)
대표전화 02) 2093-3399 **팩 스** 02) 2093-3393
출 판 부 02) 2093-3395 **영업부** 02) 2093-3396
등록번호 제315-2008-000033호

ISBN 978-89-7172-991-5 (13740)

반석출판사

달리기를 하는 사람들은 일정 시간 몸을 움직여 이룰 수 있는 행복감 또는 쾌감을 Runner's high라 표현한다. 사실 의학적으로 보면, 외부 자극이 있는 상황에서 신체에 의도적으로 다소 무리한 스트레스를 지속적으로 유발할 때 느끼는 일종의 도취감이라고 볼 수 있다. 이에 상응하는 정신적 도취감을 Reader's high라고 하는데, 같은 맥락에서 스트레스를 유발하는 정신적 연마의 과정에서 발생하는 희락이라고 말할 수 있다.

학습자가 이러한 Reader's high를 느낄 수 있도록 이끌어주는 요소는 무엇보다 학습자 정신에 가하는 의도적 스트레스를 감당할 수 있는 학습능력을 스스로 갖출 수 있도록 환경을 조성해 주는 동시에 지적 흥미를 꾸준하게 유발시킬 수 있는 일정 수준 이상의 학습적 스트레스를 제공하는 학습물(Study Material)이 중요하다. 심리치료사인 롤프 메르클레가 "천재는 노력하는 사람을 이길 수 없고 노력하는 사람은 즐기는 사람을 이길 수 없다."라고 말한 것에 빗대자면 Reader's high를 느낀 학습자의 학업 성취도는 높을 수밖에 없다.

본서는 저자가 10년에 걸쳐 외고와 자사고 내신 대비를 해 오면서 다뤘던 내용 중에서 학습의 지적 고양을 끌어올릴 수 있는 선별된 양질의 자료만을 담았다. 물론, 수록된 작품 자체만으로도 문학이 주는 순수한 즐거움(pleasure)을 느낄 수 있겠지만, 입시라는 틀의 범위에서 지적 "스트레스"를 통한 Runner's high를 느낄 수 있도록 다양한 형식의 이해도 문제와 평가문제로 알차게 구성했다.

특히, 본서는 일선의 외고와 자사고 내신에서 주/부교재와 보충자료(Supplementary Reading)를 통해 다루는 단편소설(또는 일부 발췌문), 연설문, 시, 그리고 다양한 분야의 비문학 글 중에서 필독서(Must-read)라 견줄 수 있는 글만을 엄선하고, 어휘정리, 구문분석, 배경지식, 실전 평가문제를 모두 담아낸 외고·자사고 대비에 최적화된 수험서임을 자부한다.

자신의 꿈을 실천하기 위해 한 단계 더 높은 곳을 향해 용감히 도전하는 외고·자사고 wanna-be에게 본서가 디딤돌 역할을 해 줄 수 있기를 바란다.

저자 박지성

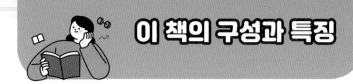

이 책의 구성과 특징

본 책은 9개의 UNIT과 각 UNIT은 5개 PART로 구성되어 있다.

PART 1 Voca Master
PART 2 Text Reading
PART 3 Voca Check
PART 4 Reading Comprehension
PART 5 Sentence Completion

각 PART의 세부 구성은 다음과 같다.

PART 1 Voca Master

PART 1에선 각 UNIT에서 다루는 작품 또는 Article에서 나오는 중요 단어를 먼저 학습할 수 있도록 구성했다. 특히, 각 단어의 영영풀이와 함께 예문 속 활용을 통해 미묘한 문맥적 뉘앙스까지 파악할 수 있도록 구성했다.

PART

1 Voca Master

- [ ] jolt — **n** shock or surprise
  - The sudden jolt of thunder scared the children.

- [ ] sack — **v** to dismiss from employment
  - The manager decided to sack the employee for repeated misconduct.

- [ ] petty — **a** trivial or of little importance
  - Don't waste your time arguing over petty issues.

- [ ] stand in the way of — to hinder or obstruct
  - Don't let obstacles stand in the way of your success.

PART 2 Text Reading

PART 2는 본문 읽기로 문단별 또는 주제별로 각 페이지를 구성하고, 특히 문제를 통해서 지문에 대한 이해도를 평가할 수 있도록 했다. 필요시, 각 문단에 중요한 개념을 묻는 문제도 실었다. 또한, 〈어구 및 표현 연구〉를 두어 본문에 대한 꼼꼼한 구문분석을 제공했다.

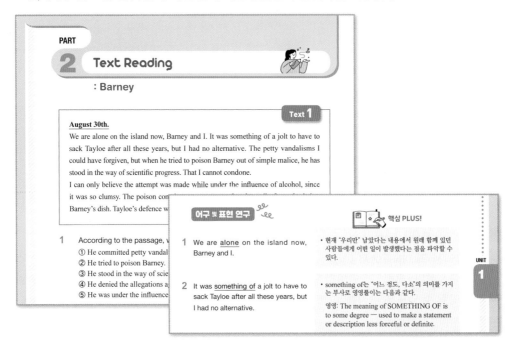

PART 3 Voca Check

PART 3에서 PART 1을 통해 학습한 본문의 어휘를 문맥 속에서 활용할 수 있는 빈칸 채우기 문제를 담았다.

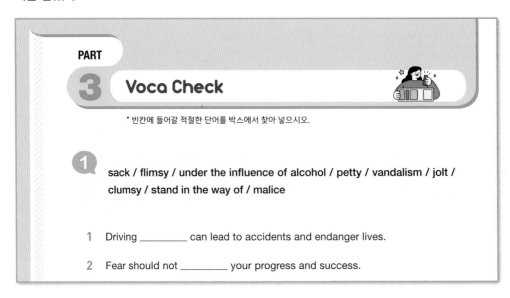

PART 4 Reading Comprehension

PART 4에서는 외고와 자사고에서 접하게 되는 실전유형의 독해 문제가 담겨 있다.

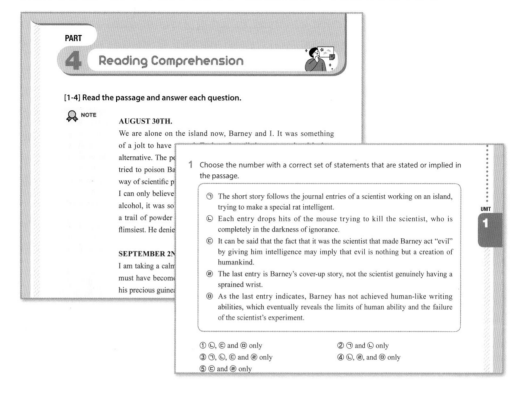

PART 5 Sentence Completion

PART 5에서 어휘의 활용과 글의 논리적 이해, 즉 문해력을 높여주는 문장완성 문제를 담았다.

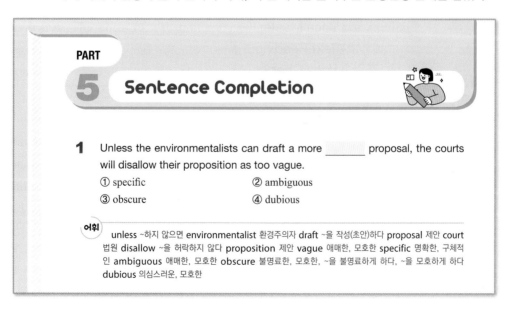

목차

문학_단편소설
Barney
by Will Stanton

그림 박예송

Voca Master

☐ **jolt**

n shock or surprise

- The sudden <u>jolt</u> of thunder scared the children.

☐ **sack**

v to dismiss from employment

- The manager decided to <u>sack</u> the employee for repeated misconduct.

☐ **petty**

a trivial or of little importance

- Don't waste your time arguing over <u>petty</u> issues.

☐ **stand in the way of**

to hinder or obstruct

- Don't let obstacles <u>stand in the way of</u> your success.

☐ **vandalism**

n the act of intentionally damaging property

- The graffiti on the walls was an act of <u>vandalism</u>.

☐ **malice**

n the intention to do harm or evil

- She spoke without <u>malice</u>, simply trying to offer constructive criticism.

☐ **under the influence of alcohol**

intoxicated by alcohol

- It's dangerous to drive <u>under the influence of alcohol</u>.
- He made a series of regrettable decisions while <u>under the influence of alcohol</u>.

☐ **clumsy**

a lacking skill or grace in physical movement

- Her <u>clumsy</u> attempt at dancing made everyone laugh.

☐ **flimsy**

a weak, lacking strength or substance

- The <u>flimsy</u> excuse he gave for being late was not convincing.

☐ **affair** **n** an event or happening

- Her personal <u>affairs</u> were a mess, and she needed to sort them out.

☐ **monastic** **a** relating to a monastery or monks

- The <u>monastic</u> lifestyle involves a commitment to prayer and simplicity.

☐ **become too much for** to overwhelm or exceed one's capacity

- The workload <u>became too much for</u> him to handle.

☐ **abandonment** **n** the act of giving up or leaving something behind

- The <u>abandonment</u> of the project was a disappointment to everyone involved.

☐ **guinea pig** **n** a person used in experiments

- The scientist needed a <u>guinea pig</u> for testing the new drug.
- He volunteered to be a <u>guinea pig</u> in the medical trial.

☐ **to the last** until the end

- He fought <u>to the last</u> to defend his honor.

☐ **clod** **n** a clumsy or foolish person

- Don't be such a <u>clod</u>; think before you act.

☐ **mute** **a** silent or unable to speak

- She stood <u>mute</u>, unable to express her emotions.

☐ **reproach** **v** to express disapproval or disappointment

- If you show poor manners at your grandmother's dinner table, she will <u>reproach</u> you.

☐ **ascribe** **v** to attribute to a particular cause or source

- They <u>ascribed</u> their success to hard work and dedication.

sport — **n** an enjoyable activity or pastime
- Reading is a <u>sport</u> that she enjoys in her free time.

glutamic acid — **n** an amino acid
- Foods rich in <u>glutamic acid</u> include meat, fish, and soy products.

drag — **v** to pull along with effort
- The boat began to <u>drag</u> anchor in the strong current.

go over — **v** to review or examine carefully
- She likes to <u>go over</u> her notes before taking an exam.

confine — **v** to keep within limits or boundaries
- The fence was built to <u>confine</u> the animals to a specific area.

do away with — **v** to eliminate or get rid of
- The company plans to <u>do away with</u> paper documents and go digital.

too great to ignore — so significant that it cannot be overlooked
- The economic impact of the new law is <u>too great to ignore</u>.

vault — **n** a secure room for storing valuables
- The museum displayed its most valuable artifacts in the <u>vault</u>.

vermin — **n** pests or nuisance animals
- Pest control measures are needed to deal with <u>vermin</u> in urban areas.

I have spoken too soon. — I made a premature statement
- He believed he had won the game, but when his opponent made a surprising move, he said, "<u>I have spoken too soon</u>."

☐ **frisk**

a to move about playfully or search someone for hidden items

- Security personnel <u>frisked</u> passengers before they boarded the plane.

☐ **commence**

v to begin or start

- Let's <u>commence</u> the meeting as soon as everyone is here.

☐ **splash**

v to scatter or cause to scatter in all directions

- Be careful not to <u>splash</u> the paint on the walls.

☐ **own**

v to admit or acknowledge

- She had to <u>own</u> up to her mistake and apologize.

☐ **retrieving**

n the act of getting something back

- The act of <u>retrieving</u> lost memories from childhood photo albums brought a sense of nostalgia to the family reunion.

☐ **insurmountable**

a unable to be overcome

- With determination, even the most <u>insurmountable</u> obstacles can be conquered.

☐ **rather**

ad somewhat or to some extent

- The movie was <u>rather</u> disappointing compared to the trailer.

☐ **shaking**

a causing tremors or vibrations

- His voice was <u>shaking</u> with emotion as he delivered the speech.

☐ **come off**

v to happen or succeed as planned

- The party didn't <u>come off</u> as expected due to bad weather.

☐ **facilitate**

v to make a process easier or smoother

- The new software is designed to <u>facilitate</u> data analysis.

☐ **descent**　　**n** the act of moving downward or coming from a higher place

- Climbing down the steep mountain was a challenging <u>descent</u>.

☐ **at intervals**　　with spaces or periods of time between

- He took short breaks <u>at intervals</u> during the long workday.

☐ **rude**　　**a** lacking manners or politeness; impolite

- His <u>rude</u> behavior offended many people at the party.

☐ **grope for**　　**v** to search for something with one's hands, especially in the dark or when unable to see

- In the blackout, he had to <u>grope for</u> the flashlight to find his way.

☐ **give out**　　**v** to stop working; to fail or break

- The old car's engine finally <u>gave out</u> after years of use.
- His patience <u>gave out</u>, and he lost his temper.

☐ **squeak**　　**n** a high-pitched, sharp sound

- The mouse emitted a tiny <u>squeak</u> as it scurried across the floor.

☐ **upon v-ing**　　immediately after doing something

- <u>Upon hearing</u> the news, she burst into tears.

☐ **sever**　　**v** to cut or separate forcefully

- The decision to <u>sever</u> ties with the business partner was difficult but necessary.

☐ **chafe**　　**v** to rub or wear away by friction; to irritate or annoy

- His constant criticism began to <u>chafe</u> on her nerves.

masonry `n` the craft of building with bricks, stones, or concrete blocks

- The cathedral's beautiful <u>masonry</u> was a testament to the craftsmanship of the builders.

plight `n` a difficult or dangerous situation

- The company's financial <u>plight</u> forced it to lay off many employees.

sacking `n` a type of fabric, often used for bags or sacks

- They made a tent out of rough <u>sacking</u> material for their camping trip.

replenish `v` to fill or make something complete again

- It's essential to <u>replenish</u> the water in your body by staying hydrated.

take off `v` to have a break or rest, often used in the context of work or a task

- Let's <u>take off</u> for a coffee break before continuing the meeting.

spell `n` a short period of rest or relaxation

- A short <u>spell</u> of meditation each morning helped him start the day with focus.

bring up to date to update or make something current

- The software company regularly <u>brings up-to-date</u> versions with new features and improvements.

fix `v` to prepare or make something quickly, often referring to food

- He offered to <u>fix</u> a sandwich for his hungry guests.

2 Text Reading

: Barney

Text **1**

August 30th.

We are alone on the island now, Barney and I. It was something of a jolt to have to sack Tayloe after all these years, but I had no alternative. The petty vandalisms I could have forgiven, but when he tried to poison Barney out of simple malice, he has stood in the way of scientific progress. That I cannot condone.

I can only believe the attempt was made while under the influence of alcohol, since it was so clumsy. The poison container was overturned and a trail of powder led to Barney's dish. Tayloe's defence was of the flimsiest. He denied it. Who else then?

1 According to the passage, why did the narrator have to sack Tayloe?
① He committed petty vandalism.
② He tried to poison Barney.
③ He stood in the way of scientific progress.
④ He denied the allegations against him.
⑤ He was under the influence of alcohol.

2 Why did the narrator say that the attempt to poison Barney was clumsy?
① The poison container was overturned.
② The poison was spilled all over the floor.
③ The poison was too weak to harm Barney.
④ Tayloe left his fingerprints on the poison container.
⑤ Tayloe did not try to hide the evidence.

3 Why did the narrator say that he could have forgiven Tayloe's petty vandalisms?
① They did not harm Barney.
② They were accidental.
③ They were done out of malice.
④ They were not intentional.
⑤ They were done while Tayloe was under the influence of alcohol.

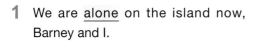

 핵심 PLUS!

1 We are <u>alone</u> on the island now, Barney and I.

- 현재 "우리만" 남았다는 내용에서 원래 함께 있던 사람들에게 어떤 일이 발생했다는 점을 파악할 수 있다.

2 It was <u>something of</u> a jolt to have to sack Tayloe after all these years, but I had no alternative.

- something of는 "어느 정도, 다소"의 의미를 가지는 부사로 영영풀이는 다음과 같다.

  영영: The meaning of SOMETHING OF is to some degree — used to make a statement or description less forceful or definite.

  ex) He is something of an expert with car repair.

  ex) The movie was something of a disappointment.

3 ①<u>The petty vandalisms</u> I could have forgiven, but ②when he tried to poison Barney <u>out of</u> simple malice, he has stood in the way of scientific progress.

- ① 목적어 도치구문으로 The petty vandalisms가 문장 앞으로 이동한 경우이다. 원래 문장은 다음과 같다. → I could have forgiven **the petty vandalisms**.
- ② out of simple malice에서 out of는 "~ 때문에" "~로 인해"라는 뜻으로 because of 의미를 가진다.

4 <u>That</u> I cannot condone.

- 목적어 도치구문이다.
  I cannot condone **that**.

5 The poison container was overturned and <u>a trail of</u> powder led to Barney's dish.

- a trail of는 "길게 늘어진"의 의미로 해석하면 된다.(a trail of powder: 길게 늘어진 가루)

6 He denied <u>it</u>.

- it은 the attempt to poison Barney를 의미한다.

7 <u>Who</u> else then?

- Literal meaning: The author's belief that Tayloe was responsible for the act of poisoning Barney
- Implication: Tayloe가 아닌 다른 범인의 가능성.

September 2nd.

I am taking a calmer view of the Tayloe affair. The monastic life here must have become too much for him. That, and the abandonment of his precious guinea pigs. He insisted to the last that they were better suited than Barney to my experiments. They were more his speed, I'm afraid. He was an earnest and willing worker, but something of a clod, poor fellow. At last I have complete freedom to carry out my work without the mute reproaches of Tayloe. I can only ascribe his violent antagonism toward Barney to jealousy. And now that he has gone, how much happier Barney appears to be! I have given him complete run of the place, and what sport it is to observe how his newly awakened intellectual curiosity carries him about. After only two weeks of glutamic acid treatments, he has become interested in my library, dragging the books from the shelves, and going over them page by page. I am certain he knows there is some knowledge to be gained from them had he but the key.

4   Where does the protagonist think Tayloe's attitude toward Barney comes from?
① He was impressed with Barney's intellectual abilities.
② He was happy to have Barney as a companion.
③ He was jealous of Barney.
④ He was indifferent towards Barney.
⑤ He was afraid of Barney.

5   According to the passage, what has happened to Tayloe's guinea pigs?
① They have been given to Barney.
② They are still living with Tayloe.
③ They have been abandoned by Tayloe.
④ They have been used in the author's experiments.
⑤ It is not mentioned in the passage.

6   What is the author's opinion of Barney's behavior after the glutamic acid treatments?
① He is disturbed by Barney's behavior.
② He is pleased with Barney's behavior.
③ He is afraid of Barney's behavior.
④ He is skeptical of the glutamic acid treatments.
⑤ It is not mentioned in the passage.

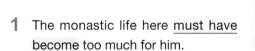 

UNIT 1

1 The monastic life here <u>must have become</u> too much for him.

- must have p.p: ~이었음에 틀림이 없다

2 He insisted <u>to the last</u> that they <u>were</u> better <u>suited</u> than Barney <u>to</u> my experiments.

- to the last = to the last minute
- be suited to N: ~에 어울리다

3 He insisted to the last that <u>they</u> were better suited than Barney to <u>my</u> experiments. <u>They</u> were more <u>his</u> speed, I'm afraid.

- 각 대명사가 지칭하는 대상을 명확히 구별할 것.
  (they = guinea pigs, my = I, They = guinea pigs, his = Tayloe)

4 I can only <u>ascribe</u> his violent antagonism toward Barney <u>to</u> jealousy.

- ascribe A to B: A의 결과를 B의 탓으로 삼다(A = 결과, B = 원인)

5 I have given / him / complete run of the place, and <u>what sport</u> it is to observe how his newly awakened intellectual curiosity carries him <u>about</u>.

- run에 대한 해석
  I의 의도: Tayloe와 그의 guinea pigs가 모두 사라진 상황에서 과학자 I는 Barney에게 여기저기 자유롭게 돌아다닐 수 있는 온전한 자유를 준다는 의미로 사용.

- sport는 본문에서 "보기에 즐거운 것 또는 행위"를 의미함.

- what sport it is to observe how his newly awakened intellectual curiosity carries him about.
  = It is a sport to observe how his newly awakened intellectual curiosity carries him around.

6 I am certain that he knows that there is some knowledge <u>to be gained</u> from them <u>had he but the key</u>.

- to부정사의 수동태 표현

- had he but the key는 가정법 생략 도치
  had he but the key = if he had but the key

- but은 only와 같은 뜻의 부사임.

September 8th.

For the past two days I have had to keep Barney confined and how he hates it. I am afraid that when my experiments are completed I shall have to do away with Barney. Ridiculous as it may sound, there is still the possibility that he might be able to communicate his intelligence to others of his kind. However small the chance may be, the risk is too great to ignore. Fortunately there is, in the basement, a vault built with the idea of keeping vermin out, and it will serve equally to keep Barney in.

7 According to the passage, why does the speaker have to confine Barney?
① Barney is a danger to others.
② Barney is too intelligent to be kept freely.
③ Barney doesn't like being confined.
④ Barney is a vermin.
⑤ Barney needs to be kept away from others of his kind.

8 What does the speaker imply about Barney's intelligence?
① Barney's intelligence is a potential threat.
② Barney's intelligence is already communicated to others.
③ Barney's intelligence is irrelevant to the experiments.
④ Barney's intelligence is exaggerated.
⑤ Barney's intelligence is impossible to communicate.

9 Where is Barney kept confined?
① In the basement vault
② In the speaker's laboratory
③ In a vermin-free room
④ In a secure cage
⑤ In Barney's natural habitat

1 For the past two days I have had to keep Barney confined and <u>how he hates it</u>.

- 지능이 높아진 Barney의 반응은 과학자에 대한 적대감(hostility).

2 I am afraid that when my experiments are completed <u>I shall have to do away with Barney</u>.

- do away with는 "제거하다"는 의미로 과학자의 속내를 지능이 높아진 Barney가 알아차렸을 가능성이 높음.

3 ①<u>Ridiculous as it may sound</u>, there is still ②<u>the possibility that he might be able to communicate his intelligence to others of his kind</u>.

- ① Ridiculous as it may sound = Though it may sound ridiculous
- ② 앞으로 일어날 일에 대한 복선이 되는 부분

4 However small the chance may be, the risk is **too** great **to** ignore.

- too ~ to 용법: 너무 ~해서 ~할 수 없는

5 Fortunately there is, in the basement, <u>a vault</u> built with the idea of keeping vermin out, and it will serve equally to keep Barney in.

- vault의 존재에 대해서 Barney는 이미 인식하고 있는 상황일 것.

September 9th.

Apparently, I have spoken too soon. This morning I let him out to frisk around a bit before commencing a new series of tests. After a quick survey of the room he returned to his cage, sprang up on the door handle, removed the key with his teeth, and before I could stop him, he was out the window. By the time I reached the yard I spied him on the coping of the well, and I arrived on the spot only in time to hear the key splash into the water below.

I own I am somewhat embarrassed. It is the only key. The door is locked. Some valuable papers are in separate compartments inside the vault. Fortunately, although the well is over 12 metres deep, there are only a few metres of water in the bottom, so the retrieving of the key does not present an insurmountable obstacle. But I must admit Barney has won the first round.

---

10 What did the speaker do before Barney escaped?

① Let Barney out to frisk around.
② Commence a new series of tests.
③ Lock the door and secure the key.
④ Remove valuable papers from the vault.
⑤ Reach the yard to check on Barney.

11 Where did the speaker find Barney after he escaped?

① Inside the vault
② On the coping of the well
③ Near the window of the room
④ On the door handle of the cage
⑤ In the yard where the tests were conducted

12 What happened to the key?

① It was locked inside the vault.
② It was thrown into the water below the well.
③ It was kept securely by the speaker.
④ It was used to open the door.
⑤ It was lost during the escape.

어구 및 표현 연구

핵심 PLUS!

1 Apparently, <u>I have spoken too soon.</u>

- 상대를 얕잡아 보고 의도치 않은 결과가 나왔을 때 쓰는 표현.

2 <u>After a quick survey of the room</u> he ~~returned~~ to his cage, ~~sprang~~ up on the door handle, ~~removed~~ the key with his teeth, and (before I could stop him), he was out the window.

- Barney는 케이지에서 나와 "주변을 꼼꼼히 정찰하는 행위"를 함. 그리고는 열쇠를 훔쳐 달아남.
- returned, sprang, removed 동사 병치

3 <u>By the time I reached the yard</u>, I spied him on the coping of the well, and <u>I arrived on the spot only in time to hear the key splash into the water below.</u>

- By the time S V, S V "~할 때쯤"의 뜻으로 by the time은 부사절을 이끄는 접속사 역할임.
- 열쇠가 우물에 빠지는 소리를 과학자가 들을 수 있도록 과학자의 접근을 몰래 기다리는 치밀한 행동.

4 <u>Some valuable papers</u> are in separate compartments <u>inside the vault.</u>

- 과학자가 열쇠를 찾아야 할 수 밖에 없는 이유를 이용해서 우물에 들어가게 만들려는 의도를 파악할 수 있다.

September 10th.

I have had a rather shaking experience, and once more in a minor clash with Barney I have come off second-best. In this instance I will admit he played the hero's role and may have saved my life.

In order to facilitate my descent into the well, I knotted a length of two-centimetre-thick rope at half-metre intervals to make a rude ladder. I reached the bottom easily enough, but after only a few minutes of groping for the key, my flashlight gave out and I returned to the surface. A few metres from the top I heard excited squeaks from Barney, and upon obtaining ground level I observed that the rope was almost completely severed. Apparently it had chafed against the edge of the masonry and the little fellow perceiving my plight had been doing his utmost to warn me.

I have now replaced that section of rope and arranged some old sacking beneath it to prevent a recurrence of the accident. I have replenished the batteries in my flashlight and am now prepared for the final descent. These few moments I have taken off to give myself a breathing spell and to bring my journal up to date. Perhaps I should fix myself a sandwich as I may be down there longer than seems likely at the moment.

13 How did the speaker make their descent into the well easier?

① Flashlight   ② Sandwich
③ Makeshift ladder   ④ Old sacking
⑤ Batteries

14 Why did Barney make excited squeaks near the top?

① He was excited about the condition of the rope ladder.
② He was anxious to find the location of the key.
③ He was happy to signal the presence of another person.
④ He requested a sandwich to ease the hunger.
⑤ He was eager to communicate a need for fresh batteries.

15 What precautions did the speaker take after the rope incident?

① Replaced the batteries in the flashlight
② Arranged old sacking beneath the rope
③ Groped for the key in the darkness
④ Climbed back to the surface easily
⑤ Resumed their journal writing

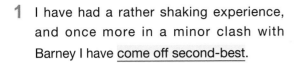

 핵심 PLUS!

1 I have had a rather shaking experience, and once more in a minor clash with Barney I have <u>come off second-best</u>.

- come off second-best = to fail to win, to be defeated in a competition

2 In this instance I will admit (that) <u>he played the hero's role and may have saved my life</u>.

- 이어지는 내용을 통해 Barney의 행동의 의도와 과학자가 받아들이는 의미가 다름을 파악.

3 I knotted a length of two-centimetre-thick rope / at half-metre intervals / <u>to make a rude ladder</u>.

- to부정사의 부사적 용법: ~하기 위해서
- rude는 "조잡한," "급조한"의 의미로 쓰이고 있다.

4 A few metres from the top I heard <u>excited squeaks</u> from Barney, and upon obtaining ground level I observed that the rope was almost completely severed..... <u>the little fellow perceiving my plight had been doing his utmost to warn me</u>.

- Barney의 "흥분된 찍찍 소리"의 의도와 과학자가 이해한 내용을 파악하도록 한다.

5 I have replenished the batteries in my flashlight and am now prepared for <u>the final descent</u>.

- the final descent의 의미: The well is going to turn into his grave.

6 ①<u>These few moments</u> I have taken off to give myself a breathing spell and to ② <u>bring my journal up to date</u>. Perhaps I should fix myself a sandwich as ③<u>I may be down there longer than seems likely at the moment</u>.

- ① 목적어 도치로 These few moments 가 문장 앞으로 이동한 형태. 원래 문장은 아래와 같다.
  I have taken off **these few moments** to give myself a breathing spell and to bring my journal up to date.
- 밑줄 친 ②와 ③의 내용으로 보아 더 이상의 journal entry가 있으면 안 됨.

September 11th.

Poor Barney is dead an soon I shell be the same. He was a wonderful ratt and life without him is know worth living. (A)If anybody reeds this please do not disturb anything on the island but leeve it like it is as a shryn to Barney, especially the old well. Do not look for my body as I will caste myself into the see. You mite bring a couple of young ratts and leeve them as a living memorial to Barney. Females – no males. I sprayned my wrist is why this is written so bad. This is my laste will. Do what I say and don't come back to disturb anything after you bring the young ratts like I said. Just females

16 Based on the entire entries of the journal, who might have written the last entry dated on September 11th?

17 Some of the words in the last paragraph are misspelled. What was the reason that the author offered?

18 What can be inferred from the underlined (A)?
① Barney especially liked the old well.
② You shouldn't drink out of the well because it is contaminated.
③ Barney tried to cover up the murder.
④ The old well is so sacred that it can't be disturbed.

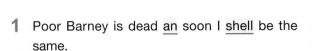

 핵심 PLUS!

1 Poor Barney is dead <u>an</u> soon I <u>shell</u> be the same.

- 단어가 misspell인 점에 주의할 것.

2 If anybody reeds this please do not disturb anything on the island but leeve it like it is as a shryn to Barney, <u>especially the old well.</u>

- 특히, 우물을 건들지 말라는 의도를 파악할 것(과학자가 죽어 있는 곳).

3 Do not look for my body <u>as I will **caste** myself into</u> the see.

- Barney의 죽음과 함께 자신도 바다에 몸을 던질 것이니 찾아도 소용없음을 강조.

4 You mite bring a couple of young ratts and leeve them as a living memorial to Barney. <u>Females – no males.</u>

- 암컷 쥐를 놓고 가라는 의도에서 Barney는 수컷이며 지적 종족 번식을 의도함을 파악할 수 있음.

5 <u>I sprayned my wrist is why this is written so bad.</u> This is my laste will.

- 자칭 과학자라 칭하는 Barney의 논리적 허점이 발견되는 곳.

3 Voca Check

* 빈칸에 들어갈 적절한 단어를 박스에서 찾아 넣으시오.

1

sack / flimsy / under the influence of alcohol / petty / vandalism / jolt / clumsy / stand in the way of / malice

1   Driving _____ can lead to accidents and endanger lives.

2   Fear should not _____ your progress and success.

3   The sudden _____ startled everyone in the room.

4   The act of intentionally damaging artwork is considered an act of _____.

5   The _____ structure of the paper made it easy to tear.

6   His _____ towards others was evident from his spiteful actions.

7   He was upset about the _____ arguments they had over trivial matters.

8   The company decided to _____ several employees due to budget constraints.

9   His _____ movements often resulted in him knocking things over.

2 reproach / take off / abandonment / become too much for / guinea pig / monastic / to the last / mute / ascribe / glutamic acid / drag / affair / spell / sport

1   The stray dog was found wandering the streets, showing signs of _____.

2   The workload has _____ him, and he feels overwhelmed.

3   The laboratory used mice as _____ for their experiments.

4   The scandalous _____ shocked the entire community.

5   _____ is an amino acid commonly found in many foods.

6   Despite his lack of words, his _____ conveyed his emotions effectively.

7   She felt a sense of _____ after realizing her mistake.

8   He took a short _____ to recharge and regain his focus.

9   The increase in crime rates was _____ to the lack of law enforcement.

10 He fought _____ breath, refusing to give up until the end.

11 The amusement park was a place of _____ and excitement for the visitors.

12 He had to _____ the heavy suitcase up the stairs.

13 After working for hours, she decided to _____ and relax for a while.

3   vault / commence / coping / frisk / go over / do away with / vermin / confine / retrieving / splash / own / insurmountable / too great to ignore

1   The prisoners were _____ in their cells for the entire day.

2   The farmer used pesticides to control the _____ that were damaging his crops.

3   The company plans to _____ outdated policies to streamline their operations.

4   The detective decided to _____ the crime scene for any potential evidence.

5   The impact of climate change is _____ and requires immediate attention.

6   The children excitedly _____ around the playground, enjoying their playtime.

7   The valuable documents were stored in a secure _____.

8   The workers installed a _____ on top of the fence for added stability.

9   The dog was trained in _____ objects and returning them to its owner.

10 The ceremony will _____ with a speech by the mayor.

11 The challenges they faced seemed _____ and impossible to overcome.

12 He had to _____ his involvement in the crime during the interrogation.

4

rather / shaking / come off / facilitate / descent / at intervals / rude / grope / give out / squeak / sever / chafe / masonry / plight / sacking / replenish / bring up to date / fix

1   The farmer used _____ to create sturdy bags for storing the harvested potatoes, ensuring they would be protected during transport.

2   The rough fabric _____ against his skin, causing irritation.

3   The website needs regular updates to _____ with the latest technology and trends.

4   The movie _____ successful, receiving positive reviews from both critics and audiences.

5   The new software update aims to _____ the user experience by improving accessibility and adding new features.

6   The hikers took breaks _____ to rest and enjoy the surrounding scenery.

7   The old flashlight batteries finally _____ and needed to be replaced.

8   The chef used a sharp knife to _____ the chicken into smaller pieces.

9   In the darkness, he _____ to find the light switch on the wall.

10 His _____ behavior during the meeting offended many of his colleagues.

11 She quickly _____ a simple dinner using the ingredients she had in the pantry.

12 The old building was made of sturdy _____.

13 The door _____ as someone pushed it open.

14 The company faced a financial _____ and had to lay off several employees.

Reading Comprehension

[1-4] Read the passage and answer each question.

 NOTE

AUGUST 30TH.

We are alone on the island now, Barney and I. It was something of a jolt to have to sack Tayloe after all these years, but I had no alternative. The petty vandalisms I could have forgiven, but when he tried to poison Barney out of simple malice, he was standing in the way of scientific progress. That I cannot condone.

I can only believe the attempt was made while under the influence of alcohol, it was so clumsy. The poison container was overturned and a trail of powder led to Barney's dish. Tayloe's defence was of the flimsiest. He denied it. ㉠Who else then?

SEPTEMBER 2ND.

I am taking a calmer view of the Tayloe affair. The monastic life here must have become too much for him. That, and the abandonment of his precious guinea pigs. ㉡He insisted to the last that they were better-suited than Barney to my experiments. They were more his speed, I'm afraid. He was an earnest and willing worker, but something of a clod, poor fellow. At last I have complete freedom to carry on my work without the mute reproaches of Tayloe. I can only ascribe his violent antagonism toward Barney to jealousy. And now that he has gone, how much happier Barney appears to be! ㉢I have given him complete run of the place, and what sport it is to observe how his newly awakened Intellectual curiosity carries him about. After only two weeks of glutamic acid treatments, he has become interested in my library, dragging the books from the shelves, and going over them page by page. I am certain he knows there is some knowledge to be gained from them had he but the key.

SEPTEMBER 8TH.

For the past two days I have had to keep Barney confined, and how he hates it. ㉣I am afraid that when my experiments are completed I shall have to do away with Barney. Ridiculous as it may sound there is still the possibility that he might be able to communicate his intelligence to others of his kind. However small the chance may be, the risk is too great to ignore. ㉤Fortunately there is, in the basement, a vault built with the idea of keeping vermin out, and it will serve equally well to keep Barney in.

SEPTEMBER 9TH.

(A)Apparently I have spoken too soon. This morning I let him out to frisk around a bit before commencing a new series of tests. After a quick survey of the room he returned to his cage, sprang up on the door handle, removed the key with his teeth, and before I could stop him, he was out the window. ㉻By the time I reached the yard I spied him on the coping of the well, and I arrived on the spot only in time to hear the key splash into the water below. I own I am somewhat embarrassed. It is the only key. The door is locked. Some valuable papers are in separate compartments inside the vault. Fortunately, although the well is over forty feet deep, there are only a few feet of water in the bottom, so the retrieving of the key does not present an insurmountable obstacle. But I must admit Barney has won the first round.

SEPTEMBER 10TH.

I have had a rather shaking experience, and once more in a minor clash with Barney. I have come off second-best. In this instance I will admit he played the hero's role and may even have saved my life. In order to facilitate my descent into the well I knotted a length of three-quarter-inch rope at one-foot intervals to make a rude ladder. I reached the bottom easily enough, but after only a few minutes of groping for the key, my flashlight gave out and I returned to the surface. A few feet from the top ⓐI heard excited squeaks from Barney, and upon obtaining ground level I observed that the rope was almost completely severed. Apparently it had chafed against the edge of the masonry and the little fellow, perceiving my plight, had been doing his utmost to warn me.

I have now replaced that section or rope and arranged some old sacking beneath it to prevent recurrence of the accident. I have replenished the batteries in my flashlight and am now prepared for ⓑ the final descent. ⓒThese few moments I have taken off to give myself a breathing spell and to bring my journal up to date. Perhaps I should fix myself a sandwich as I may be down there longer than seems likely at the moment.

SEPTEMBER 11TH.

Poor Barney is dead and soon I shell be the same. He was a wonderful ratt and life without him is knot worth livving. If anybody reeds this please do not disturb anything on the island but leeve it like it is as a shryn to Barney, espechilly the old well. Do not look for my body as I will caste myself into the see. You mite bring a couple of young ratts and leeve them as a living memorial to Barney. ⓓFemales-no males. ⓔI sprayned my wrist is why this is written so bad. This is my laste will. Do what I say an don't come back or disturb anything after you bring the young ratts like I said. Just females. Goodby.

1 Choose the number with a correct set of statements that are stated or implied in the passage.

> ㉠ The short story follows the journal entries of a scientist working on an island, trying to make a special rat intelligent.
>
> ㉡ Each entry drops hits of the mouse trying to kill the scientist, who is completely in the darkness of ignorance.
>
> ㉢ It can be said that the fact that it was the scientist that made Barney act "evil" by giving him intelligence may imply that evil is nothing but a creation of humankind.
>
> ㉣ The last entry is Barney's cover-up story, not the scientist genuinely having a sprained wrist.
>
> ㉤ As the last entry indicates, Barney has not achieved human-like writing abilities, which eventually reveals the limits of human ability and the failure of the scientist's experiment.

① ㉡, ㉢ and ㉤   ② ㉠ and ㉡
③ ㉠, ㉡, ㉢ and ㉣   ④ ㉡, ㉣, and ㉤
⑤ ㉢ and ㉣

2 Choose ONE that shows the most INAPPRORPRIATE reaction after reading the text.

① 정훈: Going over the intention of the question in ㉠, I thought that the criminal who tried to kill Barney might be someone other than Tayloe.

② 지훈: Through ㉡, I can tell that Tayloe kept urging the scientist to 'get rid of' Barney because his intelligence was increasing too fast to ignore.

③ 춘식: If the meaning of the word 'run' used in the sentence ㉢ is interpreted as 'operation' or 'management', it can be interpreted in a completely different way than the writer intended.

④ 허웅: Judging from Barney's stealing the key on September 9th, it can be seen that Barney already "smelled a rat" about the intention of the scientist mentioned in ㉣ and ㉤.

⑤ 경희: From ㉥, Barney must have been taken aback when he found out that he was being watched by a scientist, and was embarrassed to drop the key in the well.

3 Which of the following best paraphrases the underlined (A)?

① I am too proud of myself to compete with a less intelligent rat like Barney.

② I spoke so fast that Barney couldn't understand me.

③ Barney isn't smart enough yet to understand me.

④ I shouldn't have taken him lightly.

⑤ Barney belittled me too hastily.

4 Which of the following interpretations is <u>NOT</u> appropriate?

① About ⓐ, it can be inferred that the scientist perverted Barney's intention of being excitedly squeaky.

② Judging from the implication of ⓑ and ⓒ, there should be no additional entry, which means that September 10th should be the last one.

③ From ⓓ, it can be inferred that Barney is male, and that all the "precious guinea pigs" Tayloe had earlier were low-intelligence females.

④ From ⓔ, it can be identified that there is a logical flaw in Barney's cover-up.

⑤ The 'person' who wrote the last entry is not the scientist.

* pervert: to twist the meaning or sense of

PART

5 Sentence Completion

1 The ability to speak is an _____ quality that distinguishes human beings from the other animals.

① unique   ② typical   ③ passing   ④ transitory

어휘
ability 능력 the ability to speak 말할 수 있는 능력 quality 자질, 특성 distinguish A from B A와 B를 구별하다 unique 유일한, 독특한 typical 전형적인 (= representative) passing 일시적인, 한때의; 대충의, 수박 겉핥기식의 transitory 일시적인, 덧없는

2 Even though formidable winters are the norm in the Dakotas, many people were unprepared for the _____ of the blizzard of 1888.

① inevitability   ② ferocity

③ importance   ④ probability

⑤ mildness

어휘
formidable 가공할 만한, 굉장한, 만만찮은 the norm 표준, 기준, 일반적 현상 be unprepared for ~에 준비가 되어 있지 않다 blizzard 강한 눈보라 inevitability 불가피성 ferocity 사나움, 괴팍함, 잔인성 probability 있음직함, 가능성, 그럴 것 같음 mildness (날씨 등의) 온화함

3 As the first streamlined car, the Airflow represented a _____ in automotive development, and although its sales were _____, it had an immense influence on automobile design.

① milestone – disappointing   ② breakthrough – significant

③ regression – unimportant   ④ misjudgment – calculable

⑤ revolution – tolerable

어휘
streamlined 유선형의 represent 드러내다, 나타내다 automotive development 자동차 발달 immense 거대한 influence 영향력 have an immense influence on ~에 큰 영향력을 미치다 milestone 이정표, 중대한 시점, 중요한 사건 breakthrough 획기적 발전 regression 퇴보 misjudgment 오판 revolution 혁명, 혁신 disappointing 실망스러운 significant 중요한 calculable 신뢰할 수 있는 tolerable 참을 수 있는, 감당할 수 있는

4 While nurturing parents can compensate for adversity, cold or inconsistent parents may _____ it.

① exacerbate   ② neutralize

③ eradicate   ④ ameliorate

⑤ relieve

어휘 nurturing 양육하는 compensate for 보상하다 adversity 역경 inconsistent 변덕스러운, 일치하지 않는 exacerbate 악화시키다 neutralize 중립화하다 eradicate 제거하다 ameliorate 향상시키다 (= improve, alleviate) relieve 완화시키다 (= abate)

5 Social tensions among adult factions can be _____ by politics, but adolescents and children have no such _____ for resolving their conflict with the exclusive world of adults.

① intensified – attitude   ② complicated – relief

③ frustrated – justification   ④ adjusted – mechanism

⑤ revealed – opportunity

어휘 social tension 사회적 긴장감 adult faction 어른들로 구성된 당파 politics 정치 adolescent 사춘기 청소년 resolve 해결하다 conflict with ~와의 충돌 exclusive 배타적인 intensify 강화하다 complicate 복잡하게 하다 relief 완화(제), 완충장치 frustrate 좌절시키다 justification 정당화 adjust 조절하다 mechanism (해결책으로서의) 기구, 장치 reveal 드러내다

6 While to government economists the plans to stimulate the flagging economy appear _____ on paper, ministry spokesmen have expressed strong doubts about their practicability.

① feasible   ② crippling

③ flimsy   ④ unrealizable

어휘 government economists 정부 경제학자 stimulate (경제를) 활발하게 하다, 고무시키다 flagging 침체된 on paper 서류상(이론상) spokesmen 대변인 express (감정을) 드러내다 strong doubts 강한 의구심 practicability 실행 가능성 feasible 실천(실행) 가능한 crippling (절름발이로 만들 정도로) 타격을 주는 flimsy 무른, 취약한, 천박한 unrealizable 실현 불가능한, 인식(이해) 불가능한

7 The accident was a _____ lesson; I'll never drink and drive again.

① salutary   ② skeptical

③ mournful   ④ polemic

> **어휘** accident 사고 salutary 유익한 skeptical 회의적인 (= cynical, doubtful, dubious) mournful 슬픔에 잠긴, 애처로운 polemic 논쟁의, 논쟁을 좋아하는 (= belligerent, pugnacious)

8 All living things have certain _____ that are passed on from one generation to the next.

① flavor   ② energy

③ attributes   ④ circulates

> **어휘** living things 생물, 유기체 certain (어떤)일정한; 확실한 from A to B A에서 B까지(B로) generation 세대 flavor 맛, 풍미 energy 힘, 활기 attribute 특성, 특질; (attribute A to B) A를 B의 탓으로 돌리다 circulate 순환하다, 유포시키다, (신문·책자 따위를) 배부하다

9 The _____ author is lauded by all for his brilliant insights and helpful advice.

① acclaimed   ② debased

③ combined   ④ depreciated

> **어휘** author 저자, 작가 laud 찬양(칭찬)하다 brilliant 빛나는, 화려한 insight 통찰력 helpful 도움이 되는, 유용한 advice 충고 acclaimed 갈채를 받는, 인정받는 debased 타락한 (= degraded) combined 결합한 depreciated 경멸된, 무시된 (=devalued)

10 Her mind felt exceptionally clear, but it fastened on what were really quite unimportant details that it invested with an _____ significance that they did not at all possess in fact.

① obscure   ② intense

③ obscene   ④ obtuse

> **어휘** exceptionally 예외적으로, 이례적으로 clear 분명한, 또렷한 fasten on ~에 고정하다, 시선을 두다, 초점을 맞추다 quite 아주, 매우 unimportant 하찮은, 중요하지 않은 detail 세부사항 invested with ~로 둘러싸인 significance 중요성 not at all 결코 ~하지 않은 possess 소유하다 obscure 애매한, 모호한 intense 강렬한, 심한 obscene 외설적인, 불건전한 obtuse 뭉툭한, 무딘, 우둔한 (↔ acute)

UNIT 2

문학_현대시

The Road Not Taken
by Robert Frost

AI그림 달의이성

Voca Master

☐ **diverge**

v To separate or go in different directions, to branch out

• The two roads <u>diverge</u> in the forest, leading to different destinations.

☐ **bend**

v To curve or flex something, to change direction by curving

• He had to <u>bend</u> the metal rod to fit it into the desired shape.

☐ **undergrowth**

n Low-lying vegetation, such as bushes and plants, that grows beneath taller trees or in a forest

• The <u>undergrowth</u> in the jungle made it difficult to walk through.

☐ **fair**

a Having a flat, level, and smooth surface; beautiful or attractive

• The <u>fair</u> meadow stretched out before us, perfect for a picnic.

☐ **claim**

n A demand for a right or a statement of ownership
v To assert ownership or make a statement

• She filed a <u>claim</u> for the lost jewelry.
• He <u>claimed</u> that he had completed the project.

☐ **grassy**

a Covered with lush and abundant grass; having a green, grass-like quality

• The <u>grassy</u> field was ideal for playing soccer.

☐ **want**

v To lack or be deficient in something; to desire or need

- They <u>want</u> more time to finish the assignment.

☐ **wear**

v To use or have something over time, causing it to become old or damaged

- The constant use of the shoes caused them to <u>wear</u> out quickly.

☐ **lie**

v To be situated or positioned in a particular place or manner

- The book <u>lies</u> on the table.

☐ **tread**

v To step or walk on something, typically making a sound

- He <u>trod</u> lightly to avoid making noise in the library.

☐ **rhyme scheme**

n The pattern of rhymes at the end of lines in a poem, often represented with letters (eg, ABAB or AABBCC)

- The sonnet followed an ABABCDCD <u>rhyme scheme</u>.

☐ **repeat**

v To do or say something again; to replicate or duplicate

- Please <u>repeat</u> the instructions one more time for clarity.

☐ **line**

n A row of text or words in a poem, essay, or document

- The first <u>line</u> of the poem captured my attention immediately.

☐ **stanza**

n A group of lines in a poem, typically separated by spaces or indents and forming a unit of thought

- The poem had four <u>stanzas</u>, each expressing a different emotion.

☐ **face**

v To confront or deal with a difficult situation or person

- She had to <u>face</u> her fear of heights during the mountain climbing expedition.

☐ **suppose**

v To assume or believe something based on evidence or probability

- I <u>suppose</u> he'll be late again, judging by his track record.

☐ **subtle**

a Not obvious or easily detectable; delicate or refined

- The <u>subtle</u> differences in the paintings required a keen eye to notice.

☐ **fork**

n A point where a road, river, or path splits into two or more directions

- Take the left <u>fork</u> in the road to reach the lake.

☐ **dense**

a Closely packed together, having a high concentration

- The forest was so <u>dense</u> that it was difficult to see far ahead.

☐ **worn-in**

a Used or worn to the point where it fits comfortably and feels natural

- His <u>worn-in</u> sneakers were the most comfortable shoes he owned.

☐ **reinforce**

v To strengthen or support something, often by adding more material or effort

- The additional troops were sent to <u>reinforce</u> the front lines.

☐ **statement**

n A spoken or written expression of facts, opinions, or information

- The CEO issued a <u>statement</u> regarding the company's financial performance.

□ exclaim

v To cry out or shout something loudly and suddenly

- She exclaimed with joy when she received the surprise gift.

□ save

v To keep or set aside for later use; to prevent something from being wasted or lost

- He decided to save some of his earnings for a rainy day.

□ contradict

v To deny or assert the opposite of a statement or claim made by someone else

- Her testimony seemed to contradict the evidence presented in court.

□ acknowledgement

n The act of recognizing or accepting something, often with gratitude

- She received an acknowledgement for her hard work on the project.

□ recount

v To narrate or describe in detail; to tell a story or give an account of events

- He recounted the thrilling adventure of his journey through the jungle.

2 Text Reading

: The Road Not Taken

Two roads diverged in a yellow wood,
And sorry I could not travel both
And be one traveler, long I stood
And looked down one as far as I could
To where it bent in the undergrowth;

Then took the other, as just as fair,
And having perhaps the better claim,
Because it was grassy and wanted wear;
Though as for that the passing there
Had worn them really about the same,

And both that morning equally lay
In leaves no step had trodden black.
Oh, I kept the first for another day!
Yet knowing how way leads on to way,
I doubted if I should ever come back.

I shall be telling this with a sigh
Somewhere ages and ages hence:
Two roads diverged in a wood, and I—
I took the one less traveled by,
And that has made all the difference.

노란 숲속에 두 개의 길이 갈라져 있었지,
나는 한 여행자여서
둘 다 걸 수 없는 것을 아쉬워하면서
오래 서서 볼 수 있는 한 멀리 나는 한쪽 길을 내려
다 보았지
그것이 덤불 속으로 굽어 사라지는 곳까지

그리고 나서 똑같이 아름다운 다른 길을 택했지,
아마 더 나은 조건을 가진 듯해서,
그 길은 풀이 무성하고 닳은 자취가 없었기에,
비록 거기를 지나다니는 것이
사실 거의 똑같이 그들을 닳게 했겠지만,

그 날 아침 두 길은 똑같이 놓여있었지
밟아 겁게 된 적이 없었던 낙엽들 속에,
아, 나는 첫 길을 다른 날을 위해 남겨두었지!
어떻게 길이 계속 길로 이어지는지 알기에,
나는 내가 다시 돌아오지 못할 것으로 생각했지만.

나는 한숨을 쉬며 이렇게 말하고 있을 테지
그로부터 오랜 세월이 흐른 후 어디에선가
숲 속에 두 개의 길이 갈라져 있었고, 그래서 나는
사람이 덜 다닌 길을 택했고,
그리고 그것이 모든 것을 달라지게 했다고.

어구 및 표현 연구

1 Stanza별 분석

Stanza 1
Two roads diverged in a yellow w<u>ood</u>,
And sorry I could not travel <u>both</u>
And be one traveler, long I st<u>ood</u>
And looked down one as far as I c<u>ould</u>
To where it bent in the underg<u>rowth</u>;

- 타협이 불가능한 선택의 딜레마 (dilemma). 선택한 길이 어떤 결과로 이어질지 알 수 없음.
- Rhyme scheme – ABAAB

Stanza 2
Then took the other, as just as f<u>air</u>,
And having perhaps the better cl<u>aim</u>,
Because it was grassy and wanted w<u>ear</u>;
Though as for that the passing th<u>ere</u>
Had worn them really about the s<u>ame</u>,

- 어떤 길이든 공정함.
- claim = option 또는 조건
- want = lack 부재하다, 없다
- 풀이 무성하고, 사람이 다니지 않은 길 선택 ← 결국 선택한 결과의 효과가 무의미하게 되더라도
- Rhyme scheme – ABAAB

Stanza 3
And both that morning equally l<u>ay</u>
In leaves no step had trodden bl<u>ack</u>.
Oh, I kept the first for another d<u>ay</u>!
Yet knowing how way leads on to w<u>ay</u>,
I doubted if I should ever come b<u>ack</u>.

- for another day 또 다른 날을 위해

Stanza 4
I shall be telling this with a s<u>igh</u>
Somewhere ages and ages hen<u>ce</u>:
Two roads diverged in a wood, and <u>I</u>—
I took the one less traveled b<u>y</u>,
And that has made all the differen<u>ce</u>.

- ages and ages 오랜 세월

 작품해설

★ the road = 인생을 비유

★ A rhyme scheme(운율) is the pattern of sounds that repeats at the end of a line or stanza. Rhyme schemes can change line by line, stanza by stanza, or can continue throughout a poem.

2 Line별 분석

Two roads diverged in a yellow wood,

- The speaker, walking through a forest whose leaves have turned yellow in autumn, comes to a fork in the road.

  가을이 되어 노랗게 물든 숲속을 걷던 화자는 갈림길에 섰습니다.

  » a fork in the road 갈림길

And **sorry** I could not travel both

And **be one traveler**, long I stood

- The speaker, regretting that he or she is unable to travel by both roads (since he or she is, after all, just one person),

  화자는 두 길을 모두 갈 수 없는 것을 유감스럽게 생각합니다. (그나 그녀는 결국 한 사람이기 때문에),

  » regret 유감이다(나중에 후회가 남을 것이라는 의미)

And looked down one as far as I could

- The speaker stands at the fork in the road for a long time and tries to see where one of the paths leads.

  갈림길에 오래 서서 그 길 중 하나가 어디로 이어지는지 보려고 합니다.

To where it bent in the undergrowth;

- However, the speaker can't see very far because the forest is dense and the road is not straight.

  그러나 숲이 울창하고 길이 일직선이 아니기 때문에 화자는 멀리 볼 수 없습니다.

Then took the other, **as just as fair**,

- The speaker takes the other path, judging it to be just as good a choice as the first,

  화자는 첫 번째 선택만큼 좋은 선택이라고 판단하여 다른 길을 택합니다.

And having perhaps **the better claim**,

Because it was grassy and wanted wear;

- and supposing that it may even be the better option of the two, since it is grassy and looks less worn than the other path.

  잔디가 무성하고 다른 경로보다 덜 닳은 것처럼 보이기 때문에 둘 중 더 나은 옵션일 수 있다고 가정합니다.

Though **as for that the passing there**

Had worn them really about the same,

- Though, <u>now that</u> the speaker has actually walked on the second road, he or she thinks that in reality the two roads must have been more or less equally worn-in.

  그러나 화자는 실제로 두 번째 길을 걸었으므로 실제로는 두 길이 모두 거의 동등하게 닳았을 것이라고 생각합니다.

  » worn-in 닳은

And **both** that morning equally lay

In leaves no step had trodden black.

- Reinforcing this statement, the speaker recalls that <u>both roads</u> were covered in leaves, which had not yet been turned black by foot traffic.

  위의 문장을 보강하면서 화자는 두 도로가 아직 도보로 인해 검게 변하지 않은 나뭇잎으로 뒤덮인 것을 회상합니다.

Oh, I **kept** the first for another day!

- The speaker exclaims that he or she is in fact just <u>saving</u> the first road, and will travel it at a later date,

  화자는 자신이 사실은 첫 번째 길을 남겨둔 것뿐이며 나중에 밟을 것이라고 외칩니다.

  » keep (= save) 남겨두다, 아껴두다

Yet knowing how way leads on to way,

I doubted if I should ever come back.

- but then immediately contradicts him or herself with the acknowledgement that, in life, one road tends to lead onward to another, so <u>it's therefore unlikely that he or she will ever actually get a chance to return to that first road</u>.

  그러나 인생에서 한 길은 다른 길로 이어지는 경향이 있으므로 첫 번째 길로 돌아갈 기회를 실제로 얻지 못할 수도 있다는 사실을 즉시 인정합니다.

I shall be telling this with a sigh

Somewhere ages and ages hence:

- The speaker imagines him or herself <u>in the distant future</u>, recounting, with a sigh, the story of making the choice of which road to take.

  화자는 먼 미래의 자신을 상상하며 어떤 길을 택할 것인지를 한숨과 함께 이야기합니다.

Two roads diverged in a wood, and I—

I took the one **less traveled by**,

And that has made all the difference.

- Speaking as though looking back on his or her life from the future, the speaker states that he or she was faced with a choice between two roads and chose to take the road that was less traveled, and the consequences of that decision have made all the difference in his or her life.

화자는 자신의 인생을 미래에서 뒤돌아보듯 말하면서 두 길 중 하나의 선택에 직면했고 덜 가본 길을 택했다고 합니다. 그리고 그 결정의 결과는 그 사람의 삶에 큰 영향을 미쳤습니다.

 작품해설

The Road Not Taken By Robert Frost

1 평범한 소재와 언어 사용

소박하고 투명한 일상의 언어와 사고를 확장하여, 상징과 은유를 통해 우리 인생 앞에 놓인 두 갈래 길과 우리가 항상 마주치는 어려운 선택의 문제를 깊은 깨달음과 서정적 아름다움으로 승화. 이로써 평범한 일상의 순간들이 시적이고 철학적인 의미를 부여한다.

2 선택과 기회비용, 자유의지와 결정론의 문제 고찰

독자들에게 인생에서의 중요한 선택과 그로 인한 기회비용의 문제를 생각하게 하며, 우리가 내리는 선택이 자유의지에 의한 것인지, 아니면 결정론에 의해 이미 정해진 것인지에 대해 깊이 고민하게 만든다.

3 시공의 제약 속 인간이 마주치는 선택의 문제

시간과 공간이라는 제약 속에서 살아가는 인간이 항상 두 갈래 길 중 하나를 선택해야 하는 운명을 상징적으로 묘사한다. 이는 우리의 선택이 제한된 조건 속에서 이루어질 수밖에 없음을 시사한다.

4 결과에 대한 판단보단 선택 자체에 의미를 부여

시는 선택의 결과가 옳고 그름에 대해 언급하지 않고, 선택 그 자체에 의미를 부여한다.

5 선택하지 못한 길에 대한 미련과 회환

이는 우리가 선택한 길 뿐만 아니라 선택하지 않은 길에 대한 미련과 회환도 내포되어 있음을 표현한다. 이러한 방식으로 시는 인생의 복잡성과 선택의 본질을 아름답고 깊이 있게 탐구한다.

PART 3 · Voca Check

* 빈칸에 들어갈 적절한 단어를 박스에서 찾아 넣으시오.

1

undergrowth / repeat / claim / face / grassy / want / stanza / wear /
rhyme scheme / diverge / tread / fair / lie / bend / line

1   The two paths in the woods started to _____, leading us in different directions.

2   The strong wind caused the tree to _____ and sway precariously.

3   The dense _____ in the forest made it challenging to walk through.

4   The _____ maiden lived in a picturesque cottage in the countryside.

5   She wanted to _____ her rightful inheritance after her father's passing.

6   The _____ field was the perfect spot for a picnic on a sunny day.

7   I _____ for nothing when I'm in the company of my closest friends.

8   Years of use had caused the old book to _____ and lose its original charm.

9   The ancient ruins _____ hidden deep within the jungle.

10 Be careful not to _____ on the fragile flowers in the garden.

11 The poet used a unique _____ in his sonnet, which added to its beauty.

12 Please _____ your question; I didn't quite catch it the first time.

13 The teacher asked each student to read a _____ from the poem aloud.

14 The _____ consisted of four lines that conveyed the poet's emotions.

15 The mountain climbers had to _____ harsh weather conditions during their ascent.

16 The road _____ around the hill, revealing a breathtaking view of the valley below.

2 fork / suppose / dense / acknowledgement / reinforce / worn-in / subtle / recount / statement / contradict / exclaim / save

1 Let's _____ that the weather clears up for our outdoor picnic this weekend.

2 Her smile conveyed a _____ charm that captivated everyone she met.

3 At the _____ in the road, we had to decide whether to go left or right.

4 The forest was so _____ with trees that it was nearly impossible to see the sky.

5 His shoes were well-_____ from years of daily use.

6 We need to _____ the security measures to protect our data from cyber threats.

7 She made a bold _____ during the meeting, expressing her concerns about the project.

8 When he saw the surprise party, he couldn't help but _____ with joy.

9 Please _____ some of your energy for the last part of the hike; it's the most challenging.

10 His argument seemed to _____ what he had said just minutes earlier.

11 Her _____ of your efforts on the project meant a lot to the team.

12 Can you _____ the story of your adventure from start to finish?

[1-2] Read the passage and answer each question.

[가]
ⓐTwo roads diverged in a yellow wood,
And sorry I could not travel both
ⓑAnd be one traveler, long I stood
And looked down one as far as I could
To where it bent in the undergrowth;

[나]
Then took the other, as just as fair,
And having perhaps the better claim,
Because it was grassy and wanted wear;
Though as for that the passing there
Had worn them really about the same,

[다]
ⓒAnd both that morning equally lay
In leaves no step had trodden black.
Oh, I kept the first for another day!
ⓓYet knowing how way leads on to way,
I doubted if I should ever come back.

[라]
I shall be telling this with a sigh
Somewhere ages and ages hence:
Two roads diverged in a wood, and I—
I took the one less traveled by,
And that has made all the difference.

1 This is a description of the rhyme scheme for the above poem. Write the words to fill in the blanks.

> "The Road Not Taken" consists of _____ stanzas of _____ lines each. The rhyme scheme is _____; the rhymes are strict and masculine, with the notable exception of the last line (we do not usually stress the -ence of difference).

2 시의 각 행에 대한 설명 중 옳은 것을 <u>모두</u> 고르시오.

① ㉠ The two roads that diverge symbolize two important choices encountered later in life.

② ㉡ The speaker, like anyone faced with a choice, must make a choice, but can't know enough to be sure which choice is the right one. The speaker, as a result, is paralyzed: "long I stood" contemplating which road to choose.

③ ㉡ In much the same way that people are generally unable to see what the future holds, the speaker is unable to see what lies ahead on each path.

④ ㉢ The speaker rightly chose the road that was less traveled.

⑤ ㉣ By making a choice, the speaker will now never get the chance to experience the other road and can never know which was less traveled.

* contemplate 숙고하다

3 According to the poem above, which of the following statements in the box are <u>CORRECT</u>?

> I.   The title "The Road Not Taken" refers to the less-chosen path that the speaker initially takes.
>
> II. The speaker convinces himself that he can backtrack the road if efforts are made.
>
> III. In the 1st stanza, the speaker is deliberating his future between two reasonable choices.
>
> IV. In the 4th stanza, the speaker regrets his choice, because it is proven to be unreasonable, compared to the other.
>
> V. The main theme of the poem is pioneering uncultivated future and making new attempts.

① I, II, III, and IV   ② I and III

③ II, III, and IV   ④ III only

⑤ III, IV, and V

4 Which of the following is <u>NOT</u> a correct match between a literary device employed by the poem and its explanation?

① Imagery: The use of descriptive language helps to paint a vivid picture of the two roads in the yellow wood, with one road being grassy and the other being overgrown with undergrowth.

② Metaphor: The fork in the road is used as a metaphor for the choices we make in life, with each road representing a different path.

③ Hyperbole: The speaker says that he took the road less traveled by, but earlier in the poem, he admits that both roads were equally worn.

④ Repetition: The phrase "two roads diverged in a yellow wood" is repeated in the first and last stanzas, emphasizing the importance of the choice the speaker made.

⑤ Rhyme: The poem follows an ABAAB rhyme scheme.

5 Sentence Completion

1 Unless the environmentalists can draft a more _____ proposal, the courts will disallow their proposition as too vague.

① specific ② ambiguous
③ obscure ④ dubious

> **어휘**
> unless ~하지 않으면 environmentalist 환경주의자 draft ~을 작성(초안)하다 proposal 제안 court 법원 disallow ~을 허락하지 않다 proposition 제안 vague 애매한, 모호한 specific 명확한, 구체적인 ambiguous 애매한, 모호한 obscure 불명료한, 모호한, ~을 불명료하게 하다, ~을 모호하게 하다 dubious 의심스러운, 모호한

2 The relatives who received little or nothing sought to _____ the will by claiming the deceased had not been in his right mind when he had signed the document.

① obey ② submit
③ invalidate ④ acquiesce

> **어휘**
> relative 상대적인, 친척 receive ~을 받다 sought [seek의 과거·과거분사]~을 찾다, 추구하다, ~하려고 시도(노력)하다 will 유언(장), 의지 claim ~을 주장하다 the deceased 고인 be in one's right mind ~의 정상적인 상태이다 sign ~에 사인하다, 기호 document 문서 the document 여기서 the will을 가리킴 obey 따르다, 복종하다 submit 복종(굴복)하다[to], 제출하다 invalidate ~을 무효로 하다 acquiesce ~을 묵묵히 따르다[to, in]

3 The two groups were in total disagreement: in fact, their viewpoints were so _____ that there seemed no chance at all to reach an agreement of any kind.

① atomic ② polarized
③ stabilized ④ harmonious

> **어휘**
> group 그룹, 단체 total 전체의, 합계의, 완전한 disagreement 불일치, 불화 be in total disagreement 완전히 불일치 상태이다 in fact 사실상 viewpoint 관점 so ~ that - 너무 ~해서 -하다 chance 가능성, 기회, 우연 reach ~에 도달하다 agreement 합의 kind 종류 an agreement of any kind 어떠한(모든) 종류의 합의 atomic 원자의 polarize ~을 양극화시키다 stabilize ~을 안정시키다 harmonious 조화된, 균형 잡힌, 사이좋은

4 Society is like a building, which stands firm when its foundations are strong and all its timbers are sound. The man who can not be trusted is to society what a bit of ＿＿ is to a house.

① strong timber　　　　　　　　② rotten timber

③ dry brick　　　　　　　　　　④ wet brick

5 The opposition accused the government of a/an ＿＿ of responsibility.

① evasion　　　　　　② waste　　　　　　③ slip

④ lift　　　　　　　　⑤ exhaustion

6 His overly ＿＿ demeanor is what made most of the voters decide to cast a vote against him because they thought that he was not genuine and in fact too much of a politician.

① permissive　　　　　　　　② saccharine

③ candid　　　　　　　　　　④ equitable

7 The challenge of sustainable development will render passe the very idea of
_____ nation-states that scramble for markets, power and resource.

① resourceful   ② developed

③ cooperative   ④ competing

8 He may be deemed _____ who _____ considers the consequences before he
acts.

① impetuous – always   ② wary – generally

③ intrepid – casually   ④ diffident – usually

9 Heart attack patients have a _____ risk of death if they go to the hospital
on the weekend, when they are more likely to miss or wait longer for crucial
treatments.

① slightly higher   ② imperceptible

③ immediate   ④ more impending

10 Social scientists have established fairly clear-cut _____ that describe the appropriate behavior of children and adults, but there seems to be _____ about what constitutes appropriate behavior for adolescents.

① functions – rigidity

② estimates – indirectness

③ norms – confusion

④ regulations – certainty

⑤ studies – misapprehension

어휘 social scientist 사회학자 establish 확립하다, 설립하다 fairly 꽤 clear-cut 뚜렷한, 명쾌한 describe 묘사하다, 기술하다 appropriate 적합한, 적절한; 횡령하다, 사유하다 behavior 행동 constitute 구성하다, 조직하다 adolescent 청소년 function 기능 rigidity 엄격함, 단단함 estimate 평가, 판단 indirectness 간접성 norm 규범, 기준 confusion 혼동, 혼란 regulation 규칙, 규정 certainty 확실성 study 연구 misapprehension 오해, 오인

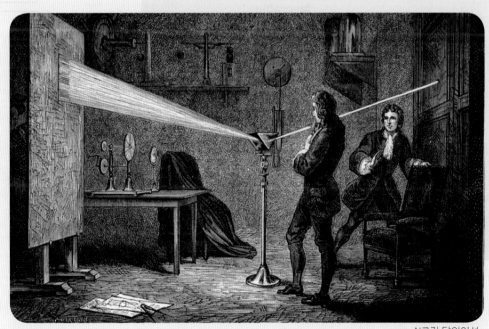 **UNIT 3**

비문학_과학철학
The Scientific Revolution in the 17th Century

AI그림 달의이성

☐ **candidate** — **n** A person or thing regarded as suitable for or likely to receive a particular position or treatment

- She is a strong <u>candidate</u> for the leadership role due to her experience and skills.

☐ **God-fearing** — **a** Having a deep religious belief and reverence for God

- The <u>God-fearing</u> community gathered at the church every Sunday for worship.

☐ **inscrutable** — **a** Impossible to understand or interpret

- The Mona Lisa's enigmatic smile remains <u>inscrutable</u> to art experts.

☐ **deity** — **n** A god or goddess in a polytheistic religion

- In Greek mythology, Zeus is considered the chief <u>deity</u> of the gods.

☐ **unpromising** — **a** Not showing the potential for success or growth; not favorable

- The barren land appeared <u>unpromising</u> for farming.

☐ **bloom** — **v** To flourish or develop rapidly and beautifully

- The garden <u>bloomed</u> with colorful flowers in the spring.

☐ **crowning** — **a** The highest or most important

- Winning the championship was the <u>crowning</u> achievement of his career.

☐ **fortitude** — **n** Courage and strength in facing adversity or difficulty

- Her <u>fortitude</u> in overcoming challenges inspired others.

☐ **make sense of** — To understand or interpret something

- It took him some time to <u>make sense of</u> the complex instructions.

☐ **deliberately** — `ad` On purpose or intentionally

- She <u>deliberately</u> chose a quiet spot to read her book.

☐ **obscure** — `a` Not clear or easily understood; hidden or vague

- The meaning of the ancient text was so <u>obscure</u> that it took years to decipher.

☐ **be struck dumb** — To be rendered speechless due to astonishment or amazement

- When she saw the breathtaking view from the mountaintop, she <u>was struck dumb</u> with awe.

☐ **with admiration** — Expressing a feeling of respect, approval, or wonder for someone or something

- He looked at the intricate artwork <u>with admiration</u> for the artist's talent.

☐ **eccentric** — `a` Unconventional and slightly strange

- The <u>eccentric</u> scientist had peculiar habits and an unconventional approach to research.

☐ **account** — `n` A narrative or record of events

- The historical <u>account</u> of the battle provided valuable insights.

☐ **stranglehold** — `n` A tight grip or control that limits freedom or progress

- The monopoly had a <u>stranglehold</u> on the market, making it difficult for competitors.

☐ **favoured** — `a` Regarded with preference or approval

- He was one of the <u>favoured</u> candidates for the prestigious award.

☐ **pagan** — `n` A person holding religious beliefs other than the main world religions

- The ancient Romans had a variety of <u>pagan</u> gods and goddesses.

❑ **exert**

v To apply or put forth effort or influence

- She had to <u>exert</u> all her energy to complete the marathon.

❑ **proto-scientist**

n Early practitioners of scientific exploration and inquiry

- The <u>proto-scientists</u> laid the groundwork for modern scientific discoveries.

❑ **spring into being**

To come into existence suddenly or rapidly

- The idea for the new invention <u>sprang into being</u> during a brainstorming session.

❑ **paid-up**

a Fully paid or up to date, often referring to memberships or subscriptions

- As a <u>paid-up</u> member of the club, he had access to all its facilities.

❑ **materialism**

n A philosophical belief that physical matter is the only reality and everything can be explained by it

- His <u>materialism</u> led him to focus solely on tangible possessions.

❑ **rationality**

n The quality of being based on reason or logic

- The decision-making process should involve <u>rationality</u> rather than emotions.

❑ **pursuit**

n The act of following or striving to achieve something

- His lifelong <u>pursuit</u> of knowledge led to groundbreaking discoveries.

❑ **arcane**

a Understood by few; mysterious or secret

- The ancient texts contained <u>arcane</u> knowledge known only to a select few scholars.

❑ **discipline**

n A branch of knowledge or field of study

- Physics is a <u>discipline</u> that explores the fundamental laws of the universe.

☐ **obsessive**

a Having an intense and irrational preoccupation with something

- His obsessive attention to detail made him an excellent detective.

☐ **numerological**

a Related to the study of the mystical significance of numbers

- Some people believe in the numerological significance of certain dates or numbers.

☐ **tribute**

n An act, statement, or gift acknowledging respect or admiration

- The monument was built as a tribute to the soldiers who fought in the war.

☐ **dazzlingly**

ad In a manner that impresses or astonishes with brightness or brilliance

- The fireworks display lit up the night sky dazzlingly.

☐ **deft**

a Skillful and quick in one's movements or actions

- The chef's deft hands created a masterpiece out of simple ingredients.

☐ **wind up**

To bring something to a conclusion or finalize it

- They had to wind up the meeting before the scheduled time.

☐ **intervention**

n The action of becoming involved in a situation to alter or prevent an outcome

- The timely intervention of the paramedics saved the accident victim's life.

☐ **dismay**

n A sudden loss of courage or resolution due to distress or fear

- In the face of unexpected setbacks, a wave of dismay washed over her, leaving her momentarily paralyzed.

UNIT

3

Text Reading

: The Scientific Revolution in the 17th Century

The 1600s were not, on the face of it, an obvious candidate for the description of the "age of genius." It was a world in which everyone was God-fearing and when everything from floods to comets was seen as the inscrutable will of a jealous, stern deity. Yet it was from this unpromising soil that the modern, scientific world-view bloomed. The crowning achievement of the age — Isaac Newton's Philosophiæ Naturalis Principia Mathematica — is among the most influential books ever written; those with the mathematical fortitude to make sense of its deliberately obscure diagrams are struck dumb with admiration. The equations derived by the eccentric genius are still used to design cars, build bridges and send spacecraft into the cosmos. But the legacy of the age is more than just a set of useful theories. The intuition of men like Newton and Johannes Kepler that, beneath the apparent chaos of everyday life, the universe is a regular, ordered machine that can be described with a few simple equations proved amazingly to be correct. It is this idea of universality that is the true legacy of the scientific revolution. The standard account tells us that the new science broke the stranglehold that the church and a few of its favoured pagan thinkers had exerted for centuries on Western thought. That is broadly true, but the reality was a good deal more complicated. The proto-scientists did not spring into being as paid-up believers in modern materialism and rationality. Newton divided his time between pursuits that today we would recognize as science and older, much more arcane disciplines such as alchemy and an obsessive search for numerological codes in the Bible. Newton intended his great system of the world as a tribute to a dazzlingly deft geometer-god. When others took it to suggest that, once the universal clockwork was wound up there would be no further need for divine intervention to keep the planets in their orbits, he was dismayed. In a sense, he was not the first of the scientists, but the last of the sorcerers.

1 본문의 내용으로 비추어 옳은 진술만으로 짝지어진 것은?

I   The 1600s were characterized by a prevailing belief in God and the attribution of natural phenomena to divine will.

II Isaac Newton's pursuits in alchemy and numerological codes in the Bible were entirely unrelated to modern materialism and rationality.

III The scientific revolution of the 1600s finally eliminated the need for divine intervention in understanding the cosmos.

IV Isaac Newton's Principia Mathematica is considered one of the most influential books ever written and contains equations still used in practical applications today.

V   The scientific revolution of the 1600s, led by figures like Newton and Kepler, introduced the idea that the universe operates according to regular, ordered principles that can be described with simple equations.

① I and II
② I, II and IV
③ II and V
④ I, IV and V
⑤ II, IV and V

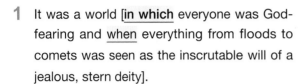

 핵심 PLUS!

1 It was a world [<u>in which</u> everyone was God-fearing and <u>when</u> everything from floods to comets was seen as the inscrutable will of a jealous, stern deity].

- 완전절을 취하는 [전치사+관계대명사]와 시간의 관계부사 when절의 병렬 구조
  [N <u>**in which** S V</u> ~ and <u>**when** S V</u> ~]

2 Yet <u>it</u> was (from this unpromising soil) <u>that</u> the modern, scientific world-view bloomed.

- 부사구 from this unpromising soil을 강조하는 It ~ that 구문

3 [those (with the mathematical fortitude <u>to make</u> sense of its deliberately obscure diagrams)] <u>are struck dumb</u> with admiration.

- 전치사구의 긴 수식어구를 가진 주어 파악.
- be struck dumb: 말문이 막힐 정도로 놀라다

4 [The equations **derived by the eccentric genius**] are still used to design cars, build bridges and send spacecraft into the cosmos.

- 과거분사의 수식을 받는 긴 주어 파악.

5 [The intuition of men (like Newton and Johannes Kepler) <u>**that**</u>, (beneath the apparent chaos of everyday life), the universe is a regular, ordered machine (<u>**that**</u> can be described with a few simple equations)] proved amazingly to be correct.

- 주어자리에 동격의 that, 주격 관계대명사와 부사구(괄호)의 수식을 받는 긴주어 파악.

6 <u>**It**</u> is this idea of universality <u>**that**</u> is the true legacy of the scientific revolution.

- 주어를 강조하는 It ~ that 구문

7 The standard account tells us that the new science broke the stranglehold [that S(the church and a few of its favoured pagan thinkers) had exerted for centuries on Western thought].

- [exert + (목적어) + on] 구조에서 목적어가 생략된 목적격 관계대명사 that

8 Newton divided his time between [pursuits that today we would recognize as science and older, much more arcane disciplines such as alchemy] and [an obsessive search for numerological codes in the Bible].

- between A and B 구조

3

3 Voca Check

* 빈칸에 들어갈 적절한 단어를 박스에서 찾아 넣으시오.

1

inscrutable / fortitude / stranglehold / exclusive / pagan / eccentric / unpromising / candidate / dumb / crowning / deity / deliberately / struck

1 The favored _____ delivered a powerful speech, earning the respect of the voters.

2 His _____ nature made it difficult for others to understand his motivations.

3 The ancient temple was dedicated to a mysterious _____.

4 Despite the _____ weather, the young plant began to bloom and flourish.

5 Her _____ achievement was winning the championship for the third year in a row.

6 It takes great _____ to face adversity with courage and resilience.

7 He _____ chose the path of living a minimalist lifestyle.

8 When he saw the breathtaking view, he was _____ with admiration.

9 The artist's _____ approach to painting led to unique works of art.

10 The corporation had a _____ on the market, controlling most of the industry.

11 The favored few were allowed entry into the _____ club.

12 The old traditions were rooted in _____ beliefs.

2　wind / deft / expertise / up / challenging / dismay / pursuit / paid-up / commitment / intervention / proto-scientist / tribute

1　He had to exert a lot of effort to complete the _____ project.

2　The _____ was a precursor to modern scientists, exploring the natural world.

3　Only _____ members of the club could attend the special event.

4　The _____ of wealth and possessions was not his primary goal in life.

5　His _____ to materialism and logic guided his decision-making.

6　His lifelong pursuit of knowledge led to _____ in a particular field.

7　The dazzling concert was a fitting _____ to the legendary musician.

8　With _____ skill, the artist crafted a beautiful sculpture.

9　If you continue down this path, you may eventually _____ in a difficult situation.

10　The _____ of the teacher improved the students' understanding of the topic.

11　The news of the disaster filled the community with _____.

[1-4] Read the passage and answer each question.

 NOTE

The 1600s were not, on the face of it, an obvious candidate for the description of the "age of genius." It was a world in which everyone was God-fearing and when everything from floods to comets was seen as the inscrutable will of a jealous, stern deity. (A) Yet it was from this unpromising soil that the modern, scientific world-view bloomed. The crowning achievement of the age — Isaac Newton's Philosophiæ Naturalis Principia Mathematica — is among the most influential books ever written; those with the mathematical fortitude to make sense of its deliberately obscure diagrams are struck dumb with admiration. The equations derived by the eccentric genius are still used to design cars, build bridges and send spacecraft into the cosmos. (B) But the legacy of the age is more than just a set of useful theories. The intuition of men like Newton and Johannes Kepler that, beneath the apparent chaos of everyday life, the universe is a regular, ordered machine that can be described with a few simple equations proved amazingly to be correct. (C) It is this idea of universality that is the true legacy of the scientific revolution. (D) The standard account tells us that the new science broke the stranglehold that the church and a few of its favoured pagan thinkers had exerted for centuries on Western thought. That is broadly true, but the reality was a good deal more complicated. (E) The proto-scientists did not spring into being as paid-up believers in modern materialism and rationality. (F) Newton divided his time between pursuits that today we would recognize as science and older, much more arcane disciplines such as alchemy and an obsessive search for numerological codes in the Bible. Newton intended his great system of the world as a tribute to a dazzlingly deft geometer-god. When others took it to suggest that, once (가)the universal clockwork was wound up there would be no further need for divine intervention to keep the planets in their orbits, he was dismayed. In a sense, (나)he was not the first of the scientists, but the last of the sorcerers.

1 When the above passage can be divided into three paragraphs, which would be the best boundary?

① (A) and (C)
② (B) and (D)
③ (B) and (F)
④ (C) and (E)
⑤ (D) and (F)

2 Choose the option that contains all the correct statements about the scientific background of 1600s?

I.   The era was marked by strong religious influence and a belief in divine intervention in natural phenomena.
II. The scientists of the era had profound insights into the underlying order of the universe, which turned out to be remarkably accurate. This insight laid the foundation for modern scientific thinking.
III. While the scientific revolution did challenge religious authority, the relationship between science and religion was complex and multifaceted during that period.
IV. Newton's dismay at the idea that his work might eliminate the need for divine intervention reflects the complex relationship between science and spirituality during that era.

① I, II and IV
② II and IV
③ II, III and IV
④ I and IV
⑤ All of the above

3 Which of the following best explains the contextual meaning of the underlined expression "the universal clockwork was wound up" in (가)?

① The universe was in a state of chaos.

② The universe had stopped functioning.

③ The universe had become predictable and orderly.

④ Divine intervention was required to keep the planets in orbit.

⑤ Isaac Newton had completed his scientific work.

4 The underlined expression (나) implies that _____.

① his conviction that the universe was an orderly place sprang from his religious belief

② he believed that the universe was something that could be comprehended by mortal minds

③ his scientific achievement was diminished by his belief in alchemy

④ he was neither a scientist nor a sorcerer

⑤ his scientific achievement kept his sorcerer persona hidden

PART

5 Sentence Completion

1 Her _____ of the stock market made her a millionaire.

① manipulation　　　　② invention

③ misinterpretation　　④ pull-out

> **어휘**　stock market 주식시장 make (+목+목·보) ~을 ~가 되게 하다(만들다) millionaire 백만장자, 대부호 manipulation 조작, 교묘한 솜씨 invention 발명, 날조 misinterpretation 오해, 오역 pull-out (자금의)회수, 빼내기

2 My uncle's letters are annoyingly _____. They are wordy and always repeating the news of previous letters.

① abundant　　　② redundant

③ hyperbolic　　④ reticent

> **어휘**　letter 편지, 글자 annoying 짜증나는 annoyingly 짜증나게 wordy 장황한 repeat 반복하다 previous 이전의 abundant 풍부한 redundant 여분의, 과다한, 불필요한 hyperbolic 과장된 reticent 말이 적은, 과묵한, 삼가는

3 His _____ makes him a rather poor farmhand.

① laziness　　　　　② enterprising spirit

③ industriousness　④ nature of hardworking

> **어휘**　make (+목+목·보) ~을 ~가 되게 하다(만들다) rather 다소 farmhand 농장 노동자 lazy 게으른 laziness 게으름 enterprising spirit 기업가적(모험적인) 정신 industrious 근면한 industriousness 근면함 nature of hardworking 근면함

4 His heavy dependency on alcohol made him a _____ person.

    ① jobless   ② congenial

    ③ workaholic   ④ amiable

어휘 heavy dependency on ~에 대한 큰 의존 make (+목+목·보) ~을 ~가 되게 하다(만들다) a jobless person 실업자 congenial 같은 성질의, 마음이 맞는 workaholic 일중독의 amiable 상냥한, 친근한

5 Our understanding of genetics will allow us to _____ many of the diseases of mankind.

    ① prevent   ② advance

    ③ invent   ④ promote

어휘 genetics 유전학 allow A to ⓡ A가 ⓡ하도록 허락하다 disease 질병 mankind 인류 prevent 막다, 예방하다 advance 진척(촉진)시키다 invent 발명하다, 날조하다 promote 승진시키다, 진척시키다, 장려하다

6 If you carry this _____ attitude to the meeting, you will _____ any supporters you may have at this moment.

    ① arrogant – attract   ② respectful – defer

    ③ defiant – alienate   ④ supercilious – attract

어휘 attitude 태도 carry ~ attitude ~한 태도를 취하다 supporter 지지자 at this moment 이 순간, 지금 arrogant 거만한, 건방진 attract ~의 마음을 끌다, 매혹하다 respectful 공손한 defer 연기하다, 미루다 defiant 반항적인, 무례한 alienate ~을 멀어지게 하다, 소원하게 하다 supercilious 거만한, 젠체하는

7 These toxic chemicals get into strands of DNA, _____ the risk of cancer and other ailments.

    ① boosting   ② diminish

    ③ dwindle   ④ tapering off

어휘 toxic 유해한, 유독한 chemical 화학제품, 화학적인 get into ~로 가다 strand 한 가닥의 실, 섬유, DNA 사슬 risk 위험 cancer 암 ailment 질병 boost 끌어올리다, 증가시키다 diminish 감소시키다, 줄이다 dwindle 작아지다, 축소되다 taper off 점점 줄다, 적어지다

8 He was an _____ treated with contempt.

① outsider　　　　　　② erudite

③ literate　　　　　　④ scholar

9 These are _____ people who utilized all of their dead prey.

① thrift　　　　　　② extravagant

③ exorbitant　　　　　　④ unrestrained

10 George spent hours in the reference library looking for facts to _____ their claims that seemed so absurd to him.

① decide　　　　　　② exaggerate

③ refute　　　　　　④ verify

UNIT 4

비문학_예술

The Gleaners
by Jean-François Millet

1 Voca Master

☐ **hardship**

n Severe suffering or adversity; a difficult or trying situation

- After losing his job, he faced financial <u>hardship</u> and struggled to make ends meet.

☐ **impoverished**

a Reduced to poverty; lacking in resources or wealth

- The <u>impoverished</u> family couldn't afford basic necessities like food and clothing.

☐ **scour**

v To clean or remove something by scrubbing or washing it vigorously

- She had to <u>scour</u> the stubborn stains from the kitchen counter.

☐ **stalk**

n The main stem of a plant, typically having leaves, buds, and flowers attached

- The sunflower's tall <u>stalk</u> held a large, vibrant blossom.

☐ **licence**

n Official permission, typically in the form of a document or a legal right

- He applied for a driver's <u>licence</u> to legally operate a vehicle.

☐ **desperate**

a Feeling or showing a sense of hopelessness or extreme urgency

- In a <u>desperate</u> attempt to save her failing business, she sought investors.

☐ **undertake**

v To take on a task, responsibility, or duty

- She decided to <u>undertake</u> the challenging project despite its complexity.

☐ **identifiable** **a** Capable of being recognized or distinguished

- The suspect's unique tattoo made him easily identifiable to the police.

☐ **or lack thereof** A phrase used to indicate the absence or absence of something

- The team's success depended on their effort, or lack thereof, in training.

☐ **be occupied with** To be engrossed or absorbed in a particular task or activity

- He was too occupied with his studies to attend the party.

☐ **seek** **v** To search for or try to obtain something

- She decided to seek professional advice to solve her legal issues.

☐ **till** **v** To prepare and cultivate land for crops

- The farmer needed to till the soil before planting the seeds.

☐ **champion** **n** A person who vigorously supports or defends a cause or belief

- She was a champion of equal rights for all citizens.

☐ **visualization** **n** The act of forming mental images or visual representations

- Visualization techniques can help reduce stress and anxiety.

☐ **hierarchy** **n** A system of ranking or organizing people or things into levels of importance or authority

- The military has a strict hierarchy with clearly defined ranks.

☐ **recede** **v** To move back or withdraw; to become more distant

- As the floodwaters began to recede, the extent of the damage became evident.

☐ **communal**   **a** Relating to or shared by a community or group

- The park provided a <u>communal</u> space for residents to gather and socialize.

☐ **workforce**   **n** The total number of workers in a specific area, industry, or country

- The company needed to hire more employees to expand its <u>workforce</u>.

☐ **oversee**   **v** To supervise or watch over a task or process

- The manager was responsible for <u>overseeing</u> the production line.

☐ **viable**   **a** Capable of working successfully; feasible

- The business plan was not <u>viable</u> due to a lack of funding.

☐ **recession**   **n** A period of economic decline characterized by a decrease in economic activity

- The 2008 financial <u>recession</u> had a significant impact on global markets.

☐ **demonstrate**   **v** To show or prove the truth or existence of something

- She used scientific experiments to <u>demonstrate</u> her theory.

☐ **marginalize**   **v** To treat someone or a group as unimportant or insignificant

- The policy had the unintended effect of <u>marginalizing</u> certain communities.

☐ **parallel**   **n** A similarity or comparison between two things

- There was a clear <u>parallel</u> between the two historical events.

☐ **sheave**   **n** A pulley or wheel with a groove for holding a rope or cable

- The ship's crew used a <u>sheave</u> to raise the heavy anchor.

diagonally

ad In a slanting or oblique direction

- She cut the fabric diagonally to create a unique pattern.

stack

n A neat pile or arrangement of objects, typically one on top of the other

- The librarian organized the books into a tidy stack on the shelves.

bounty

n Generosity or rewards, often in the form of a gift or payment

- The bounty offered for information about the missing dog encouraged people to search.

homespun

a Made or produced at home; simple and unrefined

- The homespun quilt was a cherished family heirloom.

stiffness

n The quality of being rigid or inflexible; a lack of ease or comfort

- The stiffness of the new shoes made them uncomfortable to wear.

discomfort

n A feeling of physical or emotional unease or distress

- His expression revealed his discomfort during the awkward conversation.

disunity

n Lack of unity or harmony; division or disagreement

- The disunity within the political party weakened its influence.

jar against

To clash or conflict with something, often in terms of opinions or ideas

- Her views on the topic jarred against those of her colleagues.

torturous

a Involving extreme pain, suffering, or torment

- The torturous journey through the desert was grueling.

☐ **connote**　　**v** To suggest or imply a particular meaning or feeling in addition to the literal definition

- The word "home" can <u>connote</u> feelings of comfort and belonging.

☐ **bring on**　　To cause or induce a particular situation or outcome

- Eating too much spicy food can <u>bring on</u> heartburn.

☐ **relief**　　**n** A feeling of comfort or reassurance after a period of stress, pain, or difficulty

- The news of his safe return brought great <u>relief</u> to his family.

☐ **recommence**　　**v** To begin again; to restart something

- After a brief break, the construction work will <u>recommence</u> next week.

☐ **arduous**　　**a** Involving a lot of effort and difficulty; strenuous

- Climbing the steep mountain was an <u>arduous</u> task.

☐ **thankless**　　**a** Not likely to receive thanks or appreciation; unappreciated

- Being a referee in a heated game is often a <u>thankless</u> job.

☐ **a flock of**　　A group of animals or birds, typically of the same species

- We observed <u>a flock of</u> seagulls flying over the beach.

☐ **pass over**　　To go over or across something

- The hikers had to <u>pass over</u> a narrow bridge to continue on the trail.

☐ **straggle**　　**v** To move or spread out in a scattered, disorganized manner

- The marathon runners began to <u>straggle</u> as they approached the finish line.

☐ **pathos**   **n** The power to evoke feelings of pity, sympathy, or sadness

- The movie's emotional scenes were filled with <u>pathos</u> that moved the audience to tears.

☐ **plight**   **n** A difficult or challenging situation; a predicament

- The <u>plight</u> of the refugees touched the hearts of people around the world.

☐ **empathize with**   To understand and share the feelings of another; to feel empathy for

- She could <u>empathize with</u> her friend's grief over losing a loved one.

☐ **unveil**   **v** To reveal or uncover something previously concealed

- The artist was about to <u>unveil</u> his latest masterpiece to the public.

☐ **salon**   **n** A gathering or exhibition, often related to art or culture

- The annual <u>Salon</u> in Paris showcases contemporary art from around the world.

☐ **innocuous**   **a** Harmless; not likely to cause offense or harm

- His joke was meant to be <u>innocuous</u>, but it ended up offending some people.

☐ **monarchy**   **n** A form of government where a single ruler, often a king or queen, holds supreme authority

- The United Kingdom is a constitutional <u>monarchy</u> with a parliamentary system.

☐ **turbulent**   **a** Characterized by unrest, disturbance, or disorder

- The <u>turbulent</u> protest led to clashes between demonstrators and the police.

☐ **piety**　　　**n** Deep devotion or reverence, especially in religious matters

- Her <u>piety</u> was evident through her daily prayers and acts of charity.

☐ **spirituality**　　　**n** The quality of being connected to the spiritual or non-material aspects of life

- Meditation and yoga are practices that can enhance one's <u>spirituality</u>.

☐ **abject**　　　**a** Extremely miserable, wretched, or hopeless

- The refugees lived in <u>abject</u> poverty and dire conditions.

☐ **motif**　　　**n** A recurring theme, subject, or pattern in art, literature, or music

- The use of nature as a <u>motif</u> is common in romantic poetry.

☐ **upsetting**　　　**a** Causing emotional disturbance or distress

- The news of the accident was deeply <u>upsetting</u> to the community.

☐ **tame**　　　**a** Domesticated or trained; not wild or aggressive

- The <u>tame</u> lion in the circus performed tricks for the audience.

☐ **vanish**　　　**v** To disappear suddenly or completely from sight

- The magician made the rabbit <u>vanish</u> into thin air.

☐ **poverty-stricken**　　　**a** Experiencing extreme poverty or destitution

- The charity organization aimed to help the <u>poverty-stricken</u> families in the area.

☐ **call**　　　**n** A loud cry or shout; a demand for attention or action

- Her <u>call</u> for help was heard by a passing hiker in the wilderness.

2 Text Reading

: The Gleaners

In quite typical subject matter for Millet, this painting depicts one of the hardships of the impoverished which has thankfully disappeared from modern life. Gleaning is the act of scouring the field for stalks of crop missed in the first harvesting. One needed a licence to be allowed to do this, and only the poorest, most desperate would undertake to obtain one. Thus the three main figures in the painting are immediately identifiable as of very low social status.

It is the idea of their place in society, or lack thereof, which Millet seems to be occupied with in this piece. The piece was created while Millet was in Barbizon, and one of the leaders of the Barbizon School, which sought a return to Nature in art. For most members of the group this meant landscape painting, but Millet focused on figures within landscapes, almost as if portraying what had become Nature, as humans had tilled the earth for thousands of years. A champion of the rural working class in his paintings (he was not an overtly political figure in actions), he often depicts people working in the fields, such as in The Sower (1850) or The Angelus (1857-59), but these are usually people who have found a place in society, they are part of the workforce. The Gleaners however depicts women who have no place, or have through poverty lost their place, in society.

UNIT

4

1 Which of the following is <u>TRUE</u> of the passage?

① The painting "The Gleaners" by Millet primarily focuses on the beauty of the landscape.

② Millet was a prominent political figure advocating for the rights of the rural working class.

③ Gleaning was a common practice among all social classes during Millet's time.

④ The Barbizon School mainly produced paintings featuring historical and mythological subjects.

⑤ "The Gleaners" portrays women who have fallen into poverty and have no place in society.

 핵심 PLUS!

1 In quite typical subject matter for Millet, this painting depicts <u>one of</u> the hardships of <u>the impoverished</u> <u>which</u> has, thankfully disappeared from modern life.

- [one of N(복수명사)]: ~ 중의 하나
- [the + 형용사] = 셀 수 있는 복수명사(the impoverished: 빈곤해진 사람들)
- [N which V ~]의 주격 관계대명사

2 Gleaning is the act of scouring the field for stalks of crop [(**which are**) <u>missed</u> <u>in the first harvesting</u>].

- [주격 관계대명사 + be동사]가 생략된 과거분사가 이끄는 형용사구
- miss는 "놓치다, 잡지 못하다"의 타동사임.
- in the first harvesting에서 in은 "~할 때"의 의미를 가진 전치사.

3 Thus the three main figures in the painting are immediately identifiable <u>as</u> (<u>being</u>) <u>of</u> very low social status.

- as와 of 사이에 being이 생략된 형태임.
- **be of** very low social status = **have** a very low social status

4 <u>It</u> is (the idea of their place in society, or lack thereof,) <u>which</u> Millet seems to be occupied with in this piece.

- It ~ that 강조구문
- which에 걸리는 절은 목적어가 생략된 형태임.
  <u>It</u> is (the idea of their place in society, or lack thereof,) **which** Millet seems to be occupied with **(O)** in this piece.

5 A champion of the rural working class in his paintings (he was not an overtly political figure in actions), he often depicts people [**working** in the fields, such as in The Sower (1850) or The Angelus (1857-59)], but these are usually people [**who** have found a place in society], they are part of the workforce.

- 수식어구가 달린 후치수식의 현재분사와 주격 관계대명사

As we look into the painting, we are presented with a visualisation of the rural social hierarchy. The further back we recede into the picture depth, the higher the rank of the people depicted. At first we see the gleaners themselves, then behind them is the communal workforce, cutting and reaping the harvest. Further back still they are overseen by a figure on horseback, with the large domestic buildings highlighting the figure. This was a time when owning a horse was still a major indicator of wealth: Benz did not create his automobile until the 1880s, and the gap between rich and poor had not reached a point at which it was viable for the majority of people to own horses. The low skyline of the piece, little more than half way up the canvas, emphasises this sense of recession, and of the distance between the gleaners and the rest of the community, a distance symbolic as well as physical. Millets demonstrates to us how these people's poverty has lead them to being marginalised by society, and shut out from the support of the community.

UNIT

4

2 According to the passage, what is the significance of owning a horse during the time when the painting is set?

① Owning a horse was a symbol of poverty.
② Owning a horse was an indicator of wealth.
③ Owning a horse was a requirement for communal workforce.
④ Owning a horse had no significance in the rural community.
⑤ Owning a horse was a recent development in transportation.

3 What is the symbolic and physical significance of the low skyline in the painting described in the passage?

① It represents the prosperity of the community.
② It suggests a lack of natural beauty in the landscape.
③ It highlights the distance and marginalization of the gleaners from the rest of the community.
④ It signifies the prevalence of horses in the rural society.
⑤ It emphasizes the abundance of domestic buildings.

4 Which group of people is depicted furthest back in the painting, according to the passage?

① The gleaners themselves   ② The communal workforce
③ The figure on horseback   ④ The owners of domestic buildings
⑤ People who did not own horses

1 As we look into the painting, we are presented with <u>a visualisation of the rural social hierarchy</u>.

- a visualisation of the rural social hierarchy: 시골 사회 위계질서의 시각화

2 **The further** back we recede into the picture depth, **the higher** the rank of the people depicted.

- [The 비교급 + the 비교급] 구문

3 Further back **still** they are overseen by a figure on horseback, **with** the large domestic buildings **highlighting** the figure.

- 비교급 강조 still이 further를 후치수식하고 있음.
- "~가 ~하면서"의 with N v-ing의 부대구문
  with (the large domestic buildings) highlight**ing** the figure

4 This was a time (**when** owning a horse was still a major indicator of wealth): Benz did not create his automobile until the 1880s, and the gap between rich and poor had not reached a point (**at which** it was viable for the majority of people to own horses).

- 시간의 관계부사 [a time + **when** S V] 구조
- [전치사 + 관계대명사] [a point + **at which** S V] 구조

5 The low skyline of the piece, (**which is**) little more than half way up the canvas, emphasises this sense of recession, and of the distance between the gleaners and the rest of the community, a distance symbolic as well as physical.

- [주격 관계대명사 + be동사]의 생략
- [~ of N, and of N]의 병렬구조
- 동격의 코마(,)

6 Millets demonstrates to us how these people's poverty has lead them to being marginalised by society, and shut out from the support of the community.

- lead N to N(V-ing)와 전치사에 걸리는 동명사의 수동태 병치

Millet shows this through symbolic contrasts and parallels. The small sheaves that the women have gathered are contrasted diagonally with the huge stacks that the group have gathered. Nature's bounty as visualised by the stacks, with more further in the background, and more sheaves waiting to be piled, is pitifully contrasted with the small number of sheaves gathered by the gleaners, and the stalks in their hands. The women's clothes are homespun, heavy materials, the stiffness of the red cloth tied with a piece of rope around the woman's arm portrays a feeling of discomfort. The unity of the group, working together, all bending and lifting as one, is again contrasted with the three women, one of whom is almost standing straight, creating a sense of disunity, jarring against the shared pose of the other two women.

The standing woman's pose is almost torturous; she seems to have taken a pause, connoting the aching back brought on by this repetitive physical labour, but we do not see her at the point of relief, but as she returns to her work, recommencing the arduous, virtually thankless task. In the sky above, a flock of birds passes over, with stragglers falling behind, mimicking the figures down below. Thus Millet fills the painting with pathos, and as viewers it is hard not to empathise with the plight of these women. Even Millet's use of light suggests the women's struggle, as the sun shines down on the house and the group, whilst they are nearly in shadow, on the edge of darkness.

UNIT

4

5   According to the passage, what does the contrast between the small sheaves held by the women and the massive stacks in the background symbolize in Étienne-Jules Millet's painting?

① The women's preference for smaller tasks
② The women's efficiency in gathering sheaves
③ An emphasis on the beauty of the small sheaves
④ A symbol of inequality in resources and opportunities
⑤ The women's reluctance to join the larger group

6   What is the primary purpose of mentioning the flock of birds in the passage in relation to the women in the painting?

① To highlight the women's fascination with nature
② To symbolize the women's struggle to keep up with opportunities
③ To suggest that the women often observed the birds
④ To emphasize the abundance of birds in the sky
⑤ To indicate the women's joy in mimicking the flight of birds

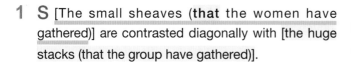

 핵심 PLUS!

1 S [The small sheaves (**that** the women have gathered)] are contrasted diagonally with [the huge stacks (that the group have gathered)].

- 주격 관계대명사의 수식을 받는 주어와 전치사 with에 걸리는 목적어

2 S [Nature's bounty as visualised by the stacks, with more further in the background, and more sheaves waiting to be piled,] is pitifully contrasted with [the small number of sheaves gathered by the gleaners, and the stalks in their hands].

- the stacks를 수식하는 [with more ~ and more ~]의 전치사구 병치
- ~ contrasted with의 전치사에 걸리는 명사구 병치

3 The women's clothes are homespun, heavy materials, (and) [the **stiffness** of the red cloth (which is) **tied with** a piece of rope around the woman's arm] **portrays** a feeling of discomfort.

- 문장과 문장을 연결하는 등위 접속사 and 삽입
- 과거분사 tied의 수식을 받는 주어의 핵 stiffness와 본동사 portrays

4 [The unity of the group, working together, **all bending and lifting as one**,] is again contrasted with the three women, **one of whom** is almost standing straight, creating a sense of disunity, jarring against the shared pose of the other two women.

- all bending and lifting as one = as they are all bending and lifting as one
- one of whom = and the three women

5 The standing woman's pose is almost torturous; she seems **to have taken** a pause, connoting the **aching** back **brought on by** this repetitive physical labour, but we do not see her at the point of relief, but as she returns to her work, recommencing the arduous, virtually thankless task.

- 완료부정사 to have taken
- 과거분사 brought의 수식을 받는 the aching back(aching은 현재분사임.)

6 In the sky above, a flock of birds passes over, (**with** stragglers **falling** behind), mimicking the figures down below.

- "N이 V한 채"의 의미를 가진 부대구문 with N V-ing

The Gleaner's was first unveiled at the Salon of 1857. While the painting may seem fairly innocuous to modern viewers, its focus on the lives of peasants and the working classes was seen as politically threatening by the middle and upper class audience who saw it at the Salon. The latest of France's revolutions was only in 1848, when in February the Orlean monarchy was overthrown only to be replaced by an increasingly conservative government in the Republic, which lead to a bloody revolt in June 1848, and the eventual election of Louis Napoleon as President (who would become Napoleon III, leader of the Second French Empire). After this turbulent recent history one can understand a certain sensitivity amongst parts of society to subjects which seemed to glorify the peasant classes.

7   According to the passage, why did the middle and upper classes perceive Étienne-Jules Millet's painting, "The Gleaners," as politically threatening at the Salon of 1857?

① Because they considered the painting unremarkable and inconsequential.
② Because the painting challenged existing social hierarchies and norms.
③ Because the painting focused on the lives of the elite rather than peasants.
④ Because the painting was devoid of any political context.
⑤ Because the painting portrayed a utopian vision of society.

8   According to the passage, why were some segments of society sensitive to depictions that seemed to glorify the peasant classes in art during the 19th century?

① Because they believed such depictions were aesthetically unappealing.
② Because they believed peasants deserved more recognition in art.
③ Because they considered peasant life unimportant.
④ Because they wanted to celebrate the working class.
⑤ Because they associated such depictions with revolutionary sentiments and challenges to the established order.

 핵심 PLUS!

1 While the painting may seem fairly innocuous to modern viewers, its focus on the lives of peasants and the working classes was seen as politically threatening by the middle and upper class audience (who saw it at the Salon).

• 수동태와 주격 관계대명사 파악.

2 The latest of France's revolutions was only in 1848, when in February the Orlean monarchy was overthrown only to be replaced by an increasingly conservative government in the Republic, which lead to [a bloody revolt in June 1848, and the eventual election of Louis Napoleon as President (who would become Napoleon III, leader of the Second French Empire)].

• 앞의 연도를 받아 "그 시기에"로 해석하는 시간의 관계부사 when
• 역접의 의미를 가지는 결과적 용법의 to부정사의 부사적 용법인 only to 파악. "그러나 결국 (또다시) ~하다"
• 계속적 용법의 관계대명사 which
• [~]의 내용은 모두 lead to의 전치사 to에 걸리는 명사구의 병치임.

3 After this turbulent recent history one can understand a certain sensitivity (amongst parts of society) to [subjects which seemed to glorify the peasant classes].

• sensitivity에 걸리는 전치사 to
• 부사구 삽입어 amongst parts of society
• 주격 관계대명사 which

However, Millet's interests were not explicitly political, he was a religious man who looked to the working classes as examples of the continuation of Old Testament piety and spirituality, rather than as the future leaders of France. His audience had more cause to be worried by Courbet's works, which were heavily influenced by Millet, and more overtly political. The Stonebreakers, of 1850, for example, actively confronts the viewer, with the cruel reality of abject poverty, with similar themes and motifs to The Gleaners, but carrying them to more upsetting extremes. By comparison Millet's pieces seem fairly tame.

While the scenes Millet depicts in The Gleaners have long since vanished from France, the ideas he presented are as eternal as he makes their actions seem. The marginalisation of the poverty stricken is an issue which remains relevant, although we can only hope that the modern middle and upper classes would react to a modern Millet in a slightly more positive way than to see it as a call to revolution.

9 According to the passage, what distinguishes Étienne-Jules Millet's artistic motivation from that of Gustave Courbet?

① Millet's art is more overtly political.
② Millet's art is influenced by Old Testament spirituality.
③ Courbet's art is less confrontational.
④ Courbet's art is primarily religious in nature.
⑤ Courbet's art focuses on the working classes.

10 What does the passage suggest about the enduring relevance of Étienne-Jules Millet's themes and ideas in his art?

① They have lost all relevance in contemporary society.
② They remain relevant only to the working classes.
③ They continue to resonate with contemporary societal concerns.
④ They are primarily concerned with political revolutions.
⑤ They have only historical significance.

11 In the passage, what is the author's hope regarding the reaction of modern middle and upper classes to artwork similar to that of Étienne-Jules Millet?

① The hope that they will interpret such art as a call to revolution
② The hope that they will view such art as irrelevant
③ The hope that they will respond with compassion and understanding
④ The hope that they will consider such art as overtly political
⑤ The hope that they will dismiss such art as inconsequential

1 However, Millet's interests were not explicitly political, (as) he was [a religious man **who looked to** the working classes **as** examples of the continuation of Old Testament piety and spirituality, **rather than as** the future leaders of France].

- 주격 관계대명사 who
- look to A as B, rather than as C

2 His audience had more cause <u>to be worried by</u> Courbet's works, (**which** <u>were heavily influenced by</u> Millet, and more overtly political).

- 형용사 용법의 to부정사의 수동태
- 계속적 용법의 관계대명사와 관계대명사에 걸리는 수동태

3 The Stonebreakers, of 1850, for example, actively confronts the viewer, with the cruel reality of abject poverty, with similar themes and motifs to The Gleaners, <u>but carrying them to more upsetting extremes</u>.

- but 이후에 이어지는 분사구문은 아래와 같이 볼 수 있음.
  but carrying them to more upsetting extremes.
  = but it(= The Stonebreakers) carries them to more upsetting extremes.
- them = similar themes and motifs

4 While the scenes Millet depicts in The Gleaners have long since vanished from France, the ideas [(<u>which</u>) he presented] are as eternal [<u>as</u> he makes their actions seem].

- 목적격 관계대명사 which의 생략
- 불완전절을 가지는 유사관계대명사 as

5 The marginalisation of <u>the poverty-stricken</u> is an issue (**which** remains relevant), although we can only hope [<u>that</u> (the modern middle and upper classes) would react to a modern Millet in a slightly more positive way than to see <u>it</u> as a call to revolution].

- [the + 형용사] = 셀 수 있는 복수명사 (the poverty-stricken: 가난한 사람들)
- although 양보절 내 타동사 hope의 목적어로 명사절 that이 위치함을 파악.
- it = a modern Millet

Voca Check

* 빈칸에 들어갈 적절한 단어를 박스에서 찾아 넣으시오.

1

stalk / undertake / hardships / be occupied with / till / champion / impoverished / identifiable / desperate / license / scour / or lack thereof

1 Overcoming personal _____ can build resilience and character in an individual.

2 The _____ conditions in the impoverished neighborhood called for immediate intervention.

3 The detective had to _____ through old case files to find a clue.

4 The majestic lion slowly moved through the savanna, its _____ blending with the tall grass.

5 You'll need a special _____ to drive a motorcycle legally.

6 In their _____ attempt to save their home, they tried every possible solution.

7 He decided to _____ the challenging task of climbing the highest mountain.

8 The suspect's distinctive tattoo made him easily _____ by the witnesses.

9 The quality of customer service, _____ was a significant concern, led to the company's decline.

10 She always seems to _____ her work, seldom taking a break.

11 Many people _____ personal growth as a lifelong journey of learning and self-improvement.

12 Farmers must carefully _____ the soil to prepare it for planting.

2

oversee / stack / diagonally / demonstrate / communal / sheave / recession / hierarchy / marginalize / workforce

1 The company's skilled _____ is the backbone of its success.

2 The CEO's responsibility is to _____ the operations of the entire organization.

3 During the economic _____ in 2008, many businesses struggled to stay afloat.

4 In the educational _____ of a school, the principal is at the top, followed by teachers, and then students.

5 The artist used vivid colors to _____ the beauty of the landscape.

6 The new policy seeks to _____ the voices of marginalized communities.

7 The workers carefully placed one box on top of another to create a stable _____.

8 The rope was threaded through the _____ to lift heavy objects.

9 She drew a line _____ across the page to create an interesting visual effect.

10 The concept of a _____ garden encourages neighbors to share and cultivate the land together.

3

disunity / jar against / bounty / pass over / pathos / homespun / recommence / bring on / connote / straggle / arduous / stiffness / a flock of / thankless / pathos

1 The _____ handwoven blankets provided a cozy warmth during the winter.

2   The _____ of the hiker's muscles after a long trek up the mountain was evident.

3   The _____ caused by the discord among team members hindered their progress.

4   Her kind actions came from the _____ of her heart, not expecting anything in return.

5   The speaker's words were filled with _____ as she shared a touching story.

6   The rugged terrain made the journey a(n _____ ordeal for the explorers.

7   The auctioneer explained that the word "vintage" can _____ the quality and age of a wine.

8   After a brief pause, the concert will _____ with a stunning musical performance.

9   The child's attempt to _____ his friends for a game of soccer gathered quite a crowd.

10 His decision to _____ the issue and not address it directly caused more confusion.

11 The actor's portrayal of the character evoked a strong sense of _____ in the audience.

12 The sailor noticed _____ seagulls in the distance.

13 The repetitive motion of the machine can _____ discomfort to the operator's hands.

14 Despite the _____ challenges, he continued his philanthropic work tirelessly.

15 The sudden noise _____ the quiet of the library, startling everyone present.

4

plight / abject / empathize / motif / turbulent / piety / vanishing / spirituality / tranquility / innocuous / poverty-stricken / upsetting / unveil

* 단 중복 사용되는 단어 있고, 필요시 형태를 변형할 것.

1   The artist chose the lotus flower as a recurring _____ in her paintings to symbolize purity and enlightenment.

2   In a time of _____ social change, the country struggled to find stability.

3   The new art exhibition will _____ the latest works by contemporary artists.

4   Her deep _____ led her to become a dedicated volunteer at the local charity.

5   It's difficult not to _____ with those who have faced such an _____ life.

6   The _____ conditions in the region were a source of concern for international aid organizations.

7   The _____ of the garden provided a space for reflection and inner _____.

8   The _____ of the magician left the audience in awe.

9   Despite its initial _____ appearance, the chemical reaction had significant consequences.

10 The president's new policy was _____ at the press conference.

11 The _____ news of the accident deeply affected the entire community.

12 Few of us can be unmoved by the _____ of the refugees.

13 The 1960s were a _____ decade, marked by significant social changes, political unrest, and numerous civil rights movements.

14 The Great Depression left millions of families in _____ poverty, struggling to survive amidst widespread unemployment and economic collapse.

Reading Comprehension

[1-4] **Read the passage and answer each question.**

 NOTE

In quite typical subject matter for Millet, this painting depicts one of the hardships of ㉠the impoverished which has, thankfully disappeared from modern life. Gleaning is the act of scouring the field for stalks of crop missed in the first harvesting. One needed a licence to be allowed to do this, and only the poorest, most desperate would undertake to obtain one. Thus the three main figures in the painting are immediately identifiable as of very low social status. (가)

It is the idea of their place in society, or lack thereof, which Millet seems to be occupied with in this piece. The piece was created while Millet was in Barbizon, and one of the leaders of the Barbizon School, which sought a return to Nature in art. For most members of the group this meant landscape painting, but Millet focused on figures within landscapes, almost as if portraying what had become Nature, as humans had ㉡tilled the earth for thousands of years. A champion of the rural working class in his paintings (he was not an overtly political figure in actions), he often depicts people working in the fields, such as in The Sower (1850) or The Angelus (1857-59). (나) The Gleaners however depicts women who have no place, or have through poverty lost their place, in society.

As we look into the painting, we are presented with a ©visualisation of the rural social hierarchy. The further back we recede into the picture depth, the higher the rank of the people depicted. At first we see the gleaners themselves, then behind them is the communal workforce, cutting and reaping the harvest. (다) Further back still they are overseen by a figure on horseback, with the large domestic buildings highlighting the figure. This was a time when owning a horse was still a major indicator of wealth: Benz did not create his automobile until the 1880s, and the gap between rich and poor had not reached a point at which it was ②unfeasible for the majority of people to own horses. (라) The low skyline of the piece, little more than half way up the canvas, emphasises this sense of recession, and of the distance between the gleaners and the rest of the community, a distance symbolic as well as physical. (마) Millets demonstrates to use how these people's poverty has lead them to being ⑥marginalised by society, and shut out from the support of the community.

Millet shows this through symbolic contrasts and parallels. The small sheaves that the women have gathered are contrasted diagonally with the huge stacks that the group have gathered. Nature's bounty as visualised by the stacks, with more further in the background, and more sheaves waiting to be piled, is pitifully contrasted with the small number of sheaves gathered by the gleaners, and the stalks in their hands. The women's clothes are homespun, heavy materials, the stiffness of the red cloth tied with a piece of rope around the woman's arm portrays a feeling of discomfort. The unity of the group, working together, all bending and lifting as one, is again contrasted with the three women, one of whom is almost standing straight, creating a sense of disunity, jarring against the shared pose of the other two women.

The standing woman's pose is almost torturous; she seems to have taken a pause, connoting the aching back brought on by this repetitive physical labour, but we do not see her at the point of relief, but as she returns to her work, recommencing the arduous, virtually thankless task. In the sky above, a flock of birds passes over, with stragglers falling behind, mimicking the figures down below. Thus Millet fills the painting with pathos, and as viewers it is hard not to empathise with the plight of these women. Even Millet's use of light suggests the women's struggle, as the sun shines down on the house and the group, whilst they are nearly in shadow, on the edge of darkness.

UNIT

4

1 Which of the following is <u>AWKWARD</u> to use in context?
① ㉠ the impoverished
② ㉡ tilled
③ ㉢ visualisation
④ ㉣ unfeasible
⑤ ㉤ marginalised

2 Where in the passage would be the best place for the sentence below?

> These are usually people who have found a place in society, they are part of the workforce.

① (가)   ② (나)
③ (다)   ④ (라)
⑤ (마)

3 Choose <u>TWO</u> that is <u>NOT</u> correct about the passage?

① Millet, through the way he has depicted the scene has represented the class structure of an urban community.

② Each woman is shown at various stages of their task. The woman furthest away has just straightened up, the middle woman is picking up the grain and the nearest woman is bending down to pick up the grain.

③ "Three women picking up the leftover" was traditionally part of the natural cycle of the agricultural calendar undertaken by the poor, and was regarded as a right to unwanted leftovers.

④ The act of gleaning is a back-breaking task for the poor and needy.

⑤ The difference in the social standing between the women and a landowner is highlighted by the large stacks of wheat in comparison to the scavenging women who just want food to live.

4 The following is an analysis of the work of the text. Which of the following is <u>AWKWARD</u> to use in context?

> This simple realism painting gave the audience an unusual solemnity. Millet generally use ①<u>horizontal</u> composition to make the figures appeared ②<u>monumental</u> in the ③<u>foreground</u>. The three main characters wore red, blue and yellow hat separately, so was their clothes, which attracted people's attention. Besides, their actions were calm and orderly, perhaps ④<u>prolonged</u> bending labor has made them feel very tired, but they were still sticking to it. Although the face was ⑤<u>protruding</u>, their movement and body became more expressive, that is tolerance, modesty and loyalty.

[5-8] Read the passage and answer each question.

UNIT

4

[A] In quite typical subject matter for Millet, this painting depicts one of the hardships of the impoverished which has, thankfully disappeared from modern life. Gleaning is the act of scouring the field for stalks of crop missed in the first harvesting. One needed a licence to be allowed to do this, and only the poorest, most desperate would undertake to obtain one. Thus the three main figures in the painting are immediately identifiable as of very low social status.

[B] It is the idea of their place in society, or lack thereof, which Millet seems to be occupied with in this piece. The piece was created while Millet was in Barbizon, and one of the leaders of the Barbizon School, which sought a return to Nature in art. For most members of the group this meant landscape painting, but Millet focused on figures within landscapes, almost as if portraying what had become Nature, as humans had tilled the earth for thousands of years. A champion of the rural working class in his paintings (he was not an overtly political figure in actions), he often depicts people working in the fields, such as in The Sower (1850) or The Angelus (1857-59), but these are usually people who have found a place in society, they are part of the workforce. The Gleaners however depicts women who have no place, or have through poverty lost their place, in society.

[C] As we look into the painting, we are presented with a visualisation of the rural social hierarchy. The further back we recede into the picture depth, the higher the rank of the people depicted. At first we see the gleaners themselves, then behind them is the communal workforce, cutting and reaping the harvest. Further back still they are overseen by a figure on horseback, with the large domestic buildings highlighting the figure. This was a time when owning a horse was still a major indicator of wealth: Benz did not create his automobile until the 1880s, and the gap between rich and poor had not reached a point at which it was viable for the majority of people to own horses. The low skyline of the piece, little more than half way up the canvas, emphasises this sense of recession, and of the distance between the gleaners and the rest of the community, a distance symbolic as well as physical. Millets demonstrates to use how these people's poverty has lead them to being marginalised by society, and shut out from the support of the community.

[D] Millet shows this through symbolic contrasts and parallels. The small sheaves that the women have gathered are contrasted diagonally with the huge stacks that the group have gathered. Nature's bounty as visualised by the stacks, with more further in the background, and more sheaves waiting to be piled, is pitifully contrasted with the small number of sheaves gathered by the gleaners, and the stalks in their hands. The women's clothes are homespun, heavy materials, the stiffness of the red cloth tied with a piece of rope around the woman's arm portrays a feeling of discomfort. The unity of the group, working together, all bending and lifting as one, is again contrasted with the three women, one of whom is almost standing straight, creating a sense of disunity, jarring against the shared pose of the other two women.

[E] The standing woman's pose is almost torturous; she seems to have taken a pause, connoting the aching back brought on by this repetitive physical labour, but we do not see her at the point of relief, but as she returns to her work, recommencing the arduous, virtually thankless task. In the sky above, a flock of birds passes over, with stragglers falling behind, mimicking the figures down below. Thus Millet fills the painting with pathos, and as viewers it is hard not to empathise with the plight of these women. Even Millet's use of light suggests the women's struggle, as the sun shines down on the house and the group, whilst they are nearly in shadow, on the edge of darkness.

5 The passage is about The Gleaners by Millet. Select all of the following that are not appropriate for what is covered in each paragraph.

① [A] The main figures and the meaning of their actions and status in society.
② [B] The writers who inspired Millet to create The Gleaners.
③ [C] How Millet depicts the existence of the urban social hierarchy.
④ [D] How Millet represents the marginalization of the poor.
⑤ [E] How Millet elicits sympathy from viewers for the three women.

* elicit: to call forth or draw out (something, such as information or a response)

6 Choose <u>TWO</u> interpretations that are <u>LEAST</u> consistent with the analysis of the painting.

① The task the three women was involved in was backbreaking.
② The contrast between abundance and scarcity, and between light and shadow, is cleverly used by Millet to emphasize the class divide.
③ For Millet, pure landscape was of the upmost important.
④ The three women, bent and toiling in the darkened foreground, are set against a warm pastoral background scene of harvesters.
⑤ The remoteness of the landlord class is "toned down" by the blurry image of the landlord's foreman, sitting on a horse in the remote distance.

7 Which of the following can be inferred from the passage?

> The Gleaner's was first unveiled at the Salon of 1857. While the painting may seem fairly innocuous to modern viewers, its focus on the lives of peasants and the working classes was seen as politically threatening by the middle and upper class audience who saw it at the Salon. The latest of France's revolutions was only in 1848, when in February the Orlean monarchy was overthrown only to be replaced by an increasingly conservative government in the Republic, which lead to a bloody revolt in June 1848, and the eventual election of Louis Napoleon as President (who would become Napoleon III, leader of the Second French Empire). After this turbulent recent history one can understand a certain sensitivity amongst parts of society to subjects which seemed to glorify the peasant classes.

① When The Gleaners was first released, the viewers were mostly working-class people.

② A series of revolutions that occurred in France in the early 1800s resulted in most painters focusing on works with a strong political orientation.

③ Millet tried to openly criticize the deep-rooted political corruption in French society through The Gleaners.

④ The painting's focus on the lowest ranks of rural society attracted considerable opposition from the upper classes.

⑤ The ruling class tried to further consolidate its political foundation by making use of Millet, who had drawn full support from the workers.

* consolidate: make (something) physically stronger or more solid

8 The following is an analysis of Millet's work on The Gleaners. Which of the underlined parts in context is the most AWKWARD?

①The entire composition is in fact a commentary on the social classes of France and, in particular, on the inability of the lower classes to rise above their station. ②The three women are shown bent over, so they do not pierce the horizon, confirming that what we are born into is where we stay. ③Meanwhile, the uppermost line of ground is occupied by peasant farmers watched over by the foreman, some of whom break the horizon, too. ④The sky symbolizes the unattainable upper class of society that looks down on its inferiors. ⑤It is as different from the other people as air is to earth.

🎗 NOTE

[A] Millet paid close attention to its composition, using every device to Ⓐ<u>imbue</u> his subjects with a simple but monumental grandeur. The angled light of the setting sun accentuates the Ⓑ<u>sculptural</u> quality of the gleaners, while their set expressions and thick, heavy features tend to Ⓒ<u>emphasize</u> the burdensome nature of their work. Furthermore, these figures, bent double and toiling in the darkened foreground, are set against a warm pastoral background scene of harvesters - with their haystacks, cart and sheaves of wheat - reaping a rich harvest in the corn fields. The contrast between abundance and Ⓓ<u>scarcity</u>, and between light and shadow, is cleverly used by Millet to emphasize the class divide. And the remoteness of the landlord class is also highlighted by the Ⓔ<u>telling</u> image of the landlord's foreman, sitting on a horse in the remote distance.

[B] The entire composition is in fact a commentary on the social classes of France and, in particular, on the inability of the lower classes to rise above their station. The three women are shown bent over, so they do not pierce the horizon, confirming that what we are born into is where we stay. Meanwhile, the uppermost line of ground is occupied by peasant farmers watched over by the foreman, none of whom break the horizon either. _____. It is as different from the other people as <u>air is to earth</u>.

9 문단 [A]의 밑줄 친 단어 Ⓐ~Ⓔ 중 쓰임이 <u>어색한</u> 것은?

① Ⓐ imbue

② Ⓑ sculptural

③ Ⓒ emphasize

④ Ⓓ scarcity

⑤ Ⓔ telling

10 문단 [B]의 빈칸에 들어갈 표현으로 가장 적절한 것은?

① The composition serves as a reminder of the beauty of rural life

② The horizon symbolizes the limitless possibilities of the lower classes

③ The sky symbolizes the unattainable upper class of society that looks down on its inferiors

④ The composition suggests that social mobility is easily achievable

⑤ The lower classes are content with their station in life

11 문단 [B]의 밑줄 친 표현 air is to earth를 언급한 목적으로 가장 적절한 것은?

① To highlight the vastness of the sky

② To emphasize the importance of the lower classes

③ To suggest that the upper class is deeply connected to the lower classes

④ To show the physical limitations of social mobility

⑤ To indicate that the upper class remains grounded in reality

5 Sentence Completion

1 We were all appalled at their attempt to _____ the reputation of the chancellor; a simple, civil protest would have been much more effective.

① fortify ② putrefy
③ equalize ④ empower
⑤ support

> **어휘**
> appall ~을 오싹 소름이 끼치게 하다, 섬뜩하게 하다 attempt 시도 reputation 명성, 명예 (= prestige) chancellor 수상, 학장 simple 단순한, 정직한 civil 시민의, 정중한 protest 항의 effective 효과적인 fortify 강화하다, 요새화하다 putrefy ~을 부패시키다 equalize 같게 하다, 평등하게 하다 empower ~에게 권력을 주다 support 지지하다, 지원하다

UNIT
4

2 The boss took decisive _____ to curb employee theft.

① ways ② devices
③ investment ④ measures

> **어휘**
> decisive 결정적인, 단호한 curb 억제하다, 구속하다 employee 직원 theft 도둑질 take ~ measure ~한 조치를 취하다 way 길; 방법 device 고안, 장치 investment 투자

3 A writer may use a(n) _____ to provide additional information about what happens to the characters after the end of the story.

① prologue ② epilogue
③ suffix ④ finale

> **어휘**
> writer 작가 use 이용(사용)하다 provide ~을 제공하다 additional 부가적인, 추가적인 information 정보 happen 일어나다, 발생하다 character 인물; 문자; 특성 prologue 머리말 epilogue 끝맺음(말) suffix 접미사 finale 피날레, 끝악장

4 His _____ attempts to _____ the reporter's questions about his inability to balance the city's budget proved effective because he was able to divert attention from fiscal matters to that of the local circus.

① guile – succumb to   ② lofty – entice   ③ dumb-founded – address
④ circuitous – dodge   ⑤ lithe – dismantle

어휘 attempt 시도 reporter 기자 question 질문 inability 무능력 balance ~의 균형을 잡다, 상쇄하다 budget 예산 prove (+보어) ~로 판명되다 effective 효과적인 divert (주의, 관심)을/를 딴 곳으로 돌리다 attention 주의, 관심 from A to B A에서 B로(B까지) fiscal 재정의, 회계의 matter 문제, 물질; 중요하다 local 그 지역의, 지방의 circus 서커스, 곡예 guile 교활 succumb to ~에 굴복하다 lofty 고상한; 거만한 entice 유혹하다, 부추기다 dumb-found ~을 놀래키다, ~을 아연실색하게 하다 address 주소, 연설; ~을 잘 다루다, 처리하다 circuitous 에두르는, 완곡한 dodge 피하다 lithe 유연한, 나긋나긋한 dismantle ~을 제거하다, 부수다

5 The _____ of North Koreans to study foreign languages and the tourism business is an indication of how capitalism is being infused into their way of thinking.

① detachment   ② aspiration   ③ aversion
④ diffidence   ⑤ abomination

어휘 study ~을 연구하다, 공부하다 foreign language 외국어 tourism business 관광사업 indication 표시, 징후 capitalism 자본주의 infuse A into B A를 B에 주입하다, 불어넣다 way of thinking 사고 방식 detachment 초연함, 분리 aspiration 열망 aversion 혐오, 반감 diffidence 자신 없음, 망설임 abomination 혐오

6 In her book, Lisa Davis exposes the way in which discrimination based on accent functions to support and _____ unequal social structures.

① perpetuate   ② suppress
③ disfavor   ④ ridicule

어휘 expose ~을 노출시키다, 폭로하다 discrimination 차별, 구별 be based on ~에 근거한 accent 강세, 억양 function 작용하다 support 지지하다, 지원하다 unequal 불평등한 social structure 사회구조 perpetuate ~을 영속화시키다 suppress ~을 억압하다, (감정을) 참다, (출판을) 금지시키다 disfavor ~을 싫어하다, 냉대하다 ridicule ~을 조롱하다

7 Philosophers assume that the _____ of wisdom is natural endowment of the human being. Potentially every man has an intense _____ to fathom the mysteries of existence.

① love – longing   ② development – doubt

③ poverty – inclination   ④ pursuit – perversity

> **어휘**
>
> philosopher 철학자 assume 가정하다, 생각하다; ~의 모습을 띄다; ~를 떠맡다; ~을 횡령하다 wisdom 지혜 natural 자연의, 타고난 자연스러운 endowment 기증; 타고난 재능, 천부의 재주 human being 인간 potentially 잠재적으로 intense 강렬한 fathom 이해하다, 헤아리다 mystery 신비, 불가사의 existence 존재 longing 열망, 갈망 doubt 의심 poverty 가난, 결핍 inclination 경향, 좋아함 pursuit 추구 perversity 외고집, 제멋대로임

8 Julius Caesar conferred citizenship on all who practiced medicine at Rome to make them more _____ of living in the city.

① desirous   ② aversive

③ inimical   ④ congenial

> **어휘**
>
> confer A on B B에게 A를 수여하다 practice medicine 의술을 실행하다 desirous 소망하는 aversive 기피하는 inimical 적의가 있는, 형편이 나쁜 congenial 동질의, 기분 좋은, 적합한

9 The changes provide an opportunity for the prime minister to _____ public esteem.

① undermine   ② recapture

③ incarcerate   ④ subvert

> **어휘**
>
> prime minister 수상 public 국민의 esteem 존중 undermine 해치다, ~의 밑을 파다 recapture 되찾다 incarcerate 투옥하다, 감금하다 subvert 전복시키다, 멸망시키다

10 Scientists' pristine reputation as devotees of the disinterested pursuit of the truth has been ＿＿＿＿＿ by recent evidence that some scientists have deliberately ＿＿＿＿ experimental results to further their own careers.

① reinforced – published

② validated – suppressed

③ exterminated – replicated

④ compromised – fabricated

⑤ resuscitated – challenged

어휘 pristine 본래의, 소박한, 초기의 reputation 명성 devotee 헌신자 disinterested 사심이 없는 pursuit 추구 deliberately 의도적으로 further 증진시키다, 돕다, 장려하다 reinforce 강화하다 validate 정당성을 입증하다, 비준하다 suppress 억압하다, 삭제하다 exterminate 근절하다 replicate 복제하다 compromise 타협하다, 더럽히다, 손상시키다 fabricate 만들다, 꾸며내다 resuscitate 소생시키다 challenge 도전하다, 신실/정당성을 의심하다

비문학_생물학

Energy Requirement and Shape

1 Voca Master

☐ **warm-blooded** **a** Having a relatively constant body temperature independent of the external environment

- Birds and mammals are <u>warm-blooded</u> animals, maintaining a relatively constant body temperature regardless of the weather.

☐ **constant** **a** Unchanging or consistent; remaining the same over time

- His unwavering dedication to his work was evident in his <u>constant</u> pursuit of excellence.

☐ **internal** **a** Located or occurring inside; inner

- The company's <u>internal</u> policies and procedures are not always visible to the public.

☐ **given** **a** Accepted or acknowledged as a fact; specified or fixed

- <u>Given</u> the current circumstances, we have no choice but to postpone the event.

☐ **retention** **n** The act of keeping or storing something

- The <u>retention</u> of important documents and records is crucial for the organization's compliance with regulations.

☐ **adapt to** To adjust or change in response to new conditions or circumstances

- In order to survive in the desert, camels have evolved to <u>adapt to</u> extreme heat and limited water sources.

☐ **dissipation** **n** The act of dispersing or wasting energy, resources, or effort

- The reckless <u>dissipation</u> of the family fortune led to financial ruin.

☐ limb   **n** An arm or leg of a person or an animal

- He injured his <u>limb</u> during the soccer match and had to be taken to the hospital for treatment.

☐ profile   **n** An outline or representation of a person's face or figure

- The artist carefully sketched the <u>profile</u> of the model's face, capturing every detail.

☐ linear   **a** Arranged in or extending along a straight or nearly straight line

- The path through the dense forest was <u>linear</u>, with no turns or deviations along the way.

☐ conceive   **v** To form or develop an idea, plan, or thought in one's mind

- She <u>conceived</u> a brilliant strategy to improve the company's efficiency.

☐ hump   **n** A rounded, raised mass or lump, often on the back of an animal

- The camel's <u>hump</u> stores fat and helps it survive in arid regions.

☐ protrude   **v** To stick out or extend beyond the usual or normal level or surface

- The tree's roots <u>protruded</u> from the ground, making it difficult to walk in that area.

☐ all too   Used to emphasize that something is more extreme or excessive than desired

- It was <u>all too</u> clear that the project was not going as planned.

☐ coarse   **a** Rough or harsh in texture or quality; lacking refinement

- The <u>coarse</u> sandpaper was used to smooth the rough surface of the wood.

UNIT

5

☐ **rhombic**

a Shaped like a rhombus, which is a quadrilateral with all sides of equal length but not necessarily right angles

- The crystal had a <u>rhombic</u> shape, reflecting its unique geometry.

☐ **stubby**

a Short and thick in a way that appears strong or sturdy

- The bulldog had a <u>stubby</u> tail and legs, giving it a distinctive appearance.

2 Text Reading

: Energy Requirement and Shape

One interesting fact is that man Ⓐhas literally been shaped by his energy requirements. We are warm-blooded animals. Such creatures must maintain a constant internal temperature, and they do this by control of their body's surface-to-volume ratio. Thus for a given species you would have in the colder areas large creatures with a large volume to surface area to maximize energy retention and in the warmer areas you would have smaller creatures with a larger surface area to volume in order to aid heat dissipation. For example, the arctic polar bear is large while the southern brown bear is smaller. In humans, populations Ⓑwho have adapted to live in extreme cold like the Inuits, tend towards high body mass index scores Ⓒwhile also having shorter limbs, giving their bodies a relatively more stubbier profile. Whereas, in the desert regions Ⓓwhich it is hot and dry you find populations with Ⓔ what we might term it as having more "linear" bodies—meaning, on the whole, they are relatively tall and thin, with a lot of surface area to volume. For much the same reasons, camels are relatively linear. We can Ⓕconceive of their humps as being an evolutionary compromise between the need to dissipate heat and the need to store fat. By protruding away from its center of their mass, the camel's tall twin humps preserve most of its linearity and large surface-to-volume ratio while providing a place to store energy for all-too-common desert food shortages.

1 본문의 내용과 일치하는 것만 바르게 짝지은 것은?

> I. The way living creatures' adapt to different climates demonstrates how nature has tailored them to thrive in specific climates through evolutionary processes.
> II. The Inuits, who have adapted to living in extreme cold environments tend to have lower body mass index (BMI) scores and shorter limbs, resulting in a more robust or "stubbier" body shape.
> III. The reference to camels and their humps exemplifies how efficiently and promptly animals in deserts use heat dissipation to maximize the energy storage.
> IV. It can be inferred from the passage that the diversity of life on Earth is a product of the ongoing struggle to balance energy requirements with the challenges posed by various climates and environments.

① I and III   ② II and IV
③ I, II and III   ④ II, III and IV
⑤ I and IV

2 Among Ⓐ~Ⓕ, choose the number of things that are grammatically INCORRECT.

① 0   ② 1   ③ 2   ④ 3   ⑤ 4

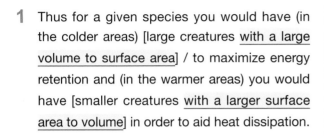

1 Thus for a given species you would have (in the colder areas) [large creatures <u>with a large volume to surface area</u>] / to maximize energy retention and (in the warmer areas) you would have [smaller creatures <u>with a larger surface area to volume</u>] in order to aid heat dissipation.

- 장소부사구와 명사를 수식하는 전치사구의 구조 파악.

2 In humans, [populations (<u>who</u> have adapted to living in extreme cold like the Inuits)] tend towards high body mass index scores [<u>while also having shorter limbs, giving their bodies a relatively more stubbier profile</u>].

- 주격 관계대명사의 수식을 받아 길어진 주어 파악.
- 분사구문
  while also having shorter limbs, giving their bodies a relatively more stubbier profile
  = while **they also have** shorter limbs, giving their bodies a relatively more stubbier profile

3 Whereas, (in the desert regions Ⓐ<u>where</u> it is hot and dry) you / find / [populations <u>with</u> (Ⓑ <u>what</u> we might term as having more "linear" bodies)]—meaning, on the whole, they are relatively tall and thin, with a lot of surface area to volume.

- Ⓐ 관계부사 where
  Ⓑ 관계대명사 what

4 We can <u>conceive of</u> their humps <u>as</u> being an evolutionary compromise between (the need <u>to dissipate</u> heat) and (the need <u>to store</u> fat).

- conceive of A as B: A를 B로 생각하다
- the need를 수식하는 to부정사의 형용사 용법

5 By protruding away from its center of their mass, the camel's tall twin humps / preserve / most of its linearity and large surface-to-volume ratio [<u>while providing a place to store energy for all-too-common desert food shortages</u>].

- 분사구문
  while providing a place to store energy for all-too-common desert food shortages
  = while **they**(= the camel's tall twin humps) **provide** a place to store energy for all-too-common desert food shortages

Voca Check

---

1 우리말을 참고하여 괄호 안의 단어를 바르게 배열하시오.

1 한 가지 흥미로운 관찰은 인간이 에너지 요구량에 따라 물리적으로 형성되었다는 것입니다.

→ One intriguing observation is that (shaped / physically / their energy requirements / human beings / by / been / have).

2 온혈동물인 우리는 몸의 표면적과 부피의 비율을 조절하여 일정한 내부 체온을 유지해야 합니다.

→ (creatures / being / warm-blooded), we must maintain a consistent internal body temperature, (we / ratio / our body's surface area to its volume / controlling / by / of / the / achieve / which).

3 반대로, 뜨겁고 건조한 사막 지역의 개체군은 우리가 더 "가느다란" 신체라고 설명할 수 있는 경향이 있습니다. 즉, 일반적으로 키가 더 크고 날씬하며 체적에 비해 표면적이 더 넓다는 의미입니다.

→ Conversely, in hot and arid desert regions, populations ("slender" / more / have / to / bodies / might / as / we / what / describe / tend), meaning they are generally taller and leaner, with a greater surface area relative to their volume.

4 낙타도 비슷한 이유로 상대적으로 날씬한 몸매를 보입니다.

→ Camels, for similar reasons, also (slender / shape / body / a / relatively / exhibit).

5 우리는 낙타의 두 혹을 열을 발산할 필요성과 지방을 저장해야 할 필요성 사이의 진화적 절충안으로 개념화할 수 있습니다.

→ We can conceptualize the two humps of the camel (the / need / an / heat / compromise / to / and / as / between / dissipate / store / the / evolutionary / need / fat / to).

2 빈칸에 들어갈 적절한 단어를 박스에서 찾아 넣으시오.

conceive / adapt to / protrude / coarse / internal / constant / retention / given / linear / warm-blooded / limb / hump / dissipation / profile

1 Many mammals are _____ creatures, maintaining a relatively constant body temperature.

2 His _____ dedication to his studies resulted in excellent academic performance.

3 The _____ organs play a crucial role in maintaining the body's equilibrium.

4 _____ the circumstances, she remained calm and composed.

5 The _____ of knowledge is essential for long-term success in education.

6 Animals have the ability to _____ their environment through evolutionary changes.

7 The _____ of energy in the form of heat is often a consequence of inefficient processes.

8 The doctor examined the patient's injured _____ to assess the extent of the damage.

9 The criminal investigator created a _____ of the suspect to aid in the search.

10 The scientist discovered that the crystals had a _____ shape with equal sides and angles.

11 She struggled to _____ a plan to improve her company's productivity.

12 The _____ of the camel is a distinct feature of its anatomy.

13 A small hill began to _____ from the desert landscape.

14 The fabric felt rough and _____ against her skin.

[1-5] Read the passage and answer each question.

NOTE

One interesting fact is that man has literally been shaped by his energy requirements. We are warm-blooded animals. Such creatures must maintain a constant internal temperature, and they do this by control of their body's surface-to-volume ratio. Thus for a given species you would have in the colder areas large creatures with a large volume to surface area to maximize energy retention and in the warmer areas you would have smaller creatures with a larger surface area to volume in order to aid heat dissipation. For example, the arctic polar bear is large while the southern brown bear is smaller. In humans, populations who have adapted to living in extreme cold like the Inuits, tend towards high body mass index scores while also having shorter limbs, giving their bodies a relatively more _____ profile. Whereas, in the desert regions where it is hot and dry you find populations with what we might term as having more "linear" bodies—meaning, on the whole, they are relatively tall and thin, with a lot of surface area to volume. For much the same reasons, camels are relatively linear. We can conceive of their humps as being an evolutionary compromise between the need to dissipate heat and the need to store fat. By protruding away from its center of their mass, the camel's tall twin humps preserve most of <u>its linearity</u> and large surface-to-volume ratio while providing a place to store energy for all-too-common desert food shortages.

1 Which of the following DIFFERS from the rest in terms of human evolution based on the passage?

① Human evolution and physical characteristics have been influenced by the energy needs of our species.

② Human evolution is not a random process but is instead driven by the necessity to meet the energy demands.

③ Our physical attributes have adapted over time to optimize energy management.

④ Human physical characteristics have evolved to facilitate the thermoregulation process of maintaining a constant internal temperature.

⑤ Warm-blooded animals like humans have evolved an "immune" system that is unaffected by the external environment.

2 Choose the one that best fills in the blank.

① coarse   ② rectangular
③ rhombic   ④ stubbier

3 Choose the option that contains all the CORRECT statements.

I.   The physical traits of animals are highly adaptable to their specific environments, ensuring their survival by either conserving or shedding heat depending on the climate they inhabit.

II. Even within the same family or species, variations in size and body shape can occur due to adaptations to specific climates.

III. Human populations in warmer regions have developed physical characteristics such as higher body mass index (BMI) and shorter limbs to adapt to their environment.

IV. Camels are relatively linear with a large volume to surface area.

① I and II
② II and III
③ I, II and III
④ I and IV
⑤ I, II and IV

4 Based on the passage, which of the following best explains the contextual meaning of camels' linearity in the underline phrase "its linearity"?

① Camels are relatively flat and wide-bodied.

② Camels have a relatively straight and narrow physical structure.

③ Camels have a circular body shape.

④ Camels have a hunched and rounded back.

⑤ Camels have a bulky and stocky appearance.

5 What is the main idea of the passage?

① Warm-blooded species are more suited to hotter climates.

② Camels store water in their humps in case of extreme drought.

③ A body's surface-to-volume ratio can fluctuate based on the current temperature.

④ The need for temperature control plays a large role in determining body shape.

⑤ Populations living in extreme cold, like the Inuits, tend to have longer limbs for better heat retention.

1 Though it would be _____ to expect Barnard to have worked out all of the limitations of his experiment, he must be _____ for his neglect of quantitative analysis.

① unjust – pardoned

② impudent – dismissed

③ unrealistic – criticized

④ pointless – examined

⑤ inexcusable – recognized

> **어휘**
> work out 해결하다 quantitative 양적인, 양에 기초를 둔 analysis 분석 unjust 부당한 pardon 용서하다 impudent 뻔뻔스러운 dismiss 해산하다, 해고하다 unrealistic 비현실적인 criticize 비판하다 pointless 무의미한 inexcusable 변명할 도리가 없는, 용서할 수 없는

2 Although Tom was aware that it would be _____ to display annoyance publicly at the sales conference, he could not _____ his irritation with the client's unreasonable demands.

① inadvisable – evince

② efficacious – suppress

③ pragmatic – counter

④ captious – express

⑤ impolitic – hide

> **어휘**
> be aware that S V ~라는 점을 인식하다 display 드러내다 annoyance 성가심, 짜증 irritation 성가심 unreasonable 말도 안 되는 demand 요구 inadvisable 권할 수 없는, 어리석은 evince 명시하다, 나타내다 efficacious 효과 있는, 효능이 잘 드는 suppress 억누르다 (= quell, subdue) pragmatic 실용적인 (= utilitarian) counter 반대하다 captious 흠잡기 잘하는, 짓궂은 impolitic 지각없는, 졸렬한

3 Candidates who oppose the present state income tax must be able to propose _____ ways to _____ the financing of state operations.

① intelligent – initiate

② individual – diversify

③ innovative – alleviate

④ arbitrary – maintain

⑤ alternate – continue

4 He felt it would be _____, in view of the intense _____ that would likely follow, to make the sacrifice required in order to gain such little advantage.

① charitable – growth

② welcomed – prejudice

③ futile – encouragement

④ academic – acclaim

⑤ unrealistic – turmoil

5 Although the fire also shocked him, Michael downplayed it to _____ his apprehensive friend.

① weaken   ② mollify

③ provoke   ④ root

UNIT

5

6 I am not attracted by the _____ life of the _____, always wandering through the countryside, begging for charity.

① proud – almsgiver

② noble – philanthropist

③ urban – hobo

④ natural – philosopher

⑤ peripatetic – vagabond

어휘
attract ~을 매혹하다, 끌어당기다 be attracted by ~에 의해 매혹당하다 wander 어슬렁거리다, 방랑하다 through ~을 통하여, ~사이를(여기저기) countryside 시골, 지방 beg (먹고 입을 것·돈·허가·은혜 따위를) 빌다, 구하다, 청하다 charity 자애, 자비, 자선 proud 오만한, 자랑으로 여기는 almsgiver 자선가 alms 자선품, 자선(행위) noble 귀족의, 고귀한 philanthropist 박애주의자 urban 도시의, 세련된 hobo 방랑자, 부랑자 natural 자연의, 타고난, 자연스러운 philosopher 철학자 peripatetic 돌아다니는, 순회하는 vagabond 부랑자, 방랑자

7 _____ longings and search for the elusive grounds of all things are _____ themes of nineteenth-and twentieth-century German literature.

① Obscure – pervasive

② Desperate – reluctant

③ Indignant – constant

④ Delicate – peaceful

⑤ Embarrassing – mobilizing

어휘
longing 동경, 갈망 search 조사, 탐색, 추구 elusive 애매한, 모호한, 파악하기 힘든 ground 땅; 기초, 근거, 이유; 외출(출장)을 금지시키다, 비행을 금지하다 thing 사물, 것 theme 주제 century 1 세기, 백년 literature 문학, 문헌 obscure 불명료한, 애매한 pervasive 널리 미치는, 충만하는 desperate 필사적인; 절망적인, 자포자기의 reluctant 마음이 내키지 않는, 꺼리는 indignant 분개한, 성난 constant 일정한, 변치 않는 delicate 섬세한, 미묘한, 가냘픈 peaceful 평화로운, 평온한 embarrassing 당혹케 하는 mobilizing 동원하는, 유통시키는

8 As a result of his bitter _____ towards his adversaries, he _____ to have their campaign funds stolen so that they could not continue with their campaigns.

① loyalty – decided   ② devotion – testified

③ resentment – plotted   ④ hatred – enumerated

⑤ love – planned

어휘 : as a result of ~의 결과로 bitter 쓰라린, 신랄한 toward ~을 향한 adversary 적, 상대 campaign 운동, 군사 행동, 선거 운동 fund 기금, 자금 stolen [steal의 과거분사] 훔쳐진 so that ~하기 위하여 continue 계속하다, 지속하다 loyalty 충성 decide 결심하다, 결정하다 devotion 헌신, 전념 testify 증명하다, 입증하다 resentment 분개, 분노 plot 음모, 계획; 줄거리; 작은 땅; 구성하다, 계획하다, 꾀하다 hatred 증오, 원한 enumerate 열거하다 plan ~을 계획하다

9 Scientists at the pharmaceutical company are currently working on the _____ of new substances that may help bring relief to sufferers of rheumatoid arthritis.

① recovery and digression   ② discovery and development

③ invention and prevention   ④ procurement and fermentation

어휘 : pharmaceutical 제약의, 조제의, (제)약학의 company 회사; 동료 currently 현재, 널리 work 일하다, 작동하다 substance 물질, 실질, 요지 bring A to B A를 B에게 가지고 오다 relief 경감, 안심 suffer (고통·변화 따위를) 겪다 sufferer 환자 rheumatoid arthritis 류머티스성 관절염 recovery 회복 digression 탈선, 벗어남 discovery 발견 development 발전, 발달, 개발 invention 발명; 날조 prevention 예방, 방지 procurement 획득, 조달 fermentatioin 발효; 동요, 소동

10 The ballet company demonstrated its _____ by putting both classical and modern works in the repertoire.

① versatility   ② mollification

③ treachery   ④ dignity

어휘 : ballet company 발레단 demonstrate ~을 증명(논증)하다; 시위운동을 하다 by ~ing ~함으로써 put 놓다, 두다; (말로) 표현하다 both 둘 다의 classical 고전적인; 표준(모범)적인 modern 현대적인, 세련된 work 작품 repertoire 레퍼토리, 상연(연주) 목록 versatility 다재다능함 mollification 완화, 경감 treachery 배반, 반역 dignity 존엄, 숭고함

UNIT 6

비문학_고전연설

Blood, Sweat, and Tears
by Winston Churchill

AI그림 달의이성

Voca Master

☐ **invade**

v To enter a country or region by force with the intent of conquest or occupation

- The enemy forces attempted to <u>invade</u> the neighboring country.

☐ **declare war on**

To officially announce that a state of war exists between one's own country and another

- The nation decided to <u>declare war on</u> its aggressor in response to the invasion.

☐ **manufacture**

v To produce goods on a large scale, typically in a factory or industrial setting

- The company plans to <u>manufacture</u> a new line of smartphones.

☐ **overrun**

v To invade and occupy a place in large numbers, overwhelming its defenses

- The enemy forces managed to <u>overrun</u> the border town in a matter of hours.

☐ **give a speech**

To deliver a formal address or presentation to an audience

- The president will <u>give a speech</u> addressing the nation's current economic situation.

☐ **newly elected**

a Referring to individuals who have recently been chosen or appointed to a position through an election

- The <u>newly elected</u> mayor promised to bring positive changes to the city.

☐ **oppose**

v To be against or in disagreement with something or someone

- Many citizens <u>oppose</u> the proposed changes to the healthcare system.

☐ **the Houses of Parliament**

The two houses of the United Kingdom's legislative body, consisting of the House of Commons and the House of Lords

- The Houses of Parliament play a crucial role in the country's governance.

☐ **meet**

v To confront or face a challenge, difficulty, or problem

- The team had to meet the unexpected obstacles head-on.

☐ **the House of Commons**

The lower house of the United Kingdom's Parliament, consisting of elected Members of Parliament (MPs)

- The House of Commons debates and passes legislation.

☐ **His Majesty**

A formal title used to address a reigning king

- His Majesty the King addressed the nation in a televised speech.

☐ **commission**

n An official task, duty, or responsibility assigned to a person or group

- The government formed a commission to investigate the issue.

☐ **evident**

a Clearly visible or easily perceived; obvious

- The effects of climate change are becoming increasingly evident.

☐ **will**

n A person's intent or determination to do something

- With a strong will, she overcame many obstacles in her life.

☐ **Administration**

n The governing body responsible for managing a country, organization, or institution

- The current Administration has proposed several policy changes.

UNIT

6

parties of the Opposition

Political parties that are not in power and typically oppose the policies of the ruling party

- The parties of the Opposition criticized the government's budget proposal.

conceive

v To form an idea, plan, or concept in one's mind; to become pregnant

- The inventor conceived the idea for the new technology.

war cabinet

A committee formed by a government during wartime to efficiently manage military affairs and strategic decisions

- The war cabinet met regularly to discuss the progress of the conflict.

represent

v To act or speak on behalf of a person, group, or entity

- The ambassador was chosen to represent her country at the international summit.

high executive office

A position of high authority and responsibility within an organization or government

- The CEO holds a high executive office in the company.

Fighting Services

Military units or branches responsible for combat operations

- The Fighting Services played a crucial role in defending the nation.

on account of

Because of; due to

- The event was canceled on account of bad weather.

urgency

n The state of being urgent or requiring immediate attention

- The urgency of the situation called for swift action.

rigor

n Extreme severity or harshness

- The rigor of the training program pushed the athletes to their limits.

☐ submit

v To present or deliver a document, proposal, or application for consideration

- He had to <u>submit</u> his research paper by the deadline.

☐ appointment

n The act of officially assigning someone to a particular position or role

- Her <u>appointment</u> as the company's new CEO was announced.

☐ in all respects

In every way; considering all aspects or factors

- The new policy was evaluated and found to be beneficial <u>in all respects</u>.

☐ in the public interest

In a way that benefits or serves the welfare of the general public

- The decision to reduce pollution was made <u>in the public interest</u>.

☐ summon

v To officially call or order someone to appear, often before a court or authority

- The judge will <u>summon</u> the witnesses to testify in the trial.

☐ in accordance with

In agreement or compliance with a particular rule, law, or guideline

- The project was completed <u>in accordance with</u> the established specifications.

☐ confer A upon B

To grant or bestow a particular honor, title, or responsibility to someone

- The university decided to <u>confer</u> an honorary degree <u>upon</u> the distinguished professor.

☐ Mr. Speaker

A title used to address the presiding officer in a legislative assembly, often the Speaker of the House of Commons in the UK

- <u>Mr. Speaker</u> called the session to order.

☐ **the Resolution of the House**
A formal decision or statement adopted by a legislative body, such as the House of Commons

- Members of Parliament debated and passed <u>the Resolution of the House</u>.

☐ **proceeding**
n A formal event or process, especially in a legal or legislative context; also refers to the minutes or records of such events

- The <u>proceedings</u> of the trial were recorded for review.

☐ **adjournment**
n The act of suspending or postponing a meeting, session, or gathering to a later time

- After a long and intense debate, the chairman called for an <u>adjournment</u> of the meeting, allowing the participants to take a brief break and gather their thoughts.

☐ **provision**
n The act of preparing or planning for future needs; a clause or condition in a document or agreement

- The <u>provision</u> of emergency supplies was essential during the disaster.

☐ **if need be**
If it is necessary or required

- We will work overtime <u>if need be</u> to meet the deadline.

☐ **notify**
v To inform or give notice to someone about something

- Please <u>notify</u> the team about the change in schedule.

☐ **at the earliest opportunity**
As soon as possible; without unnecessary delay

- The report will be reviewed <u>at the earliest opportunity</u>.

☐ **stand**
v To be valid or effective

- The contract is still <u>standing</u>, and its terms are binding.

☐ **approval**
n The act of officially agreeing to or accepting something, often after evaluation or consideration

- The board granted <u>approval</u> for the new project.

☐ **undertaking**　**n** ① A task, project, or enterprise, often of some difficulty or magnitude ② The act of taking on a responsibility or commitment

- The construction of the new bridge is a significant <u>undertaking</u> for the city.

☐ **preliminary**　**a** Pertaining to something done as a preparation or initial step before the main action or event

- The team conducted a <u>preliminary</u> investigation before launching the full inquiry.

☐ **in action**　Engaged in an operation or activity, especially a military or combat operation

- The soldiers were <u>in action</u> on the front lines.

☐ **the Mediterranean**　**n** A large sea located between Southern Europe, North Africa, and Western Asia

- Many tourists enjoy sailing in <u>the Mediterranean</u> during the summer.

☐ **here at home**　In one's own country or place of residence

- The company is expanding its operations <u>here at home</u>.

☐ **pardon**　**v** To forgive or excuse someone for an offense or wrongdoing; to grant clemency

- The president decided to <u>pardon</u> the political prisoners.

☐ **make allowance for**　To consider and accommodate specific factors or circumstances

- You should <u>make allowance for</u> possible delays in your travel plans.

☐ **ceremony**　**n** A formal and often religious or cultural event or ritual, typically with specific traditions and procedures

- The wedding <u>ceremony</u> was beautiful and meaningful.

☐ **blood, toil, tears, and sweat**

A metaphorical reference to the sacrifices, effort, and hardships required for a challenging endeavor

- The construction of the bridge demanded <u>blood, toil, tears, and sweat</u> from the workers.

☐ **ordeal**

n A severe or difficult experience or trial, often involving suffering or hardship

- Surviving in the wilderness was a true <u>ordeal</u>.

☐ **grievous**

a Extremely serious, severe, or painful

- The earthquake caused <u>grievous</u> damage to the city.

☐ **struggle**

n A vigorous effort or fight, often involving conflict or difficulties

- The <u>struggle</u> for civil rights was a defining moment in history.

☐ **wage**

v To engage in or carry out (eg, war, battle)

- The country decided to <u>wage</u> war against the invading forces.

☐ **might**

n Great physical or military strength or power; authority or control

- The nation's <u>might</u> was unmatched in the region.

☐ **monstrous**

a Extremely wicked, cruel, or inhuman; abominable

- The dictator's actions were deemed <u>monstrous</u> by the international community.

☐ **tyranny**

n The cruel and oppressive exercise of power or authority

- The people rose up against the <u>tyranny</u> of the oppressive regime.

☐ **surpass**

v To exceed or go beyond in quality, degree, or achievement

- Her performance <u>surpassed</u> all expectations.

☐ **lamentable**

a Deserving of regret, sorrow, or pity; unfortunate

- The loss of innocent lives in the accident was truly lamentable.

☐ **catalogue**

n A list or record of items, often organized systematically

- The library's catalogue made it easy to find books.

☐ **at all costs**

Regardless of the price or sacrifice involved

- They were determined to protect their homeland at all costs.

☐ **terror**

n Intense fear or extreme anxiety often resulting from a perceived threat

- The sudden sound of an explosion struck terror into the hearts of the villagers.

☐ **stand for**

To support or defend a particular principle, cause, or belief

- The organization stands for human rights and equality.

☐ **buoyancy**

n The ability to recover quickly from setbacks or remain cheerful in difficult situations

- Her natural buoyancy helped her maintain a positive outlook during tough times.

☐ **take up one's task**

To assume or start a particular duty, responsibility, or job

- She was ready to take up her task as the new team leader.

☐ **cause**

n A principle, aim, or movement that one supports or advocates for

- The environmental cause attracted many passionate volunteers.

☐ **suffer**

v To allow or tolerate something

- In order to maintain a peaceful and inclusive community, we cannot suffer discrimination or prejudice of any kind.

UNIT

6

☐ **feel entitled to**   To believe or have the perception that one has a right or qualification to something

....

- She <u>feels entitled to</u> a promotion after years of dedicated work.

 Logos, ethos, pathos 구별

★ Logos, ethos, and pathos are three persuasive techniques used in rhetoric, communication, and argumentation:

1. Logos

Logos refers to the use of logical reasoning and evidence to persuade an audience. It involves presenting facts, statistics, data, and well-structured arguments to support a claim. Logos is the appeal to the audience's sense of logic and reason, convincing them through rational and sound arguments.

2. Ethos

Ethos is the appeal to the credibility, authority, and ethical character of the speaker or author. It involves establishing the speaker's or author's expertise, trustworthiness, and moral integrity. Ethos seeks to persuade the audience by making them believe in the character and qualifications of the person delivering the message.

3. Pathos

Pathos is the appeal to the emotions and feelings of the audience. It aims to evoke sympathy, empathy, or strong emotional responses in the audience. Pathos can be used to create a connection with the audience, make them feel a particular way, or motivate them to take action based on their emotions.

2 Text Reading

: Blood, Sweat, and Tears

Text **1**

On Friday evening last I received His Majesty's commission to form a new Administration. It was the evident wish and will of Parliament and the nation that this should be conceived on the broadest possible basis and that it should include all parties, both those who supported the late Government and also the parties of the Opposition. I have completed the most important part of this task. A War Cabinet has been formed of five Members, representing, with the Opposition Liberals, the unity of the nation. The three Party Leaders have agreed to serve, either in the War Cabinet or in high executive office. The three Fighting Services have been filled.

It was necessary that this should be done in one single day, on account of the extreme urgency and rigor of events. A number of other positions, key positions, were filled yesterday, and I am submitting a further list to His Majesty tonight. I hope to complete the appointment of the principal Ministers during tomorrow. The appointment of the other Ministers usually takes a little longer, but I trust that, when Parliament meets again, this part of my task will be completed, and that the administration will be complete in all respects.

UNIT

6

1 What is the main idea of Churchill's first paragraph?

① The urgency of forming a War Cabinet
② The inclusion of all parties in the formation of a coalition government
③ The completion of key positions in one single day
④ The submission of a further list to His Majesty
⑤ The appointment of principal Ministers

2 Which group of individuals has agreed to serve in the War Cabinet or high executive office according to the passage?

① The Three Fighting Services
② The Opposition Liberals
③ The Principal Ministers
④ The Party Leaders
⑤ Members of Parliament

 핵심 PLUS!

1 On Friday evening last I received ①His Majesty's commission <u>to form</u> a new Administration.

- ① The king at the time was George VI; after his party is elected, the Prime Minister is officially appointed by the monarch.
- to부정사의 형용사 용법

2 <u>It</u> was the evident wish and will of Parliament and the nation <u>that</u> this should be conceived on the broadest possible basis and <u>that</u> it should include all parties, both those who supported the late Government and also ② <u>the parties of the Opposition</u>.

- 가주어/진주어 It ~ that 병치구조
- ② Political parties in the parliament other than the one(s) making up the ruling administration

3 A War Cabinet has been formed of five Members, [<u>representing</u>, (with ③<u>the Opposition Liberals</u>), the unity of the nation].

- 분사구문
- ③ Churchill was a member of the Conservative Party; those belonging to the Liberal Party were in the opposition, not the government.

4 The three Party Leaders have agreed to serve, <u>either</u> in the War Cabinet <u>or</u> in high executive office.

- either [전치사구] or [전치사구]의 병치구조

5 <u>It</u> was necessary <u>that</u> this should be done in one single day, <u>on account of</u> the extreme urgency and rigor of events.

- 가주어/진주어 It ~ that 구조
- on account of: ~로 인해, ~ 때문에

6 The appointment of the other Ministers usually takes a little longer, but I trust that, when Parliament meets again, this part of my task will be ④<u>completed</u>, and that the administration will be ⑤<u>complete</u> in all respects.

④의 complete는 동사로 "완성시키다"의 의미이고, ⑤의 complete는 내각 구성이 "온전하게 완성되었다"의 의미로 "전부 갖춘"의 의미로 쓰이고 있음.

I considered it in the public interest to suggest that the House should be summoned to meet today. Mr. Speaker agreed, and took the necessary steps, in accordance with the powers conferred upon him by the Resolution of the House. At the end of the proceedings today, the Adjournment of the House will be proposed until Tuesday, 21st May, with, of course, provision for earlier meeting if need be. The business to be considered during that week will be notified to Members at the earliest opportunity. I now invite the House, by the Resolution which stands in my name, to record its approval of the steps taken and to declare its confidence in the new Government.

To form an Administration of this scale and complexity is a serious undertaking in itself, but it must be remembered that we are in the preliminary stage of one of the greatest battles in history, that we are in action at many other points in Norway and in Holland, that we have to be prepared in the Mediterranean, that the air battle is continuous, and that many preparations have to be made here at home. In this crisis I hope I may be pardoned if I do not address the House at any length today. I hope that any of my friends and colleagues, or former colleagues, who are affected by the political reconstruction, will make all allowance for any lack of ceremony with which it has been necessary to act. I would say to the House, as I said to those who have joined this Government: "I have nothing to offer but blood, toil, tears and sweat."

UNIT

6

3 각 발췌 문장에 대한 설명으로 옳지 <u>않은</u> 것을 <u>한 개</u> 고르면?

① "To form an Administration of this scale and complexity is a serious undertaking in itself..."

→ This sentence presents a logical assertion that forming an Administration of this scale and complexity is a serious task.

② "I now invite the House, by the Resolution which stands in my name, to record its approval of the steps taken and to declare its confidence in the new Government."

→ In this sentence, the speaker is establishing credibility (ethos) by inviting the House to express approval and confidence in the new Government, which implies trust and reliability.

③ "I have nothing to offer but blood, toil, tears and sweat."

→ In this sentence, the speaker is appealing to the emotions (pathos) by invoking a sense of sacrifice and determination, creating an emotional connection with the audience.

④ "...that we have to be prepared in the Mediterranean, that the air battle is continuous, and that many preparations have to be made here at home."

→ These sentences provide a logical explanation of the various preparations and responsibilities in different regions.

⑤ "In this crisis, I hope I may be pardoned if I do not address the House at any length today."

→ In this sentence, the speaker is appealing to the emotions (pathos) based on the crisis, explaining why the speaker won't address the House at length.

핵심 PLUS!

1 I considered **it** in the public interest **to suggest** that the House **should** be summoned to meet today.

- 가목적어 it/진목적어 to V 구문
- suggest that S (should) V 구문

2 Mr. Speaker agreed, and took the necessary steps, in accordance with [the powers <u>conferred upon him</u> by the Resolution of the House].

- confer A upon B에서 과거분사 conferred가 선행사 the powers 수식.

3 At the end of the <u>proceedings</u> today, the Adjournment of the House will be proposed until Tuesday, 21st May, <u>with</u>, of course, <u>provision for</u> earlier meeting <u>if need be</u>.

- proceeding의 복수형은 "절차" 라는 의미.
- with provision for: ~라는 조건 과 함께
- if need be: 필요시

4 The business <u>to be considered</u> during that week will be notified to Members at the earliest opportunity.

- to부정사의 수동표현의 형용사 후치

5 To form an Administration of this scale and complexity is a serious undertaking in itself, but **it** must be remembered |that| we are in the preliminary stage of one of the greatest battles in history, |that| we are in action at many other points in Norway and in Holland, |that| we have to be prepared in the Mediterranean, |that| the air battle is continuous, and |that| many preparations have to be made here at home.

- 가주어it/진주어that 구문의 병치 구조

UNIT

6

6 In this crisis I hope I may be pardoned if I do not address the House <u>at any length</u> today.

- at any length = at great length or for an extended period

7 I hope that any of my friends and colleagues, or former colleagues, (**who** are affected by the political reconstruction), will <u>make all allowance for</u> any lack of ceremony **with which** it has been necessary to act.

- 주격 관계대명사 who
- make (all) allowance for: ~을 고려해 주다, 용인하다
- with which = with ceremony (형식 또는 예의를 갖춰)

We have before us an ordeal of the most grievous kind. We have before us many, many long months of struggle and of suffering. You ask, What is our policy? I will say: "It is to wage war, by sea, land and air, with all our might and with all the strength that God can give us; to wage war against a monstrous tyranny, never surpassed in the dark, lamentable catalogue of human crime. That is our policy." You ask, What is our aim? I can answer in one word: It is victory, victory at all costs, victory in spite of all terror, victory, however long and hard the road may be; for without victory, there is no survival. Let that be realized; no survival for the British Empire, no survival for all that the British Empire has stood for, no survival for the urge and impulse of the ages, that mankind will move forward towards its goal. But I take up my task with buoyancy and hope. I feel sure that our cause will not be suffered to fail among men. At this time I feel entitled to claim the aid of all, and I say, "Come, then, let us go forward together with our united strength."

4 In this final paragraph, Churchill uses parallelism, or repetition of and emphasis on sentence structures and key words. What is the effect of this parallelism?

① The passage does not contain any instances of parallelism.
② It creates a sense of confusion and disorganization in the message.
③ It helps to simplify the complex message and make it more accessible to the audience.
④ It adds a sense of unpredictability to the message.
⑤ It reinforces and emphasizes the message, making it more impactful.

5 In this final paragraph, what kind of persuasive appeal does Churchill use?

① Logos (logical reasoning and evidence)　② Ethos (credibility and authority)
③ Pathos (emotional appeal)　④ Rhetorical questions
⑤ Irony

6 Which of the following is NOT an appropriate explanation for the contextual meaning of each underlined word?

① ordeal: a difficult or painful experience
② wage: to carry on or engage in
③ lamentable: regrettable; unfortunate
④ urge and impulse: strong desires or motivations
⑤ buoyancy: the ability to stay afloat or rise in a fluid

핵심 PLUS!

1 We have (before us) an ordeal of the most grievous kind. We have (before us) many, many long months of struggle and of suffering.

• [타동사 + (부사구) + 목적어] 구조

2 I will say: "It is to wage war, by sea, land and air, [with all our might and with all the strength (**that** God can give us)]; to wage war against a monstrous tyranny, never surpassed in the dark, lamentable catalogue of human crime.

• 보어 자리에 위치한 to부정사의 명사적 용법
• 병치와 목적격 관계대명사
 ① to V ~ ; to V ~
 ② with N and with N (that V)

3 That is our policy." You ask, What is our aim? I can answer in one word: It is victory, victory (at all costs), victory (in spite of all terror), victory, (however long and hard the road may be); for without victory, there is no survival.

• N + 전명구의 반복 구조
• 복합관계부사절 확인

4 Let that be realized; no survival for the British Empire, no survival for (all **that** the British Empire has stood for), no survival for **the urge and impulse** of the ages, **that** mankind will move forward towards its goal.

• no suvival for 어구의 반복
• 목적격 관계대명사: all(선행사) that S V
• 동격의 that: the urge and impulse = that S V

5 I feel sure that our cause will not be suffered to fail among men.

• suffer는 여기서 "(묵묵히) …하게 내버려두다"의 의미로 다음과 같이 재진술 가능.
 I feel sure that our cause will not be **suffered** to fail among men.
 = I feel sure that our cause will not be **allowed** to fail among men.

UNIT
6

Voca Check

* 빈칸에 들어갈 적절한 단어를 박스에서 찾아 넣으시오.

1

commission / will / meet / manufacture / invade / evident / oppose / newly elected / declare war on / overrun

1   The president had to _____ the nation's economic issues head-on.

2   When the enemy forces decided to _____ our borders, it led to a declaration of war.

3   The company's decision to _____ their products locally contributed to job creation.

4   The city was _____ by hordes of tourists during the holiday season.

5   The _____ mayor gave a speech at the inauguration ceremony.

6   It was _____ that the candidate was determined to win the election.

7   The environmental group decided to _____ the construction of the new factory.

8   The committee was tasked with a crucial _____ to investigate the matter.

9   Despite the challenges, the team was determined to _____ the project's objectives.

10 His strong _____ to protect the environment was evident in his actions.

2

urgency / notify / submit / adjournment / summon / represent / rigor / confer / summons / proceeding

1   The board decided to _____ a committee to investigate the issue.

2   With a sense of _____, the rescue team rushed to the scene of the accident.

3   The lawyer was appointed to _____ the interests of the defendant during the trial.

4   The professor demanded _____ in order to address the academic matters.

5   The judge issued a _____ for the witness to testify in court.

6   The students had to _____ their research proposals before the deadline.

7   The president had to _____ a press conference to address the nation's concerns.

8   The _____ of the meeting was marked by intense discussions and debates.

9   The court decided to _____ the case until further evidence could be presented.

10 The mayor had to _____ the city council members to discuss the budget.

UNIT

6

3

approval / preliminary / pardon / stand / struggle / ordeal / undertaking / ceremony / grievous

* 단 중복 사용되는 단어 있음.

1   The _____ of starting a new business can be challenging but rewarding.

2   After the long and exhausting _____ of the marathon, he finally crossed the finish line.

3   She requested a _____ for the minor offense, hoping to avoid a legal penalty.

4   The students received _____ from their teacher for their outstanding performance.

5   The _____ to find a solution to the problem was met with determination and effort.

6   The _____ of planning a traditional wedding involves many customs and rituals.

7   The _____ process involves several steps to assess the project's feasibility.

8   The community came together for a _____ to celebrate a special cultural event.

9   The news of the accident was _____ and deeply saddened the entire community.

10 He had to _____ tall in the face of adversity and never give up.

4

for / wage / terror / buoyancy / monstrous / stands / cause / bravery / suffer / might / lamentable

1 The nation took a resolute stance, deciding to _____ a war of liberation against the encroaching invading forces.

2 Her _____ in the field of science and innovation was widely recognized.

3 The _____ creature from the legend was said to haunt the villagers' dreams.

4 Many people _____ from seasickness due to the ship's movement.

5 The advocate passionately explained the _____ of environmental conservation.

6 The crew's knowledge of _____ helped them stay afloat during the storm.

7 The _____ of the attack spread fear and panic throughout the city.

8 It's _____ to witness the heart-wrenching suffering of innocent people during times of conflict evokes profound empathy and compassion.

9 The symbol on the flag _____ the enduring principles of freedom and unity.

10 The soldiers displayed unwavering valor and dauntless _____ as they gallantly confronted the enemy on the battlefield.

4 Reading Comprehension

1 Find <u>TWO</u> that are <u>INCONSISTENT</u> with the passage.

[가] ⊙<u>On Friday evening last I received His Majesty's commission to form a new Administration.</u> It was the evident wish and will of Parliament and the nation that this should be conceived on the broadest possible basis and that it should include all parties, both those who supported the late Government and also the parties of the Opposition. I have completed the most important part of this task. A War Cabinet has been formed of five Members, representing, with the Opposition Liberals, the unity of the nation. The three Party Leaders have agreed to serve, either in the War Cabinet or in high executive office. The three Fighting Services have been filled.

[나] It was necessary that this should be done in one single day, on account of the extreme urgency and rigor of events. A number of other positions, key positions, were filled yesterday, and I am submitting a further list to His Majesty tonight. I hope to complete the appointment of the principal Ministers during tomorrow. The appointment of the other Ministers usually takes a little longer, but I trust that, when Parliament meets again, this part of my task will be completed, and that the administration will be complete in all respects.

[다] I considered it in the public interest to suggest that the House should be summoned to meet today. Mr. Speaker agreed, and took the necessary steps, in accordance with the powers conferred upon him by the Resolution of the House. At the end of the proceedings today, the Adjournment of the House will be proposed until Tuesday, 21st May, with, of course, provision for earlier meeting if need be. The business to be considered during that week will be notified to Members at the earliest opportunity. I now invite the House, by the Resolution which stands in my name, to record its approval of the steps taken and to declare its confidence in the new Government.

① ㉠ in [가] implies that the Prime Minister was officially appointed by the monarch at the time.

② From [가] it can be inferred that all the positions in the new administration have finally been filled.

③ In [나], Churchill explains what actions he has taken thus far and what plans he has for the coming days.

④ In [나], Churchill alerts his listeners to the possibility that there will be many difficulties in appointing the remaining ministers for the new government.

⑤ From [가] to [다], Churchill is consistent in staying factual and logical throughout his speech, rather than appealing to emotion.

[2-5] Read the passage and answer each question.

NOTE

[가] On Friday evening last I received His Majesty's commission to form a new Administration. It was the evident wish and will of Parliament and the nation that this should be conceived on the broadest possible basis and that it should include all parties, both those who supported the late Government and also the parties of the Opposition. I have completed the most important part of this task. A War Cabinet has been formed of five Members, representing, with the Opposition Liberals, the unity of the nation. The three Party Leaders have agreed to serve, either in the War Cabinet or in high executive office. The three Fighting Services have been filled.

[나] It was necessary that this should be done in one single day, on account of the extreme urgency and rigor of events. A number of other positions, key positions, were filled yesterday, and I am submitting a further list to His Majesty tonight. I hope to complete the appointment of the principal Ministers during tomorrow. The appointment of the other Ministers usually takes a little longer, but I trust that, when Parliament meets again, this part of my task will <A>_____, and that the administration will <B>_____ in all respects.

[다] I considered it in the public interest to suggest that the House should be summoned to meet today. Mr. Speaker agreed, and took the necessary steps, in accordance with the powers conferred upon him by the Resolution of the House. At the end of the proceedings today, the Adjournment of the House will be proposed until Tuesday, 21st May, with, of course, provision for earlier meeting if need be. The business to be considered during that week will be notified to Members at the earliest opportunity. I now invite the House, by the Resolution which stands in my name, to record its approval of the steps taken and to declare its confidence in the new Government.

[라] To form an Administration of this scale and complexity is a serious undertaking in itself, but it must be remembered that we are in the preliminary stage of one of the greatest battles in history, that we are in action at many other points in Norway and in Holland, that we have to be prepared in the Mediterranean, that the air battle is continuous, and that many preparations have to be made here at home. In this crisis ⓒI hope I may be pardoned if I do not address the House at any length today. I hope that any of my friends and colleagues, or former colleagues, who are affected by the political reconstruction, will ⓛ make all allowance for any ⓒlack of ceremony ⓔ_____ it has been necessary to act. I would say to the House, as I said to those who have joined this Government: ⓜ"I have nothing to offer but blood, toil, tears and sweat."

2 Find <u>TWO</u> that are <u>NOT</u> true in paragraph [가].

① Winston Churchill had just become prime minister, appointed by the monarch just a few days earlier.

② The Administration that Churchill hopes to achieve is non-partisan.

③ The War Cabinet consists mainly of ministers from the ruling party in order to expedite work.

④ The main Army, Navy, and Air Force positions have been assigned to suitable people.

⑤ Churchill was a member of the Liberal Party.

* expedite (일을) 신속히 처리하다

3 Which of the following is an appropriate expression to fill in the blanks <A> and <B> in paragraph [나]?

	<A>	<B>
①	be completed	be complete
②	have been completed	be completing
③	complete	complete
④	be complete	be completed
⑤	be completing	be complete

4 Which of the following statements about [가] ~ [다] is <u>NOT</u> correct?

① [가] Churchill is outlining what has happened in his brand-new government over the past few days.

② [나] Part of Churchill's job is to pull together members of Parliament to form a government made up of politicians from all parties, to be truly representative of the entire nation.

③ [나] Because of the urgent need to deal with the upcoming crisis of war with Germany, Churchill carried out his homework basically overnight.

④ [다] Churchill suggests that the urgency of the matter should also eliminate the minimum procedure for convening the House.

⑤ [다] Churchill is talking about how he called Parliament to session to formalize the new government, and how it will be called again soon.

* convene 소집하다 call Parliament to session 의회를 소집하다 formalize 모양을 갖추다

5 Which of the following is <u>NOT</u> correct about the underlined ㉠ to ㉤ in paragraph [라]?

① From ㉠, it can be inferred that Churchill is a person who usually does not consider formal procedures very important.

② ㉡ means *to pardon or excuse*.

③ ㉢ means *lack of formality*.

④ The expression to fill in ㉣ is *with which*.

⑤ By saying ㉤, Churchill is tell the British that he has to work hard to win this war, just as everyone else will.

[6-7] Read the passage and answer each question.

🏅 NOTE

(A) On Friday evening last I received (a)the King's commission to form a new Administration. It was the evident wish and will of Parliament and the nation that this should be conceived on the broadest possible basis and that it should include all parties, both those who supported the late Government and also the parties of the Opposition. I have completed the most important part of this task. (b)A War Cabinet has been formed of five Members, representing, with the Opposition Liberals, the separation of the nation. The three Party Leaders have agreed to serve, either in the War Cabinet or in high executive office. The three Fighting Services have been filled.

(B) It was necessary that this should be done in one single day, on account of the extreme _____(c)_____ and rigor of events. A number of other positions, key positions, were filled yesterday, and I am submitting a further list to His Majesty tonight. I hope to complete the appointment of the principal Ministers during tomorrow. The appointment of the other Ministers usually takes a little longer, but I trust that, when Parliament meets again, this part of my task will be completed, and that the administration will be complete _____(d)_____.

(C) I considered it in the public interest to suggest that the House should be summoned to meet today. Mr. Speaker agreed, and took the necessary steps, in accordance with the powers _____(e)_____ upon him by the Resolution of the House. At the end of the proceedings today, the Adjournment of the House will be proposed until Tuesday, 21st May, with, of course, provision for earlier meeting if need be. The business to be considered during that week will be notified to Members at the earliest opportunity. I now invite the House, by the Resolution which stands in my name, to record its approval of the steps taken and to declare its confidence in the new Government.

UNIT

6

6 Which of the following statements is true?

> I. In (A), (a) can be replaced with 'His Majesty.'
>
> II. In (A), (b) contains a word that is NOT appropriate in context.
>
> III. The main idea of (A) is NOT clearly stated but implied.
>
> IV. In (B), blank (c) can be filled in with 'urgency.'

① I and IV   ② II and III

③ III and IV   ④ I, II and IV

⑤ II, III and IV

7 In (B) and (C), choose the option that best fills in blanks (d) and (e).

	(d)		(e)
①	for respect	-	granted
②	with respect	-	conferred
③	in all respects	-	dismissed
④	in a few respects	-	granted
⑤	in all respects	-	conferred

[8-9] Read the passage and answer each question.

On Friday evening last I received His Majesty's commission to form a new Administration. It was the evident wish and will of Parliament and the nation that this should be conceived on the broadest possible basis and that it should include all parties, both those who supported the late Government and also the parties of the Opposition. I have completed the most important part of this task. A War Cabinet has been formed of five Members, representing, with the Opposition Liberals, the unity of the nation. The three Party Leaders have agreed to serve, either in the War Cabinet or in high executive office. The three Fighting Services have been filled.

ⓐIt was necessary that this should be done in one single day, on account of the extreme urgency and rigor of events. A number of other positions, key positions, were filled yesterday, and I am submitting a further list to His Majesty tonight. I hope to complete the appointment of the principal Ministers during tomorrow. The appointment of the other Ministers usually takes a little longer, but I trust that, when Parliament meets again, this part of my task will be completed, and that the administration will be complete in all respects.

I considered it in the public interest to suggest that the House should be summoned to meet today. Mr. Speaker agreed, and took the necessary steps, in accordance with the powers conferred upon him by the Resolution of the House. ⓑAt the end of the proceedings today, the Adjournment of the House will be proposed until Tuesday, 21st May, with, of course, provision for earlier meeting if need be. The business to be considered during that week will be notified to Members at the earliest opportunity. I now invite the House, by the Resolution which stands in my name, to record its approval of the steps taken and to declare its confidence in the new Government.

To form an Administration of this scale and complexity is a serious undertaking in itself, but it must be remembered that we are in the preliminary stage of one of the greatest battles in history, that we are in action at many other points in Norway and in Holland, that we have to be prepared in the Mediterranean, that the air battle is continuous, and that many preparations have to be made here at home. ⓒ<u>In this crisis I hope I may be pardoned if I do not address the House at any length today</u>. I hope that any of my friends and colleagues, or former colleagues, who are affected by the political reconstruction, will make all allowance for any lack of ceremony with which it has been necessary to act. I would say to the House, as I said to those who have joined this Government: "I have nothing to offer but blood, toil, tears and sweat."

We have before us an ordeal of the most grievous kind. We have before us many, many long months of struggle and of suffering. You ask, What is our policy? I will say: "It is to wage war, by sea, land and air, with all our might and with all the strength that God can give us; to wage war against a monstrous tyranny, never surpassed in the dark, lamentable catalogue of human crime. That is our policy." You ask, What is our aim? I can answer in one word: It is victory, victory at all costs, victory in spite of all terror, victory, however long and hard the road may be; for without victory, there is no survival. Let that be realized; no survival for the British Empire, no survival for all that the British Empire has stood for, no survival for the urge and impulse of the ages, that mankind will move forward towards its goal. ⓔ<u>But I take up my task with buoyancy and hope. I feel sure that our cause will not be suffered to fail among men. At this time I feel entitled to claim the aid of all, and I say, "Come, then, let us go forward together with our united strength."</u>

8 Choose all that are <u>CORRECT</u> about the passage.

> I From ㉠, it can be inferred that the speaker suggests that while there is a pressing need to create the new government, the process should take a form of "a snail's pace."
>
> II. From ㉡, it can be inferred that the possibility exists that the House of Commons will be summoned if there is a pressing reason to meet earlier.
>
> III. Through ㉢, the speaker is asking for leniency from the House of Commons due to the urgency of the situation.
>
> IV. The underlined part of ㉣ can be categorized as ethos as it appeals to the speaker's legitimate claim to the aid of others based on their personal qualities and leadership abilities, as well as to the sense of shared values and community spirit.

① I and IV   ② II and III
③ II, III and IV   ④ III and IV
⑤ IV only

9 Below is the explanation about the last paragraph of Churchill's speech. Which of the literary devices is this talking about?

> The last paragraph of Churchill's speech is clearly a rousing appeal to the audience's emotion. You don't refer to "monstrous tyranny, never surpassed in the dark and lamentable catalogue of human crime" unless you're trying to evoke an emotional response.

① Logos (logical reasoning and evidence)
② Ethos (credibility and authority)
③ Pathos (emotional appeal)
④ Rhetorical questions
⑤ Irony

1 Kuwait is a _____ country with enormous reserves of oil and cash, boasting an excellent port on Persian Gulf.

① bulging
② patching
③ familiar
④ inflicted

어휘 enormous 거대한, 매우 큰 reserve (석유·석탄 등의) 매장량, 비축; (미래 혹은 어떤 목적을 위하여) 떼어두다, 비축하다; ~을 예약하다 oil 석유 cash 현금, 돈 boast ~을 자랑하다 excellent 훌륭한, 뛰어난 port 항구, 항구 도시 Persian Gulf 페르시아 만 bulge 부풀다; 우세, 유리 patch 헝겊조각; ~에 헝겊을 대고 깁다 familiar 친밀한, 잘 알고 있는 inflict (타격·상처·고통 따위를) 주다, 입히다, 가하다 (= wreak)

2 Employers who retire people who are willing and able to continue working should realize that _____ age is not an effective _____ in determining whether an individual is capable of working.

① Physical – barrier
② chronological – factor
③ intellectual – criterion
④ chronological – criterion
⑤ deteriorating – value

어휘 employer 고용주 retire ~을 퇴직시키다; 은퇴하다 willing 기꺼이~ 하는, 자발적인, 의지가 있는 able ~할 수 있는, 능력 있는 continue ~을 계속하다 realize ~을 깨닫다, 알아차리다 effective 효과적인, 효율적인 in ~ing ~할 때 determine ~을 결정하다, 결심하다 whether ~인지 아닌지 individual 개개의, 개인의, 독특한 capable 유능한, ~할 능력이 있는 be capable of ~ing ~할 수 있다 physical 육체의, 신체의, 물리적인 barrier 장벽, 방해(물) chronological 연대기적인, 연대순인 factor 요소, 요인 intellectual 지적인, 두뇌를 쓰는 criterion 기준, 표준 deteriorate ~을 타락시키다, 나쁘게 하다 value 가치, 평가; 평가하다, 소중히 하다

3 The sea floor remains a place for nervous transient visits. That has led to an astonishing _____ between humanity's knowledge of the one-third of the Earth's surface that is above sea level and the two-thirds below it.

① fusion
② discretion
③ discrepancy
④ correlation

어휘 sea floor 해저 remain ~이다, ~로 남아있다 place 장소 nervous 신경 과민한, 초조한 transient 일시적인, 덧없는, 변하기 쉬운 visit 방문, 구경 lead to ~로 이끌다, ~을 초래하다 astonishing 놀라운 between (둘 중) ~사이에 humanity 인류 knowledge 지식 surface 표면, 외관 above ~위에 sea level 해수면 below ~아래에 fusion 혼합, 용해 discretion 자유재량, 사려분별 discrepancy 불일치, 차이, 어긋남 correlation 상호관계

4 South Korean golfer Shin Ji-Ae, who won the LPGA's top rookie prize this year, received _____ with her moving speech, which she delivered in English.

① a stifled giggle
② roaring laughter
③ a mere hiss
④ standing ovation

어휘 win 이기다, 얻다 rookie 신인 선수, 신병 prize 상; 높이 평가하다, 존중하다 receive ~을 받다 moving 감동적인 speech 연설, 말 deliver (편지 등을) 배달하다; (의견을) 말하다, 연설을 하다; 아이를 받다; 잘해 내다 in English 영어로 stifle ~을 숨 막히게 하다, 방해하다, (웃음·하품 따위를) 참다 giggle 킥킥 웃다 stifled giggle 참는 웃음소리 roaring 포효하는, 떠들어대는 laughter 웃음 mere 단순한, 단지 ~에 지나지 않는 hiss 쉿 하는 소리, 쉬쉬 소리 standing ovation 기립박수

5 Our narrative begins in _____ times before the invention of reading and writing when our ancestors transmitted their culture orally from one generation to the next.

① reflective
② generative
③ antiquarian
④ emergent
⑤ preliterate

어휘 narrative 이야기; 이야기의 begin 시작하다 times 시대 before ~ 전에 invention 발명; 날조 reading 읽기 writing 쓰기 when ~할 때 ancestor 조상, 선조 transmit ~을 보내다, 전달하다 culture 문화 orally 구두로, 입으로 from A to B A에서 B까지(B로) generation 세대 reflective 숙고하는; 반사하는 generative 발생하는, 생식의 antiquarian 골동품 수집(연구)의 emergent 떠오르는, 불시에 나타나는 preliterate 문자사용 이전의

6 In the tournament of the last World Cup games, there was a disappointing _____ of new ideas at dead ball situations and a number of controversial refereeing decisions. In a tournament where entertaining soccer was at such _____, it seemed appropriate the final should be a tight, exciting affair.

① lack – a premium   ② profusion – a premium

③ lack – high tide   ④ profusion – high tide

어휘 tournament 토너먼트 경기 lack 결여 a number of 수많은 referee 심판원; 심판을 보다 premium 우수한, 최고의; 액면 초과액, 할증금, 우수한 제품 profusion 풍부 prosperity 번창, 번성

7 Disturbed by the _____ nature of the plays being presented, the Puritans closed the theaters in 1642.

① mediocre   ② fantastic

③ moribund   ④ salacious

⑤ witty

어휘 disturb 방해하다, 혼란시키다 disturbed by ~에 의해 마음이 동요된, 혼란스러운 nature 자연; 성질 play 연극, 놀이 present (연극을) 상연하다; 제출하다 being presented 상연되고 있는 Puritan 청교도(엄격함, 근엄함) close ~을 닫다; 가까운, 친밀한 theater 극장 mediocre 보통의, 평범한; 2류의 fantastic 환상적인, 굉장한 moribund 죽어가는, 소멸해가는 salacious 외설적인 witty 재치 있는

8 The actor was upset by the _____ criticism of the gossip columnist who seemed out to ruin his reputation.

① soothing   ② phenomenal

③ mordant   ④ fictitious

어휘 actor 배우 upset [upset-upset-upset]뒤집어엎다, 전복시키다; 당황케 하다 criticism 비난 gossip 남의 소문 이야기, 험담, 잡담 columnist (신문의) 특별 기고가 seem ~처럼 보이다 ruin ~을 파멸시키다 reputation 명성, 평판 soothing 누그러뜨리는, 진정시키는 phenomenal 놀라운, 경이적인, 굉장한 mordant 신랄한 fictitious 허구의, 가짜의, 거짓의

9 Although there was little question that he was guilty, the charge was _____ for lack of evidence because there were no witnesses to testify.

① dismissed
② sustained
③ nullified
④ overruled

10 Although the drive to pass the bills has been _____ by the opposition party, the ruling party is set to press ahead with its stalled reform bills. The party is planning to create another team to focus on the repeal of anticommunist law.

① deterred
② emulated
③ intensified
④ deduced
⑤ taken in

문학_단편소설

Emancipation

by Kate Chopin

PART

Voca Master

☐ **confine**
v To limit or restrict something within certain boundaries or limits

- She decided to <u>confine</u> her study time to just two hours a day to avoid burnout.
- The wildlife sanctuary was created to <u>confine</u> the animals to their natural habitat.

☐ **invisible**
a Unable to be seen; not visible

- The microscopic organisms in the water are <u>invisible</u> to the naked eye.
- The ninja moved silently and <u>invisible</u> in the shadows.

☐ **at hand**
Physically or readily available or close in time

- The solution to the problem is <u>at hand</u>, and we can implement it immediately.
- With the exam <u>at hand</u>, he focused on his last-minute revisions.

☐ **lick**
v To touch or pass over something with the tongue; to defeat or surpass someone easily

- The cat would often <u>lick</u> its paws after a meal.
- In the race, he managed to <u>lick</u> his competition and win by a considerable margin.

☐ **flanks**
n The sides of a person's or animal's body between the ribs and the hips; the sides of an object

- The knight protected his <u>flanks</u> during the battle to avoid being attacked from the sides.
- She placed the vases on the <u>flanks</u> of the table to create a symmetrical arrangement.

□ bask

v To lie exposed to warmth and light, typically from the sun, for relaxation or pleasure

- Tourists often <u>bask</u> in the sun on the beautiful beaches of the island.
- The cat loves to <u>bask</u> in the sunbeam coming through the window.

□ lighten

v To make or become lighter in color or weight; to brighten

- The artist used lighter shades to <u>lighten</u> the background of the painting.
- Her smile never failed to <u>lighten</u> up the room.

□ slothful

a Lazy; showing a lack of effort or motivation

- The <u>slothful</u> student rarely completed his assignments on time.
- After a long day at work, she felt too <u>slothful</u> to do any household chores.

□ crouch

v To lower one's body close to the ground by bending one's legs

- The cat began to <u>crouch</u> in preparation for pouncing on its prey.
- He had to <u>crouch</u> to enter the small, low-ceilinged room.

□ dread

v To fear greatly; to be very afraid or anxious about something

- She <u>dreaded</u> the thought of public speaking and would do anything to avoid it.
- The child <u>dreaded</u> going to the dentist because of the pain.

□ limb

n A major appendage of the human or an animal body, specifically an arm or a leg

- The accident resulted in a broken <u>limb</u>, and he had to use crutches for a while.
- Birds have wings as their <u>forelimbs</u>, which allow them to fly.

☐ purposeless   **a** Lacking a clear goal or objective; without purpose or aim

- Wandering around the city with no destination in mind felt <u>purposeless</u> to him.
- He felt <u>purposeless</u> after retiring and decided to take up a new hobby.

☐ canopy   **n** An overhead cover, typically consisting of a cloth or other material, often used for shade or protection from the elements

- The wedding ceremony took place under a beautiful <u>canopy</u> of flowers and fabric.
- The rainforest <u>canopy</u> is home to a variety of unique species.

☐ wound   **v** Past tense of "wind," meaning to turn or twist something, typically a road or path

- The road <u>wound</u> through the picturesque countryside, offering breathtaking views.
- The river <u>wound</u> its way through the valley, creating a stunning landscape.

☐ sleek   **a** Smooth, shiny, and well-groomed in appearance

- Her <u>sleek</u> black car turned heads as it cruised down the street.
- The cat's <u>sleek</u> fur made it look elegant and regal.

☐ noxious   **a** Harmful, poisonous, or unpleasant, especially to the environment or health

- The <u>noxious</u> fumes from the factory were a major concern for the nearby residents.
- Invasive species can have <u>noxious</u> effects on native ecosystems.

☐ from without   From the outside; originating externally

- The damage to the building was caused <u>from without</u> when a tree fell on it during the storm.
- It's important to protect your computer <u>from without</u> threats such as viruses and malware.

☐ **from within**   From the inside; originating internally
....
- The company faced challenges <u>from within</u> as employees struggled with low morale.
- The strength to overcome adversity often comes <u>from within</u> oneself.

☐ **lo!**   `int` An archaic word used to draw attention or exclamation, often indicating surprise or wonder
....
- <u>Lo</u>! Behold the magnificent sunrise over the mountains!
- <u>Lo</u> and behold! There was a hidden treasure buried in the backyard.

2 Text Reading

: Emancipation

Text

There was once an animal born into this world, and opening his eyes upon Life, he saw above and about him confining walls, and before him were bars of iron through which came air and light from without; this animal was born in a cage.

Here he grew, and throve in strength and beauty under the care of an invisible protecting hand. Hungering, food was ever at hand. When he thirsted water was brought, and when he felt the need to rest, there was provided a bed of straw on which to lie; and here he found it good, licking his handsome flanks, to bask in the sun beam that he thought existed but to lighten his home.

Awaking one day from his slothful rest, lo! the door of his cage stood open: accident had opened it. In the corner he crouched, wondering and fearingly. Then slowly did he approach the door, dreading the unaccustomed, and would have closed it, but for such a task his limbs were purposeless. So out the opening he thrust his head, to see the canopy of the sky grow broader, and the world waxing wider.

Back to his corner but not to rest, for the spell of the Unknown was over him, and again and again he goes to the open door, seeing each time more Light.

Then one time standing in the flood of it; a deep in-drawn breath – a bracing of strong limbs, and with a bound he was gone.

On he rushes, in his mad flight, heedless that he is wounding and tearing his sleek sides – seeing, smelling, touching of all things; even stopping to put his lips to the noxious pool, thinking it may be sweet.

Hungering there is no food but such as he must seek and often times fight for; and his limbs are weighted before he reaches the water that is good to his thirsting throat.

So does he live, seeking, finding, joying and suffering. The door which accident had opened is opened still, but the cage remains forever empty!

1 The following is an analysis of the text. Which proverb best reflects the content of the analysis?

> The passage tells the story of an animal born in a cage who, when presented with an opportunity for freedom, ventures out into the wider world. However, the outcome is not all positive; the animal encounters difficulties and challenges, such as the lack of food and the need to fight for it. The achievement of freedom warns against assuming a positive outcome before it has been achieved, as the animal in the passage experiences both joy and suffering on its journey to freedom.

① A watched pot never boils.
② All that glitters is not gold.
③ Don't count your chickens before they hatch.
④ Every cloud has a silver lining.
⑤ Where there's a will, there's a way.

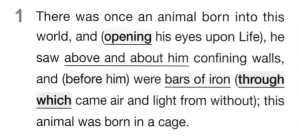

 핵심 PLUS!

1 There was once an animal born into this world, and (<u>opening</u> his eyes upon Life), he saw <u>above and about him</u> confining walls, and (before him) were <u>bars of iron</u> (<u>through which</u> came air and light from without); this animal was born in a cage.

- 분사구문: <u>opening</u> his eyes upon Life = when he opened his eyes upon Life
- above and about him: 그의 위에 주변
- 장소/방향의 부사 도치구문: (before him) were S(bars of iron) ~ 원문: <u>bars of iron</u> were before him ~
- [전치사 + 관계대명사 V S] 도치구문 확인
- which = bars of iron

2 <u>Here he grew</u>, and throve in strength and beauty under the care of an invisible protecting hand. **Hungering**, food was ever at hand.

- [Here + 대명사주어 + 동사] 구조
- 분사구문: Hungering = When he hungered

3 When he thirsted water <u>was brought</u>, and when he felt the need to rest, <u>there was provided</u> a bed of straw <u>on which to lie</u>; and here he found it good, (licking his handsome flanks), <u>to bask</u> in the sun beam that he thought existed but to lighten his home.

- 수동태
- There was provided의 주어는 a bed of straw임.
- on which to V = on which S V there <u>was provided</u> a bed of straw <u>on which to lie</u> = there <u>was provided</u> a bed of straw <u>on which he could lie</u>

4 Then slowly **did he approach** the door, dreading the unaccustomed, and would have closed it, but for such a task his limbs were purposeless.

- slowly의 부사가 문두로 이동하면서 문장이 도치됨.

5 So out the opening he thrust his head, to see the canopy of the sky **grow broader**, and the world waxing wider.

- "grow boarder"의 표현에서 동물은 지금껏 cage 안의 하늘이 세상의 전부라 생각해 온 것.

6 Hungering there is no food but such as he must seek and often times fight for; and his limbs are weighted before he reaches the water (**that** is good to his thirsting throat). **So does he live**, seeking, finding, joying and suffering. The door **which** accident had opened is opened still, but the cage remains forever empty!

- 주격 관계대명사 that과 which
- So 도치: So does he live.

UNIT

7

다음은 Kate Chopin의 "Emancipation"에 대한 작품 분석이다. 빈칸에 들어갈 보기의 단어를 박스에서 찾아 넣으시오. (단, 필요시 문맥에 맞게 단어의 형태를 변형할 것)

1

leave / beyond / constraints / impose / meet / spectrum / complacent

1 **Allegory of Life and Freedom**: The central narrative of the caged animal serves as an allegory for human existence. The cage represents the _____ and limitations _____ by societal norms, expectations, and the comfort of the known. The opening of the cage door symbolizes the opportunity for liberation or a change in one's life circumstances.

2 **The Comfort of Confinement**: Initially, the caged animal lives a life of comfort, where its basic needs are _____ without effort. This can be seen as a commentary on individuals who become _____ in their comfort zones, often fearing change or the unknown.

3 **The Temptation of Freedom**: When the cage door is accidentally opened, the animal is both curious and fearful of the unknown world _____. This mirrors the human experience of encountering opportunities for change or personal growth. The hesitation and fear before venturing out are relatable to the challenges faced when _____ one's comfort zone.

4 **The Thrill of Discovery**: As the animal explores the world outside the cage, it experiences the full _____ of life, from joy to suffering. This reflects the human condition, where personal growth and self-discovery often come with both pleasure and pain.

2

revert / remain / confines / sustenance / irreversibility / previous / ignorance / challenge / irreversible / unpredictability / transformative

1   The _____ of Change: The story highlights the _____ nature of change. Once the animal experiences the freedom of the outside world, it can never return to the _____ of the cage, even if the door remains open. This underscores the idea that once an individual gains insight, knowledge, or a new perspective, they cannot _____ to their former state of _____ or confinement.

2   **The Embrace of Uncertainty**: The story suggests that life outside the cage is uncertain and _____. The animal must seek _____ and face adversity, symbolizing the _____ of life's journey. This can be interpreted as a call for individuals to embrace uncertainty and adversity as integral parts of personal growth.

3   **The Empty Cage**: The story concludes with the cage _____ forever empty, signifying that once a person experiences personal growth and change, they can never return to their _____ state of ignorance or confinement. This echoes the idea that knowledge and self-discovery are irreversible and _____.

UNIT

7

4 Reading Comprehension

[1-5] Read the passage and answer each question.

 NOTE

There was once an animal born into this world, and opening his eyes upon Life, he saw above and about him confining walls, and before him were bars of iron through which came air and light from without; this animal was born in a cage.

Here he grew, and throve in strength and beauty under the care of an invisible protecting hand. Hungering, food was ever at hand. When he thirsted water was brought, and when he felt the need to rest, there was provided a bed of straw on which to lie; and here he found it good, licking his handsome flanks, to bask in the sun beam that he thought existed but to lighten his home.

Awaking one day from his slothful rest, lo! the door of his cage stood open: accident had opened it. In the corner he crouched, wondering and fearingly. Then slowly did he approach the door, dreading the unaccustomed, and would have closed it, but for such a task his limbs were purposeless. So out the opening he thrust his head, to see the canopy of the sky grow broader, and the world waxing wider.

Back to his corner but not to rest, for the spell of the Unknown was over him, and again and again he goes to the open door, seeing each time more Light.

Then one time standing in the flood of it; a deep in-drawn breath – a bracing of strong limbs, and with a bound he was gone.

On he rushes, in his mad flight, heedless that he is wounding and tearing his sleek sides – seeing, smelling, touching of all things; even stopping to put his lips to the noxious pool, thinking it may be sweet.

Hungering there is no food but such as he must seek and often times fight for; and his limbs are weighted before he reaches the water that is good to his thirsting throat.

So does he live, seeking, finding, joying and suffering. The door which accident had opened is opened still, but the cage remains forever empty!

1 Which of the following is <u>NOT</u> correct about the protagonist?

① He was born in a cage and was unaware of the world outside.

② An invisible caretaker provided with all his needs.

③ He felt comfortable in his cage and grew up strong and handsome.

④ He accidentally opened the cage while playing.

⑤ When the cage was open, he was scared and wanted to close it, only to find himself helpless.

2 Which of the following is <u>NOT</u> correct about the passage?

① The passage metaphorically depicts the journey of an individual who starts life in a confined and sheltered environment.

② The "invisible protecting hand" represents the care and provisions that are provided without effort or struggle.

③ The individual's needs are met with much effort — food, water, and rest are readily available.

④ A turning point occurs when the cage door is accidentally left open, which represents the unexpected opportunity for the individual to break free from their confined reality.

⑤ The transition from the cage to the outside world is depicted as a bold leap of courage and curiosity.

UNIT

7

3 Which of the following is <u>neither</u> stated <u>nor</u> implied about protagonist?

① He was unhappy with his own little world.

② He was put in a situation where he had to decide whether to stay or to leave.

③ He saw, smelt, and touched many things, even harmful ones too.

④ Unlike inside the cage, he had to seek and fight for food and water.

⑤ He preferred freedom to comforts in a cage.

4 본문의 내용과 일치하도록 빈칸을 들어갈 단어를 채워 넣으시오. (각 빈칸엔 한 단어만 넣을 것)

When the animal finds the door of his cage opened, he has to decide whether to stay or to leave. The former choice guarantees him a safe, c_____ life even if depending on "_____ _____ _____", while the latter will oblige him to seek his own food and shelter day by day for the rest of his life. He chooses the second one because he wants to be _____.

5 본문을 통해서 얻을 수 있는 교훈(moral)은 무엇이라고 생각하는지 한 문장의 영어로 쓰시오.

Sentence Completion

1 My ex-best friend tried to _____ my reputation with her vicious gossip.

① rack up   ② compliment

③ besmirch   ④ exalt

> **어휘** ex- 전 ex-best friend 예전에 가장 친했던 친구 try to ⓡ ~하려고 노력하다, 애쓰다 reputation 명성, 평판 vicious 사악한, 악의 있는 gossip 험담, 잡담 rack up 이기다, 달성하다 compliment ~을 칭찬(찬양)하다 besmirch ~을 더럽히다, (명예·인격 따위를) 손상시키다 exalt (명예·품위 등을) 높이다, 승진시키다; 칭찬하다, 찬양하다

2 His musical ability has been _____ by his other accomplishments.

① revealed   ② obscured

③ popularized   ④ exposed

> **어휘** musical 음악적인 ability 재능 other 다른, 다른 사람(것) accomplishment 성취, 업적 reveal ~을 드러내다, 나타내다 obscure ~을 무색하게 하다, ~을 덮어 감추다 popularize ~을 대중화하다; 보급시키다 expose ~을 노출시키다, 진열하다

3 It is surprising, but unruly people often times become _____ if they are treated with _____ by their peers, friends, and neighbors.

① tidy – honesty

② serene – compassion

③ biblical – love

④ sublime – pomposity

⑤ ruthless – juxtaposition

> **어휘** surprising 놀라운 unruly 제멋대로 구는 often times 자주, 종종 become ~이 되다; ~에 어울리다 if 만약~라면 treat ~을 다루다, 대접하다 peer 동료; 귀족 neighbor 이웃 tidy 단정한, 깔끔한 honesty 정직 serene 고요한, 차분한 compassion 동정 biblical 성경의 sublime 장대한, 장엄한, 최고의, 숭고한 pomposity 거만함, 호화로움, 과장 ruthless 무자비한, 가차 없는 juxtaposition 병렬, 나란히 놓기

4 The soldiers held out for a while, but in the end were overwhelmed by _____ numbers.

① sheer   ② considerable

③ mere   ④ major

⑤ widespread

5 The police _____ the suspected murderer for further questioning.

① cordoned   ② smuggled

③ detained   ④ deduced

⑤ probed

6 A great many animals and plants are threatened with _____. Dolphins and whales, gorillas and wild elephants are now classified as _____ animals.

① existence – distinguished   ② environment – survival

③ destruction – phenomenal   ④ extinction – endangered

⑤ termination – adapted

7 Frustrated by the many _____, the scientist reluctantly _____ his experiment.

① successes – finished

② dangers – extended

③ liabilities – studied

④ complications – terminated

8 By buying directly from fishing boats, the restaurant keeps its lobster menu _____.

① shabby

② effortless

③ expensive

④ affordable

UNIT

7

9 One way to show our _____ to our mentors is by the achievements we have made.

① gravity

② gratitude

③ insomnia

④ immortality

10 Though it would be _____ to expect Barnard to have worked out all of the limitations of his experiment, he must be _____ for his neglect of quantitative analysis.

① unjust – pardoned

② impudent – dismissed

③ unrealistic – criticized

④ pointless – examined

⑤ inexcusable – recognized

어휘 work out 해결하다 neglect 무시, 간과, 방치, 태만, 부주의 quantitative 양적인, 양에 관한 unjust 부당한 pardoned 용인된 impudent 뻔뻔스러운, 철면피의 dismiss 해산시키다, 해고하다, 깨끗이 잊어버리다 pointless 뾰족한 끝이 없는, 무딘, 무의미한, 요령 없는 inexcusable 변명이 서지 않는, 용서할 수 없는

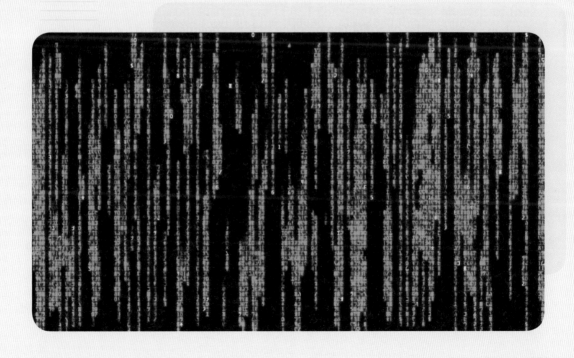

비문학_철학과 영화

The Matrix Is
The Real World

Voca Master

☐ **cast**

v To create a shadow

- The tall building <u>cast</u> a long shadow across the park.

☐ **perception**

n The process of becoming aware of or understanding something through the senses

- Our <u>perception</u> of beauty varies from person to person.

☐ **mere**

a Used to emphasize that something is small, slight, or insignificant

- It's not just a <u>mere</u> coincidence; there's a deeper connection.

☐ **reflection**

n The throwing back of light, sound, or heat by a surface

- The <u>reflection</u> of the mountains in the lake was breathtaking.

☐ **hypothesize**

v To suggest a possible explanation or idea based on limited evidence

- Scientists often <u>hypothesize</u> before conducting experiments.

☐ **meditation**

n The practice of focusing one's mind for relaxation, introspection, or spiritual purposes

- <u>Meditation</u> can help reduce stress and improve mental clarity.

☐ **Meditations on First Philosophy**

A philosophical work by René Descartes in which he explores the nature of knowledge and existence

- "<u>Meditations on First Philosophy</u>" is a seminal text in modern philosophy.

☐ **orchestrate**

v To arrange or coordinate elements, often for a specific purpose

- The conductor will <u>orchestrate</u> the music for the symphony.

☐ **deceitful**　　　**a** Intending to deceive or mislead; dishonest

- His deceitful behavior was revealed when the truth came out.

☐ **if you will**　　　A phrase used to suggest that something could be described in a certain way

- He was a visionary, an artist, if you will, of the culinary world.

☐ **devoid**　　　**a** Completely lacking in something; empty or without

- The desert appeared devoid of any signs of life.

☐ **platonic**　　　**a** Relating to the philosophy of Plato or characterized by non-sexual, idealized relationships

- Their friendship was purely platonic, with no romantic involvement.

☐ **Cartesian**　　　**a** Relating to the philosophy or ideas of René Descartes

- Descartes' Cartesian dualism distinguishes between mind and body.

☐ **explore**　　　**v** To investigate or inquire into a subject or area of interest

- The scientists will explore the deep ocean to study marine life.

☐ **simulation**　　　**n** The imitation of a real-world process or system using a model or computer program

- Flight simulations are used to train pilots in a safe, simulated environment.

☐ **enlightenment**　　　**n** The state of gaining knowledge, understanding, or spiritual insight

- The Enlightenment era led to advancements in science and philosophy.

UNIT

8

☐ **skepticism** **n** Doubt or a questioning attitude, especially towards accepted beliefs or claims

- Scientific <u>skepticism</u> encourages critical thinking and inquiry.

☐ **forefront** **n** The leading or most important position or place

- The company strives to be at the <u>forefront</u> of technological innovation.

☐ **unto oneself** Independently or self-sufficiently

- He lived <u>unto himself</u>, free from external influences.

☐ **in large part** To a significant extent; mainly or mostly

- The success of the project was due <u>in large part</u> to their dedication.

☐ **embodiment** **n** The physical representation or personification of an idea, quality, or concept

- Martin Luther King Jr. was seen as the <u>embodiment</u> of civil rights.

☐ **reflect** **v** To think deeply or consider carefully

- He needed time to <u>reflect</u> on his decision before making a choice.

☐ **adjust to** To adapt or get used to a new situation or environment

- It may take some time to <u>adjust to</u> the culture of a foreign country.

☐ **double-life** Leading two separate and often conflicting lives or identities

- He maintained a <u>double-life</u>, appearing normal by day and living a secret life by night.

alias

An alternative name or pseudonym used by a person

- The author, using an _alias_, published controversial stories anonymously.

deem

v To consider or judge something in a particular way

- The committee will _deem_ the proposal acceptable if it meets the criteria.

plunge

v To suddenly or rapidly descend or immerse oneself into something

- She decided to _plunge_ into the icy water for a refreshing swim.

apocalyptic

a Relating to the end of the world or a catastrophic event

- The movie portrayed an _apocalyptic_ scenario where humanity faced extinction.

dystopia

n An imaginary society characterized by oppressive and undesirable conditions

- The novel described a _dystopia_ where individual freedoms were severely restricted.

supreme

a Having ultimate authority or being the highest in rank, power, or quality

- The _supreme_ leader held absolute control over the nation.

no more than = nothing but = only

Expressing that something is limited to a specific extent and nothing more

- This task requires _no more than_ patience and dedication, nothing more.

be akin to

To be similar to or share characteristics with something else

- Her talent for music _is akin to_ her father's, as they both play multiple instruments.

UNIT

8

☐ **transcendent**　　**a** Going beyond ordinary limits; surpassing; exceeding

- The beauty of the painting was transcendent, leaving viewers in awe.

☐ **manipulate**　　**v** To control or influence something or someone, often in a dishonest or skillful manner

- The politician was accused of trying to manipulate public opinion through false statements.

☐ **resurrect**　　**v** To bring something back to life, figuratively or literally

- The old theater was resurrected and became a popular cultural venue.

☐ **iconic**　　**a** Widely recognized and admired as a symbol of something; representing a significant meaning

- The Eiffel Tower is an iconic symbol of Paris and France.

☐ **cascade**　　**v** To fall, flow, or hang in a way that resembles a waterfall

- Her long hair cascaded down her back in graceful waves.

☐ **realization**　　**n** The act of becoming aware of something or achieving a goal

- His realization of the importance of education led him to pursue a college degree.

☐ **enlightened**　　**a** Having gained knowledge, insight, or understanding, often in a spiritual or intellectual sense

- The enlightened philosopher believed in the power of reason and critical thinking.

☐ **transcendence**　　**n** The act or state of surpassing or going beyond normal limits or boundaries

- The music reached a level of transcendence, touching the souls of the audience.

☐ **abet**

v To encourage or assist someone, typically in a wrongdoing or harmful act

- He was arrested for <u>abetting</u> the thieves in their criminal activities.

☐ **Cartesian Skepticism**

A form of philosophical skepticism associated with René Descartes, characterized by doubting the validity of one's beliefs

- <u>Cartesian Skepticism</u> challenges traditional beliefs and seeks to establish a foundation of knowledge based on indubitable truths.

☐ **chart**

v To make a visual record of data or events; to plot or graph

- The scientist <u>charted</u> the growth of the plants over several months.

☐ **scatter**

v To disperse or spread something in different directions

- The wind caused the leaves to <u>scatter</u> across the yard.

☐ **retrieve**

v To recover or find something and bring it back

- The search and rescue team worked tirelessly to <u>retrieve</u> the lost hikers.

☐ **engineer**

v To design, plan, or oversee the construction or operation of something

- He will <u>engineer</u> the new bridge project to ensure its structural integrity.

☐ **allusion**

n A brief and indirect reference to a person, place, thing, or idea

- The novel contains an <u>allusion</u> to a famous historical event.

UNIT
8

☐ **bring A into B**
To introduce or involve something (A) in a particular situation or context (B)

- The speaker will <u>bring</u> humor <u>into</u> the presentation to engage the audience.

☐ **ponder**
v To think deeply or carefully about something

- She took a moment to <u>ponder</u> the implications of his words.

☐ **reference**
n Mention or citation of a source, idea, or piece of information

- The research paper included a <u>reference</u> to a famous scientific study.

☐ **devise**
v To invent, plan, or create something, especially a complex system or idea

- The team had to <u>devise</u> a new strategy to overcome the competition.

☐ **malicious**
a Intending to harm, annoy, or cause trouble for someone

- The <u>malicious</u> email contained a virus that damaged the recipient's computer.

☐ **sentinel**
n A guard or watchman, often assigned to keep watch and protect a place

- The <u>sentinel</u> stood watch at the entrance to the palace.

☐ **nought**
n Another term for "zero," indicating the absence of quantity or value

- The temperature dropped to <u>nought</u> degrees Celsius during the winter storm.

☐ **avail oneself**
To make use of something or take advantage of an opportunity

- She decided to <u>avail herself</u> of the resources at the library for her research.

☐ **lay a trap**

To set up a situation or plan in order to deceive, capture, or harm someone

- The detective had to <u>lay a trap</u> to catch the cunning criminal.

☐ **credulity**

n Willingness to believe or trust too readily, especially without proper evidence or justification

- His <u>credulity</u> led him to fall for various scams.

☐ **paragon**

n A person or thing regarded as a perfect example of a particular quality or trait

- She was considered a <u>paragon</u> of honesty among her colleagues.

☐ **endorse**

v To express approval or support for something, such as a plan, idea, or product

- The famous athlete agreed to <u>endorse</u> the new sports drink.

☐ **crew member**

n A person who is part of a team operating or working on a vehicle, vessel, or aircraft

- The <u>crew members</u> of the ship worked together to navigate through rough seas.

☐ **Nebuchadnezzar**

n A reference to Nebuchadnezzar, an ancient Babylonian king who reigned from 605 to 562 BC

- Known for his ambitious construction projects, <u>Nebuchadnezzar</u> is credited with the construction of the Hanging Gardens of Babylon, one of the Seven Wonders of the Ancient World.

☐ **hack**

v To gain unauthorized access to computer systems or data, often with malicious intent

- The cybersecurity expert was hired to prevent hackers from attempting to <u>hack</u> into the company's network.

☐ **in return**　　　In exchange for something; as a reciprocal action or response

- She helped him with his project, and in return, he offered his assistance with her research.

☐ **wipe**　　　**v** To clean or remove something by rubbing or drying with a cloth, paper, or one's hand

- She used a tissue to wipe the spill from the table.

☐ **juicy**　　　**a** Having a lot of juice or liquid content, often used to describe fruits or meat

- The watermelon was ripe and juicy, making it perfect for a hot summer day.

☐ **ignorance is bliss**　　　A proverbial phrase suggesting that not knowing certain information can lead to greater happiness

- Sometimes, ignorance is bliss, and it's better not to know all the details.

☐ **call into question**　　　To doubt, challenge, or raise doubts about the truth or validity of something

- The new evidence called into question the accuracy of the previous findings.

☐ **ontology**　　　**n** The branch of philosophy that deals with the nature of existence and being

- Ontology explores questions about what it means for something to exist.

☐ **projection**　　　**n** The act of projecting or casting something forward, often in a visual or symbolic sense

- The artist used perspective to create a realistic sense of projection in the painting.

☐ **bring life**　　To give vitality, energy, or excitement to something

- The talented actor's performance on stage can <u>bring life</u> to any character.

☐ **representation**　　**n** The act of depicting, symbolizing, or portraying something through various means

- The painting was a beautiful <u>representation</u> of the natural landscape.

☐ **amalgam**　　**n** A mixture or combination of different elements, often forming a unified whole

- The recipe was an <u>amalgam</u> of various culinary traditions.

☐ **attach**　　**v** To connect, fasten, or join one thing to another

- He used glue to <u>attach</u> the pieces of the broken vase.

☐ **gaze**　　A steady or intent look or stare; to look steadily at something

- They shared a romantic <u>gaze</u> at the sunset.

☐ **sentiment**　　**n** A view, opinion, or attitude, often expressed emotionally

- Her <u>sentiment</u> on the matter was clear: she believed in the importance of protecting the environment.

☐ **linger**　　**v** To stay in a place longer than necessary or expected, often unwilling to leave

- The memories of their vacation <u>lingered</u> in their minds long after they returned home.

☐ **summate**　　**v** To calculate or add up the sum or total of something

- She had to <u>summate</u> all the expenses for the project report.

UNIT

8

☐ **consequence**   **n** A result or effect of an action or condition; an outcome

- The <u>consequence</u> of his decision to quit his job was a period of financial instability.

☐ **inkling**   **v** To lead to (something) as a result

- His actions may <u>inkling</u> a change in the company's policies.

☐ **goop**   **n** A sticky or viscous substance that clings to things

- The spilled syrup turned into a sticky <u>goop</u> on the kitchen floor.

☐ **inhibit**   **v** To hinder, restrain, or prevent something from happening or progressing

- Fear can <u>inhibit</u> a person's ability to take risks.

2 Text Reading

: The Matrix Is The Real World

Text **1**

"And now," Plato says, "let me show in a figure how far our nature is enlightened or unenlightened."

Plato personifies this 'unenlightenment' of human nature through his famous "allegory of the cave" — the allegory of prisoners chained in a cave whose entire perception of reality is but shadows cast on a wall in front of them. For Plato, the shadows on the wall are not reality but rather mere reflections of more real objects. 17th-century French philosopher René Descartes similarly hypothesized in the early meditations of his "Meditations on First Philosophy" that all of the human world is but a world of shadows orchestrated by a deceitful "evil genius." For both Descartes and Plato, this world of shadows, the cave, the simulation, or Matrix if you will, is illusory and devoid of value.

UNIT

8

 **핵심 PLUS!**

1 "And now," Plato says, "let me <u>show</u> (in a figure) <u>how far our nature is enlightened or unenlightened</u>."

- show의 목적어로 의문사가 이끄는 명사절 확인: how far our nature is enlightened or unenlightened

2 Plato personifies this 'unenlightenment' of human nature through his famous "allegory of the cave" — the allegory of prisoners <u>chained</u> in a cave (<u>**whose**</u> entire perception of reality is but shadows <u>**cast**</u> on a wall in front of them).

- chained와 cast는 바로 앞의 명사를 각각 수식하는 과거분사
- 소유격 관계대명사 whose의 선행사는 prisoners로 chained와 함께 이중수식을 받고 있음.

3 For Plato, the shadows on the wall are <u>**not**</u> reality <u>**but**</u> rather mere reflections of more real objects.

- not A but B 구문

4 17th-century French philosopher René Descartes similarly **hypothesized** (in the early meditations of his "Meditations on First Philosophy") **that** all of the human world is but a world of shadows (<u>**orchestrated**</u> by a deceitful "evil genius)."

- 타동사 hypothesize의 목적어 that절: hypothesize (부사구) that S V
- orchestrated는 shadows를 수식하는 과거분사

The 1999 film The Matrix by the Wachowskis is largely Platonic and Cartesian; the film explores the journey of one man from the Matrix, a simulation ruled by deceitful robots, into the enlightenment of the 'real world.' While Plato and Descartes' skepticism of the existence of the external world seems to be at the <u>forefront</u> of the film, The Matrix also argues the anti-Platonic possibility that perhaps the Matrix isn't any less real than the 'real world'. Through analyzing Descartes' later meditations, the work of anti-Platonic philosopher Stanley Cavell, and the motivations of the character Cypher in the film, one may argue that the Matrix is indeed reality unto itself and retains the same value as the "real world."

1 본문에서 언급된 영화 The Matrix에 관한 옳은 진술만으로 짝지어진 것은?

> I. The film is likely to explore the characters' doubts about the reality of their world, echoing the philosophical skepticism of Plato and Descartes.
> II. The film challenges traditional Platonic thought by considering the idea that the Matrix may have equal reality and significance compared to the 'real world.'
> III. The film seems to encourage viewers to consider the Matrix as a legitimate reality, conforming to the traditional binary distinction between reality and illusion.

① I and II   ② I and III
③ II   ④ III
⑤ All of the above

2 본문의 밑줄 친 단어 <u>forefront</u>의 문맥적 의미를 가장 표현한 것은?

① the primary focus   ② the physical barrier
③ the historical reference   ④ the hidden agenda
⑤ the secondary concern

UNIT

8

 핵심 PLUS!

1 the film explores the <u>journey</u> of one man <u>from</u> the Matrix, (<u>a simulation ruled by deceitful robots</u>), <u>into</u> the enlightenment of the 'real world.'

- journey from A into B
- 동격의 코마(,): the Matrix = a simulation
- 과거분사 ruled의 수식을 받는 명사구: **<u>a simulation</u>** ruled by deceitful robots

2 [While Plato and Descartes' skepticism of the existence of the external world seems to be at the forefront of the film], The Matrix also argues the anti-Platonic possibility that perhaps the Matrix <u>isn't any less real than</u> the 'real world'.

- A is not any less real than B
  = A and B are equally real
  = Neither A is more real or substantial than B

3 [Through analyzing Descartes' later meditations, the work of anti-Platonic philosopher Stanley Cavell, and the motivations of the character Cypher in the film]], one may argue that the Matrix is indeed reality <u>unto itself</u> and retains the same value as the "real world."

- Through에 걸리는 명사구 병치: A, B, and C
- unto itself: 그 자체로

The Matrix and Plato's Allegory of The Cave

The Matrix, in large part, is an embodiment of Plato's "Allegory of the Cave." Plato's allegory is reflected through a dialogue between fictional versions of Glaucon, Plato's brother, and Socrates. Plato, speaking through Socrates, explains the allegory: In a cave, there are prisoners chained so that all they have ever known is a wall in front of them Ⓐ_____ _____ shadows of objects moving in front of a fire behind them are cast. Socrates says, "For them…the truth would be literally nothing but the shadows of images." Socrates then explains the various reactions of the prisoners when they are released — their trouble Ⓑ(adjust) physically and mentally to their new reality. In The Matrix, Thomas Anderson is a computer programmer who leads a double-life as a hacker under the alias Neo. After Ⓒ(deem) "The One" by Morpheus, Neo is presented with two choices; either take the blue pill and stay in his illusory world; or take the red pill and be reborn into the truth of reality. Neo chooses the red pill and plunges into the 'real world' — a post-apocalyptic dystopia Ⓓ_____ the human race is grown and harvested for energy by a supreme class of artificial intelligence. Neo realizes that his previous 'reality' was no more than a simulation. Through a Platonic lens, the Matrix, and all the humans in it are akin to the prisoners Ⓔ(watch) shadows on the cave wall. Plato says of a freed prisoner, "When he approaches the light his eyes will be dazzled, and he will not be able to see anything at all of what are now called realities." When Neo first leaves the Matrix, he asks Morpheus, " Why do my eyes hurt?" Ⓕ_____ _____ Morpheus replies, "Because you've never used them before."

3 본문의 내용에 비추어 옳지 <u>않은</u> 진술만으로 짝지어진 것은?

> I. The passage explores the concept of reality and illusion from the perspectives of Plato and René Descartes.
>
> II. Plato uses the allegory of the cave to illustrate the concept of enlightened human nature.
>
> III. According to Plato, prisoners in a cave mistake shadows for reality due to their limited perspective, which implies that humans can be unaware of the true nature of reality and may mistake illusions for truth.
>
> IV. Descartes' hypothesis questions the reliability of our perceptions and proposes that skepticism serves as a tool to differentiate the truthfulness of things we encounter through our senses.
>
> V. Both philosophers regarded the world of illusions as lacking genuine value or significance.

① I and II   ② I and IV
③ II   ④ II, III and IV
⑤ II and V

4 Ⓐ~Ⓕ의 괄호의 바른 표현 또는 밑줄에 들어갈 표현으로 적절하지 <u>않은</u> 것의 총 개수는?

> Ⓐ onto which
> Ⓑ to adjust
> Ⓒ being deemed
> Ⓓ where
> Ⓔ watching
> Ⓕ about which

① 0개   ② 1개
③ 2개   ④ 3개
⑤ 4개

어구 및 표현 연구

핵심 PLUS!

1 Plato, speaking through Socrates, explains the allegory: In a cave, there are prisoners **chained so that** [all (that) they have ever known] is a wall in front of them [**onto which** S (shadows of objects **moving** in front of a fire behind them) are cast].

- There구문의 주어 prisoners를 수식하는 과거분사 chained
- 부사절을 이끄는 접속사 so that: S V ~ so that S V
- [전치사 + 관계대명사 + S V]의 구조 파악: 주어 자리의 objects는 현재분사 moving의 수식을 받고 있음.

2 Socrates says, "For them...the truth would be literally **nothing but** the shadows of images."

- nothing but = no more than = only

3 Socrates then explains the various reactions of the prisoners when they are released — their trouble adjusting physically and mentally to their new reality.

- 동격의 dash(-): the various reactions = their trouble adjusting physically and mentally to their new reality

4 In The Matrix, Thomas Anderson is a computer programmer (**who** leads a double-life as a hacker under the alias Neo).

- 주격 관계대명사 who

5 (After **being deemed** "The One" by Morpheus), Neo **is presented with** two choices; **either** take the blue pill and stay in his illusory world; **or** take the red pill and **be reborn into** the truth of reality.

- 5형식 수동태 deem의 구조 이해: deem A B → A is deemed B
- be V-ed with의 수동표현
- 세미콜론(;)은 two choices에 대한 부연 진술: two choices = either A or B

UNIT

8

6 Neo chooses the red pill and plunges into the 'real world' — a post-apocalyptic dystopia (**where** the human race **is grown and harvested** (for energy) **by** a supreme class of artificial intelligence).

- 동격의 dash(-): the 'real world' — a post-apocalyptic dystopia
- 장소의 관계부사 where와 be p.p and p.p by의 수동태

Text Reading | 207

7 Through a Platonic lens, the Matrix, and all the humans in it are akin to (the prisoners **watching** shadows on the cave wall).

- the prisoners를 후치수식하는 현재분사 watching

8 Plato says of a freed prisoner, "When he approaches the light his eyes will be dazzled, and he will **not** be able to see [anything **at all** of (**what** are now called realities)]."

- not ~ at all과 전치사 of에 걸리는 명사절 관계대명사 what

9 "Why do my eyes hurt?" **to which** Morpheus replies, "Because you've never used them before."

- reply to의 to가 관계대명사 앞으로 전치된 to which 파악. [전치사 + 관계대명사 + 완전절(S + V)]

그림 박예송

Plato and the "Divided Line"

The Divided Line

A Picture of Plato's Ontology

Eternal Invisible Immaterial	World of Being	Being/ Goodness	Reason
	World of Numbers	Numbers Shapes Universals Souls	Intellect
Temporal Sensory Material	World of Objects	tables dogs trees cars birds etc.	Belief
	World of Images	painting sculpture shadow reflection theater fiction unicorn	Imagination

UNIT
8

Plato's notion of the "Divided Line" reveals within his allegory the hierarchy of truth and reality. In the cave, the empirical world of our senses/images, the shadows on the wall are the least real things there are. More real than the shadows are the objects that cast them — the men, statues, and animals passing in front of the fire. Both the shadows and the objects, however, are still illusions of the cave. Reality (or at least a more real-world) exists outside of the cave and is known as the intelligible world or the world of numbers and forms. This is the transcendent world of the intellectual mathematics behind the objects of the physical world. At the highest end of the divided line is the idea of The Good, or God.

When Neo leaves the Matrix, it can be said that he leaves the cave and enters the world of forms in which the objects of the Matrix, the cave, can be manipulated. Neo, being The One, represents the closest to "The Good". This is reflected at the end of the film where after being resurrected, Neo is able to see beyond the shadows of the Matrix, the ideas/forms behind them and sees the world as numbers, mathematical objects. The iconic green numbers cascading down the screen are the realization of Plato's view of enlightened transcendence from the human world of the senses.

5   Choose the number that contains all the correct statements.

I.   Plato's 'Divided Line' is a philosophical concept that he uses in his allegory of the cave to depict different levels of reality and knowledge.
II. According to Plato, there is a deeper, more authentic reality that lies beyond what we perceive with our sense.
III. There are different levels of reality, with the shadows representing a higher level of reality compared to the mere objects.
IV. Even the objects in the cave are just a step closer to truth than the shadows.

① I and II   ② II and III
③ I, II and IV   ④ I, III and IV
⑤ II, III and IV

어구 및 표현 연구

 **핵심 PLUS!**

1 In the cave, the empirical world of our senses/images, the shadows on the wall are the least real things (that) there are.

- 동격의 코마: the cave = the empirical world of our senses/images
- 주격 관계대명사의 생략

2 (More real than the shadows) are [the objects that cast them] — the men, statues, and animals **passing** in front of the fire.

- 보어도치: S [the objects that cast them] are (more real than the shadows)
- 동격의 dash: the objects = the men, statues, and animals
- the men, statues, and animals를 후치수식 하는 현재분사 passing

3 When Neo leaves the Matrix, it can be said that he leaves the cave and enters the world of forms (**in which** the objects of the Matrix, the cave, can be manipulated).

- [전치사 + 관계대명사 + S V] 파악. which = the world
- 동격의 코마: the Matrix = the cave

4 This is reflected at the end of the film [**where** (after being resurrected), Neo is able to see (beyond the shadows of the Matrix) the ideas/forms behind them and sees the world as numbers, mathematical objects].

- 장소 관계부사 where의 선행사는 the end
- [see + (부사구) + 목적어] 구조

UNIT
8

5 [The iconic green numbers **cascading** down the screen] are the realization of Plato's view **of** enlightened transcendence from the human world of the senses.

- 후치수식의 현재분사 cascading
- 동격의 of: Plato's view = enlightened transcendence from the human world of the senses

Descartes "Meditations on First Philosophy"

The Platonic philosophy of the Matrix is abetted by Cartesian skepticism. Rene Descartes's "Meditations on First Philosophy" chart Descartes' philosophical journey from doubting the existence of the external world to finally arriving at his conclusion that God, the external world, and minds do indeed exist.

Before Neo is exposed to the 'real world' there are several Cartesian hints scattered throughout. When the goth punks arrive at Neo's door to retrieve the illegal software Neo engineered, one of the punks assures Neo, "Don't worry, this never happened. You don't exist." This is a direct (가)_____ to Neo's Cartesian doubts of his own existence.

Descartes' first Meditation deals with the "things which may be brought into the sphere of the doubtful." (나)Among these things to be doubted is the existence of one's own mind. Descartes ponders over the idea that perhaps nothing is real, even himself. In the same scene, Neo asks, "Have you ever had the feeling where you're not sure if you're awake or still dreaming?" This is another direct reference to Descartes' first Meditation where he similarly asks, "How often has it happened to me that in the night I dreamt that I found myself in this particular place, that I was dressed and seated near the fire, whilst in reality, I was lying undressed in bed!"

6   본문의 빈칸 (가)에 들어갈 단어로 가장 적절한 것은?

① paradox   ② allusion
③ pipe dream   ④ contradiction
⑤ skepticism

7   According to the text, which of the following best explains Descartes' conclusion about "the existence of one's own mind" mentioned in underlined (나)?

① Descartes concluded that the existence of one's own mind is beyond doubt.
② Descartes concluded that one's mind is an illusion and does not exist.
③ Descartes concluded that the existence of one's own mind is as doubtful as the existence of the external world.
④ Descartes concluded that the existence of one's mind is the only certainty, while everything else can be doubted.
⑤ Descartes did not reach any specific conclusion regarding the existence of one's mind.

핵심 PLUS!

1 The Platonic philosophy of the Matrix <u>is abetted by</u> Cartesian skepticism. Rene Descartes's "Meditations on First Philosophy" <u>chart</u> Descartes' philosophical <u>journey from</u> doubting the existence of the external world <u>to</u> finally arriving at his conclusion that God, the external world, and minds do indeed exist.

- 수동태 be abetted by
- chart journey from A to B

2 (Before Neo is exposed to the 'real world') there are <u>several Cartesian hints</u> (**scattered** throughout).

- 과거분사 scattered가 There구 문의 주어인 several Cartesian hints 수식.

3 [When the goth punks arrive at Neo's door <u>to</u> <u>retrieve</u> the illegal software (**that**) Neo engineered], one of the punks assures Neo, "Don't worry, this never happened.

- to부정사의 부사적 용법: ~하기 위해서
- 생략된 목적격 관계대명사 that 또 는 which

4 Descartes' first Meditation deals with the "things **which** may be brought into the sphere of the doubtful."

- 주격 관계대명사

5 (Among these things <u>to be doubted</u>) is **S** [the existence of one's own mind].

- 1형식 부사구 도치구문으로 원문 으로 아래와 같다.
  → The existence of one's own mind is among these things to be doubted
- to부정사 수동태

6 Descartes ponders over the idea **that** perhaps nothing is real, even himself.

- 동격의 that: the idea = perhaps nothing is real, even himself

7 This is another direct reference to Descartes' first Meditation **where** he similarly asks, "How often has it happened to me that (in the night) I dreamt ⌜that I found myself in this particular place⌝, ⌜that I was dressed and seated near the fire⌝, whilst in reality, I was lying undressed in bed!"

- 선행사 Descartes' first Meditation을 수식하는 관계부사 where
- 타동사 dreamt의 목적어 자리에 명사절 that의 병치

Descartes argues that if we can feel as if we are awake during sleep, it is quite possible that we could always be in a sleep state and are merely imagining (가)_____, like those in the Matrix. Neo's skepticism proves true after he takes the red pill and discovers his old world was a simulation devised by malicious artificial intelligence known as sentinels. Descartes had a similar inkling about his world. In Meditation 1, Descartes supposes,

"I shall consider that the heavens, the earth, colours, figures, sound, and all other external things are nought but the illusions and dreams of which this evil genius has availed himself in order to lay traps for my (나)_____."

The sentinels are to Neo as the "evil genius" is to Descartes.

8 (가)와 (나)의 빈칸에 들어갈 표현으로 바르게 짝지어진 것은?

① reality – contradiction
② consciousness – credulity
③ illusion – senses
④ perception – doubts
⑤ skepticism – understanding

어구 및 표현 연구   핵심 PLUS!

1 Descartes argues that (if we can feel as if we are awake during sleep), **it** is quite possible **that** we could always be in a sleep state and are merely imagining consciousness, like **those** in the Matrix.

- 가주어it/진주어that
- those = 앞서 언급된 "we could always be in a sleep state and are merely imagining consciousness" 상황들을 지칭.

2 Neo's skepticism proves true [after he **takes** the red pill and **discovers** (that) his old world was a simulation **devised** by malicious artificial intelligence **known** as sentinels].

- 전체적으로 2형식 문장으로 수식어구인 부사절 after 내 구조 파악.
- 후치수식의 과거분사 devised와 known

3 Descartes had a similar inkling about his world. In Meditation 1, Descartes supposes, "I shall consider that the heavens, the earth, colours, figures, sound, and all other external things are **nought but** the illusions and dreams **of which** this evil genius has availed himself in order to lay traps for my credulity."

- nought but = nothing but
- [전치사 + 관계대명사]
~ the illusions and dreams **of which** this evil genius has availed himself in order to lay traps for my credulity
= ~ the illusions and dreams. This evil genius has availed himself **of the illusions and dreams** in order to lay traps for my credulity
» avail oneself of ~을 이용하다

4 The sentinels **are to** Neo **as** the "evil genius" **is to** Descartes.

- A is to B as C is to B: A는 C가 D의 관계처럼 B와 관련된다

216 | Part 2

Enter: Cypher

By Platonic and early-meditation-Cartesian standards, the Matrix is the Ⓐparagon of the illusion and deception of our sensible world. For Plato and Descartes, reality has a particular value that shadows on the wall or dreams do not. In the Matrix, one character in particular, argues Ⓑfor the Platonic and Cartesian skepticism that the film seems to endorse.

Cypher is a crew member on the Nebuchadnezzar who betrayed the last human city, Zion, by helping Agent Smith hack into its' mainframe. In return, Cypher wanted to go back to the Matrix with his memory Ⓒwiped of the 'real world'. In one of the film's most important scenes, Cypher meets with Agent Smith over a steak dinner. Cypher says,

"You know, I know this steak doesn't exist. I know that when I put it in my mouth, the Matrix is telling my brain that it is juicy and delicious. After nine years, you know what I realize? ⒹIgnorance is bliss."

This line not only calls into question how we experience 'reality' and 'existence' but also the value we attach to it. For Cypher, the Matrix and its blissful ignorance are Ⓔ more valuable than the 'real world'.

9 글의 흐름으로 보아 밑줄 친 어휘 Ⓐ~Ⓔ의 쓰임이 어색한 것은?

① Ⓐ paragon
② Ⓑ for
③ Ⓒ wiped
④ Ⓓ Ignorance
⑤ Ⓔ more

10 본문의 이해로 가장 적절한 것은?

① Platonic and Cartesian philosophers considered the Matrix to be a representation of the true reality.
② Cypher values the illusion of the Matrix over the reality of the 'real world.'
③ The passage suggests that Cypher is a heroic character who defends Zion against Agent Smith.
④ The Matrix is portrayed in the passage as a place of great intellectual stimulation.
⑤ The passage implies that the Matrix is a symbol of knowledge and enlightenment.

1 For Plato and Descartes, reality has a particular value (**that** shadows on the wall or dreams do not). In the Matrix, one character in particular, argues against the Platonic and Cartesian skepticism (**that** the film seems to endorse).

- 생략 가능한 목적격 관계대명사

2 Cypher is a crew member on the Nebuchadnezzar [**who** betrayed the last human city, Zion, (by helping Agent Smith hack into its' mainframe)].

- 주격 관계대명사 who
- 동격의 코마(,): the last human city = Zion
- betray를 수식하는 전치사구 파악

3 In return, Cypher wanted to go back to the Matrix (**with** his memory **wiped** of the 'real world').

- with N v-ed의 부대상황 구문으로 "N 가 V된 채"로 해석.

4 This line **not only** calls into question (how we experience 'reality' and 'existence') **but also** the value (**that** we attach to it).

- not only A but also B 구문과 생략 가능한 목적격 관계대명사 that
- 보통 [call + (목적어) + into question] 에서 목적어(how we experience 'reality' and 'existence')가 후치된 것 으로 볼 수 있지만, 구 또는 절의 긴 목 적어가 온 경우 call into question을 하나의 타동사구로 볼 수 있음.

Descartes believes the matrix is real

In the 5th and 6th meditations, Descartes proves that not only do other minds exist but so does the external world and himself. This conclusion is summated by the infamous phrase, "I think therefore I am." This sentiment can be seen lingering under the film's veil of Platonic philosophy.

The Platonic Morpheus claims Ⓐthe Matrix to be but shadows and like shadows on a cave wall, the Matrix can bear consequences to the real world. After Neo leaves a training module in the Matrix and finds himself bleeding Ⓑhe asks Morpheus, "I thought it wasn't real." ⒸMorpheus says, "Your mind makes it real."

Neo then asks, "If you're killed in the Matrix, you die here?" and ⒹMorpheus answers, "The body cannot live without the mind." Just as Descartes disproves himself in his later meditations, ⒺMorpheus contradicts his Platonic argument of the artificiality of the Matrix. We see that not only can one perceive the Matrix with all senses but consequences of the Matrix translate into the 'real world.' It would seem that the Matrix then, is literally just as real as the real world, or even as Cypher says, "The Matrix can be more real than the real world."

11 밑줄 친 Ⓐ~Ⓔ의 글의 흐름을 방해하는 내용을 담은 것은?

① Ⓐ

② Ⓑ

③ Ⓒ

④ Ⓓ

⑤ Ⓔ

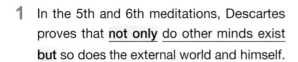

 핵심 PLUS!

1 In the 5th and 6th meditations, Descartes proves that **not only** do other minds exist **but** so does the external world and himself.

- not only와 so 도치

= Other minds not only exist, but the external world and himself also exist.

2 This sentiment can be seen lingering under the film's veil of Platonic philosophy.

- 5형식 지각동사 see의 수동태: be p.p V-ing

3 The Platonic Morpheus claims the Matrix to be but shadows and like shadows on a cave wall, the Matrix can bear no consequences to the real world.

- 5형식 동사로 쓰이고 있는 claim과 목적보어 자리에 to V
- but = only

4 (After Neo leaves a training module in the Matrix and finds himself bleeding) he asks Morpheus, "I thought it wasn't real."

- find oneself V-ing: (자기도 모르게) ~함을 깨닫다

5 **Just as** Descartes disproves himself in his later meditations, (**so**) Morpheus contradicts his Platonic argument of the artificiality of the Matrix.

- Just as S V, so S V 구문에서 so가 생략된 형태.

6 We see that **not only** can one perceive the Matrix with all senses but consequences of the Matrix translate into the 'real world.'

- [not only + V + S]의 도치

3 Voca Check

* 빈칸에 들어갈 적절한 단어를 박스에서 찾아 넣으시오.

1

orchestrate / hypothesize / deceitful / reflection / mere / perception / meditation / cast / devoid

1 The artist used a unique technique to _____ shadows on the canvas, creating a three-dimensional effect in the painting.

2 His _____ of the situation was influenced by his personal experiences and beliefs.

3 The _____ act of kindness brightened her day and lifted her spirits.

4 When looking at his _____ in the mirror, he contemplated the changes that time had brought.

5 Scientists _____ about the origins of the universe and its expansion through extensive research.

6 Regular _____ can help reduce stress and promote mental well-being.

7 The director had to _____ the complex performance, coordinating all aspects of the play.

8 His _____ behavior made it challenging to trust him in business dealings.

9 The old house was _____ of modern conveniences and required extensive renovation.

UNIT

8

2

embodiment / supreme / alias / double-life / plunge / reflect / adjust / deem / skepticism / to / forefront / apocalyptic

1   The scientist's _____ about the experiment's results led to further investigation.

2   The new technology is at the _____ of modern innovation.

3   In his novel, the protagonist serves as the _____ of resilience in the face of adversity.

4   When you _____ on your actions, you can gain valuable insights into your decisions.

5   Many people have to _____ a demanding work schedule and personal life.

6   The spy lived a _____, using different names and identities.

7   The criminal used an _____ to hide their true identity from the authorities.

8   Some may _____ the film's dark and _____ vision of the future.

9   The brave firefighter had to _____ into the burning building to save lives.

10 She held a _____ position in the company, overseeing all major decisions.

3

realization / transcendence / enlightened / transcendence / cascade / abet / akin / chart / resurrect / manipulate

1   The artist's work was a _____ of colors and forms, evoking a sense of wonder and awe.

2   The spiritual guru led his followers on a path of _____ and self-discovery.

3   With the help of advanced technology, scientists can now _____ ancient DNA to study long-extinct species.

4   She worked diligently to _____ her way through the complex data and present it in a clear, organized manner.

5   The teacher's guidance _____ her students' understanding of the subject.

6   Their collaboration was _____ to the success of the project.

7   The _____ of the philosopher's ideas led to a profound shift in societal values.

8   The criminal was charged with attempting to _____ his partner in committing the crime.

9   The bond between the two siblings was so strong that they felt _____ to each other.

10 The _____ between art and science is evident in his innovative creations.

UNIT
8

4

engineer / allusion / devise / retrieve / ponder / reference / ponder / malicious

1   The detective had to _____ the evidence scattered throughout the crime scene.

2   The novel's title is a direct _____ to Shakespeare's famous tragedy.

3   The team of engineers worked together to _____ a new, innovative solution to the problem.

4   She couldn't help but _____ the meaning behind the cryptic message.

5   He needed to _____ a plan to address the company's financial challenges.

6   The _____ remark hurt her feelings and left her upset for days.

7   When writing a research paper, it's essential to provide proper _____ to your sources.

8   He took a moment to _____ the complex math problem before attempting to solve it.

5 credulity / endorse / ontology / projection / representation / sentinel / hack / paragon / wipe

1   The security system included a digital _____ to monitor and protect the facility.

2   His belief in conspiracy theories was a result of his extreme _____, making him susceptible to various unfounded claims.

3   The company decided to _____ the new software after thorough testing and positive feedback.

4   She is regarded as a _____ of virtue and integrity in her community.

5   The hacker attempted to _____ sensitive data from the company's database.

6   In the field of philosophy, _____ explores the nature of existence and reality.

7   The artist's painting was a striking _____ of the natural world's beauty.

8   The student's report included a detailed _____ of the country's economic situation.

9   The janitor had to _____ the whiteboard clean after the lecture.

UNIT

8

6   goop / amalgam / apocalyptic / linger / sentiment / consequences / suppress / inkling / gaze / inhibit

1   The painting was a beautiful _____ of various art styles and techniques.

2   As he read the letter, an _____ of sadness and nostalgia overcame him.

3   The scientist had only a vague _____ of the breakthrough discovery until further research confirmed it.

4   He couldn't help but _____ at the stars in the night sky, captivated by their beauty.

5   The chef accidentally spilled some _____ into the soup, ruining the flavor.

6   The long-term _____ of smoking on one's health can be severe.

7   Her shyness would often _____ her from speaking up in class.

8   After the accident, the car was left to _____ by the side of the road.

9   He couldn't _____ the urge to laugh when his friend told a funny joke.

10   The author's novel had an _____ theme, portraying a bleak future for humanity.

4 Reading Comprehension

1 아래 그림에 대한 설명 중 가장 <u>어색한</u> 것은?

 NOTE

In the allegory "The Cave," Socrates describes ①<u>a group of people who have lived chained to the wall of a cave all their lives, facing a blank wall.</u> ②<u>The people watch shadows projected on the wall from objects passing in front of a fire behind them and give names to these shadows.</u> ③<u>The shadows are the prisoners' reality, but are not accurate representations of the real world.</u> ④<u>The shadows represent the fragment of reality that we can normally perceive through our senses.</u> ⑤<u>On the other hand, the objects under the sun represent the true forms of objects that we can only perceive through senses.</u> Three higher levels exist: the natural sciences; mathematics, geometry, and deductive logic; and the theory of forms.

[2-3] Read the passage and answer each question.

 NOTE

〈제시문〉

Plato begins by having Socrates ask Glaucon to imagine a cave where people have been imprisoned from childhood, but not from birth. These prisoners are chained so that their legs and necks are fixed, forcing them to gaze at the wall in front of them and not to look around at the cave, each other, or themselves. Behind the prisoners is a fire, and between the fire and the prisoners is a raised walkway with a low wall, behind which people walk carrying objects or puppets "of (A) men and other living things." The people walk behind the wall so their bodies do not cast shadows for the prisoners to see, but the objects they carry do("just as puppet showmen have screens in front of them at which they work their puppets"). The prisoners cannot see any of what is happening behind them, they are only able to see the shadows cast upon the cave wall in front of them. The sounds of the people talking echo off the walls, and the prisoners believe these sounds come from the shadows.

Socrates suggests that the shadows are reality for the prisoners because they have never seen anything else; they do not realize that what they see are shadows of objects in front of a fire, much less that these objects are inspired by real things outside the cave which they do not see. The fire, or human-made light, and the puppets, used to make shadows, are done by (B)the artists. Plato, however, indicates that the fire is also the political doctrine that is taught in a nation state. The artists use light and shadows to teach the dominant doctrines of a time and place. Also, few humans will ever escape the cave. This is not some easy task, and only a true philosopher, with decades of preparation, would be able to leave the cave, up the steep incline. Most humans will live at the bottom of the cave, and a small few will be the major artists that project the shadows with the use of human-made light.

〈그림: The Divided Line〉

The Divided Line

(A Picture of Plato's Ontology)

Eternal Invisible Immaterial	World of Being	Being/ Goodness	Reason
	World of Numbers	Numbers Shapes Universals Souls	Intellect
Temporal Sensory Material	World of Objects	tables dogs trees cars birds etc.	Belief
	World of Images	painting sculpture shadow reflection theater fiction unicorn	Imagination

UNIT

8

2 Which of the following statements regarding the underlined (A)men and other living things is not correct?

① They refer to "objects" in the cave.

② They belong to the temporal sensory realm where they exist in the form of tables, dogs, trees and so on.

③ They belong to the world that are more real than the world of images.

④ The prisoners in the cave regard numbers as more valuable than objects.

⑤ The prisoners remain unrecognizable of objects throughout their lives unless there happen unusual circumstances.

3 When defining arts based on Plato's view of the underlined (B) in the text, which analysis is most appropriate?

① Plato suggests that art gives people meaning and helps them understand the world around them. Art appreciation improves the quality of life and makes people feel good.

② Plato suggests that arts stimulate learning and improve overall academic performance. There is a powerful relationship between knowledge of the arts and success in scientific endeavors.

③ Plato argues that painting, sculpture, music, literature and the other arts are the repository of a society's collective memory.

④ Plato holds that the arts are representational, or mimetic. Artworks are ontologically dependent on, imitations of, and therefore inferior to, ordinary physical objects.

⑤ Plato claims that art is a representation of life itself. It is a perfect copy of the changeless original.

4 Which of the following is TRUE?

〈제시문 1〉

"And now," Plato says, "let me show in a figure how far our nature is enlightened or unenlightened." Plato personifies this 'unenlightenment' of human nature through his famous "allegory of the cave" — the allegory of prisoners chained in a cave whose entire perception of reality is but shadows cast on a wall in front of them. For Plato, the shadows on the wall are not reality but rather mere reflections of more real objects. 17th-century French philosopher René Descartes similarly hypothesized in the early meditations of his "*Meditations on First Philosophy*" that all of the human world is but a world of shadows orchestrated by a deceitful "evil genius." For both Descartes and Plato, this world of shadows, the cave, the simulation, or Matrix if you will, is illusory and devoid of value.

〈제시문 2〉

Plato's notion of the "Divided Line" reveals within his allegory the hierarchy of truth and reality. In the cave, the empirical world of our senses/images, the shadows on the wall are the least real things there are. More real than the shadows are the objects that cast them — the men, statues, and animals passing in front of the fire. Both the shadows and the objects, however, are still illusions of the cave. Reality (or at least a more real-world) exists outside of the cave and is known as the intelligible world or the world of numbers and forms. This is the transcendent world of the intellectual mathematics behind the objects of the physical world. At the highest end of the divided line is the idea of The Good, or God.

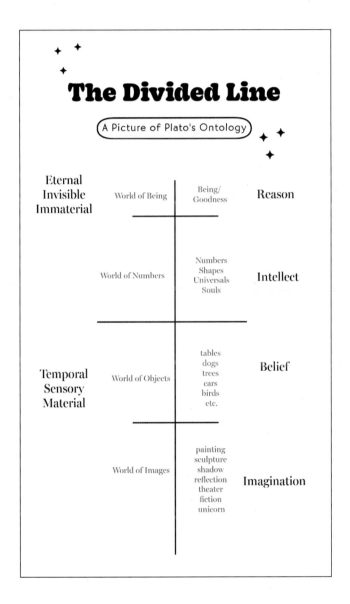

The Divided Line

A Picture of Plato's Ontology

Eternal Invisible Immaterial	World of Being	Being/ Goodness	Reason
	World of Numbers	Numbers Shapes Universals Souls	Intellect
Temporal Sensory Material	World of Objects	tables dogs trees cars birds etc.	Belief
	World of Images	painting sculpture shadow reflection theater fiction unicorn	Imagination

① Plato's divided line is an analogy that establishes and orders two realms of being that a person never comes to think about.

② According to Plato's dividing line, there is a degree of reality between "objects" in the cave.

③ As people become more and more enlightened, they experience that what they previously perceive as a shadow gradually gets closer to the Goodness.

④ According to Descartes, human beings are born evil and doomed that way, therefore ultimately impossible to perceive the Good.

⑤ Descartes was directly influenced by Plato's ideas.

5 Among ① to ⑤, which of the underlined sentences in [B] undermines the argument of the underlined ㉠ in [A]?

 NOTE

[A] The 1999 film The Matrix by the Wachowskis is largely Platonic and Cartesian; the film explores the journey of one man from the Matrix, a simulation ruled by deceitful robots, into the enlightenment of the 'real world.' While Plato and Descartes' skepticism of the existence of the external world seems to be at the forefront of the film, The Matrix also argues ㉠the anti-Platonic possibility that perhaps the Matrix isn't any less real than the 'real world'. Through analyzing Descartes' later meditations, the work of anti-Platonic philosopher Stanley Cavell, and the motivations of the character Cypher in the film, one may argue that the Matrix is indeed reality unto itself and retains the same value as the "real world."

[B] In the 5th and 6th meditations, Descartes proves that not only do other minds exist but so does the external world and himself. ①This conclusion is summated by the infamous phrase, "I think therefore I am." This sentiment can be seen lingering under the film's veil of Platonic philosophy. ②The Platonic Morpheus claims the Matrix to be but shadows and like shadows on a cave wall, the Matrix can bear no consequences to the real world. After Neo leaves a training module in the Matrix and finds himself bleeding he asks Morpheus, "I thought it wasn't real." Morpheus says, "③Your mind makes it real." Neo then asks, "If you're killed in the Matrix, you die here?" and Morpheus answers, "The body cannot live without the mind." Just as Descartes disproves himself in his later meditations, Morpheus contradicts his Platonic argument of the artificiality of the Matrix. ④<u>We see that not only can one perceive the Matrix with all senses but consequences of the Matrix translate into the 'real world.'</u> ⑤<u>It would seem that the Matrix then, is literally just as real as the real world, or even as Cypher says, "The Matrix can be more real than the real world."</u> Cypher says, "I'm tired, Trinity. Tired of this war, tired of fighting… I'm tired of the ship, being cold, eating the same goddamn goop every day." The post-apocalyptic dystopia of the 'real world' that Cypher and the others live in inhibits agency and freedom so much that it resembles more clearly the imprisonment of Plato's cave.

① This conclusion is summated by the infamous phrase, "I think therefore I am."

② The Platonic Morpheus claims the Matrix to be but shadows and like shadows on a cave wall, the Matrix can bear no consequences to the real world.

③ "Your mind makes it real."

④ We see that not only can one perceive the Matrix with all senses but consequences of the Matrix translate into the 'real world.'

⑤ It would seem that the Matrix then, is literally just as real as the real world, or even as Cypher says, "The Matrix can be more real than the real world."

6 Which of the following best describes the contextual meaning of the underlined sentence?

 NOTE

To understand the ideology behind Cypher's thinking, one need only look to the very art form that most resembles the Matrix — film, itself. Pioneering film philosopher Stanley Cavell discusses the ontology of the cinematic image in his essay "What Becomes of Things on Film." For Cavell, the cinematic image (the projections of people, places, and objects on film) are not only reflections of the "real world" but the mere fact of their filming brings life into those projections themselves. When a person is filmed, their essence is radically changed by their on-film representation. Cavell would argue that a popular actor, Jimmy Stewart for instance, is but an amalgam of his various on-screen appearances as L.B. Jefferies, Rans Stoddard, John Ferguson, etc. As humans, we attach value to what and who is seen or perceived. Philosopher George Berkeley argued that in fact, "To be is to be perceived." Film is perceived and thus, is. When Cypher is requesting to be put back into the Matrix, he adds, "And I want to be someone important, like an actor." As an audience, this line makes us aware of our own gaze; we watch the projection of an actor playing a character who exists in a fictional cinematic world who wishes to be placed in a simulation of that fictional world where he wants to make a living as an actor. In other words, <u>we watch a projection seeking to go back into a world of projections so that he can be a projection</u>. For Cypher, like Berkeley and Cavell, reality is dependent upon our perception of it to which we attach its value.

① Humans are social animals that live in harmony with other human beings.
② The existence of an object can be recognized only when the fundamental properties that lie behind the object are grasped.
③ Being perceived precedes being.
④ Existence precedes knowledge.
⑤ Being and awareness are never compatible.

[7-9] Read the passage and answer each question.

NOTE

"And now," Plato says, "let me show in a figure how far our nature is enlightened or unenlightened."

Plato personifies this 'unenlightenment' of human nature through his famous "allegory of the cave" — the allegory of prisoners chained in a cave whose entire perception of reality is but shadows cast on a wall in front of them. For Plato, the shadows on the wall are not reality but rather mere reflections of more real objects. 17th-century French philosopher René Descartes similarly hypothesized in the early meditations of his "*Meditations on First Philosophy*" that all of the human world is but a world of shadows orchestrated by a deceitful "evil genius." For both Descartes and Plato, this world of shadows, the cave, the simulation, or Matrix if you will, is illusory and devoid of value.

The 1999 film The Matrix by the Wachowskis is largely Platonic and Cartesian; the film explores the journey of one man from the Matrix, a simulation ruled by deceitful robots, into the enlightenment of the 'real world.' While Plato and Descartes' skepticism of the existence of the external world seems to be at the forefront of the film, The Matrix also argues the anti-Platonic possibility that perhaps the Matrix isn't any less real than the 'real world'. Through analyzing Descartes' later meditations, the work of anti-Platonic philosopher Stanley Cavell, and the motivations of the character Cypher in the film, one may argue that the Matrix is indeed reality unto itself and retains the same value as the "real world."

Plato's allegory is reflected through a dialogue between fictional versions of Glaucon, Plato's brother, and Socrates. Plato, speaking through Socrates, explains the allegory: In a cave, there are prisoners chained so that all they have ever known is a wall in front of them onto which shadows of objects moving in front of a fire behind them are cast. Socrates says, "For them…the truth would be literally nothing but the shadows of images." Socrates then explains the various reactions of the prisoners when they are released — their trouble adjusting physically and mentally to their new reality.

7 Which of the following is <u>NOT</u> correct about the passage?

① In Plato's cave metaphor, he is conveying human nature as unenlightened.

② The shadows reflected on the wall of the cave are the prisoners' reality, but are not accurate representations of the real world.

③ The movie The Matrix leaves open the possibility that 'the cave' could be just as real as the real world.

④ Stanley Cavell is strongly opposed to the assertion that the Matrix is every bit as real as the real world.

⑤ It is safe to say that the film The Matrix is an embodiment of Plato's "Allegory of the Cave."

8 Choose the number of correct statements about the "Allegory of the Cave".

> ㉠ The Greek Philosopher, Plato, conducted the "Allegory of the Cave" as a reflection on the nature of human beings, knowledge, and truth.
>
> ㉡ The shadows reflected on the wall were not anything but real objects.
>
> ㉢ Not all of the prisoners are chained by their inability to see the world's truth.
>
> ㉣ All the prisoners freed would soon realize that what they thought were real were nothing but the shadows.
>
> ㉤ Plato's setting up of prisoners getting free is to represent one's innate ability to change and willingness to accept new truths.

① 1   ② 2   ③ 3   ④ 4   ⑤ 5

9 본문에서 언급되는 동굴의 비유의 철학을 반영하는 영화 The Matrix에 대한 소개의 내용이다. 문맥상 어색한 것은?

The Matrix, Thomas Anderson is a computer programmer who leads a double-life as a hacker under the alias Neo. After being deemed "The One" by Morpheus, Neo is presented with two choices; either take the blue pill and stay in his illusory world; or take the red pill and be reborn into the truth of reality. Neo chooses the red pill and plunges into ⓐthe 'real world' — a post-apocalyptic dystopia where the human race is grown and harvested for energy by a supreme class of artificial intelligence. Neo realizes that his previous 'reality' was ⓑno more than a simulation. Through an ⓒanti-Platonic lens, the Matrix, and all the humans in it are akin to the prisoners watching shadows on the cave wall. Plato says of a freed prisoner, "When he approaches the light his eyes will be dazzled, and he will be ⓓunable to see anything at all of what are now called realities." When Neo first leaves the Matrix, he asks Morpheus, "Why do my eyes hurt?" to which Morpheus replies, "ⓔBecause you've never used them before."

[10-11] Read the passage and answer each question.

 NOTE

Plato's notion of the "Divided Line" reveals within his allegory the ⓐ <u>hierarchy</u> of truth and reality. In the cave, the ⓑ<u>metaphysical</u> world of our senses/images, the shadows on the wall are the least real things there are. More real than the shadows are the objects that cast them — the men, statues, and animals passing in front of the fire. Both the shadows and the objects, however, are still illusions of the cave. Reality (or at least a more real-world) exists outside of the cave and is known as the intelligible world or the world of numbers and forms. This is the ⓒ<u>transcendent</u> world of the intellectual mathematics behind the objects of the physical world. At the highest end of the divided line is the idea of The Good, or God.

When Neo leaves the Matrix, it can be said that he leaves the cave and enters the world of forms in which the objects of the Matrix, the cave, can be manipulated. Neo, being The One, ⓓ<u>represents</u> the closest to "The Good". This is reflected at the end of the film where after being resurrected, Neo is able to see beyond the shadows of the Matrix, the ideas/forms behind them and sees the world as numbers, mathematical objects. The iconic green numbers cascading down the screen are the ⓔ<u>realization</u> of Plato's view of enlightened transcendence from the human world of the senses.

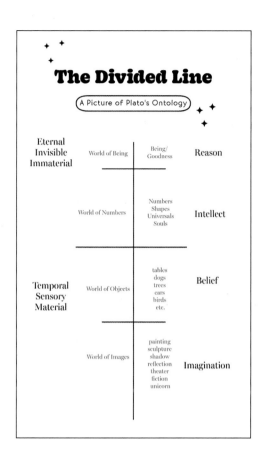

10 Which of the following is <u>NOT</u> correct about the "Divided Line"?

① The divided line is a line divided into two unequal sections.

② The division of the line is between what is visible and what is intelligible, with the visible portion being equal to the intelligible portion.

③ The objects that cast the shadows are more real than the shadows are.

④ The concept of likenesses and imitations belongs to the World of images.

⑤ At the lowest end of the visible are mere images of objects.

11 Which of the following is the most <u>AWKWARD</u> in context?

① ㉠ hierarchy

② ㉡ metaphysical

③ ㉢ transcendent

④ ㉣ represents

⑤ ㉤ realization

[12-14] Read the passage and answer each question.

 NOTE

[A] The Platonic philosophy of the Matrix is ⓐabetted by Cartesian skepticism. Rene Descartes's "Meditations on First Philosophy" ⓑ chart Descartes' philosophical journey from doubting the existence of the external world to finally arriving at his conclusion that God, the external world, and minds do indeed exist.

[B] Before Neo is exposed to the 'real world' there are several hints scattered throughout. When the goth punks arrive at Neo's door to retrieve the illegal software Neo engineered, one of the punks assures Neo, "Don't worry, this never happened. You don't exist." This is a direct ⓒallusion to Neo's Cartesian doubts of his own existence.

[C] Descartes' first Meditation deals with the "things which may be brought into the sphere of the doubtful." Among these things to be doubted is the existence of one's own mind. Descartes ⑦ponders over the idea that perhaps nothing is real, even himself. In the same scene, Neo asks, "Have you ever had the feeling where you're not sure if you're awake or still dreaming?" This is another direct reference to Descartes' first Meditation where he similarly asks, ⓛ"How often has it happened to me that in the night I dreamt that I found myself in this particular place, that I was dressed and seated near the fire, whilst in reality, I was lying undressed in bed!"

[D] Descartes argues that if we can feel as if we are awake during sleep, it is quite possible that we could always be in a sleep state and are _____, like those in the Matrix. Neo's skepticism proves true after he takes the red pill and discovers his old world was a simulation devised by malicious artificial intelligence known as sentinels. Descartes had a similar ⓓinkling about his world. In Meditation 1, Descartes supposes, "I shall consider that the heavens, the earth, colours, figures, sound, and all other external things are ⓔ nought but the illusions and dreams of which this evil genius has availed himself in order to lay traps for my credulity." The sentinels are to Neo as the "evil genius" is to Descartes.

12 Which of the following best explains the purpose of the author to mention 'the goth punks' in paragraph [B]?

① To demonstrate that the uncertainty of one's existence leads to doubting everything around him or her everything is doubtful

② To show that all events that occur in reality has innate associations with the truth

③ To show the Cartesian skepticism

④ To show that reality and perception do not sometimes converge on a harmonious point

⑤ To show that when you start facing reality, you get psychosis

13 Among ⓐ ~ ⓔ, which of the following pairs is not a synonym?

① ⓐ abetted — encouraged

② ⓑ chart — show

③ ⓒ allusion — reference

④ ⓓ inkling — certainty

⑤ ⓔ nought but — no more than

14 Choose all the correct statements about paragraphs [C] and [D].

① For Descartes, the existence of one's own mind is the only thing that need be doubted and illusory in the end.

② Considering the context, ㉠ can be replaced with 'contemplates.'

③ ㉡ shows that Neo is experiencing the very Cartesian skepticism.

④ One possible filler for the blank in paragraph [D] is 'merely imagining consciousness.'

⑤ When Neo takes the red pill as mentioned in paragraph [D], 'reality' remains elusive to him forever.

[15-16] Read the passage and answer each question.

 NOTE

⊙By Platonic and early-meditation-Cartesian standards, the Matrix is the paragon of the illusion and deception of our sensible world. For Plato and Descartes, reality has a particular value that shadows on the wall or dreams do not. In the Matrix, one character in particular, ⓛis epistemologically in tune with the Platonic and Cartesian skepticism that the film seems to endorse.

Cypher is a crew member on the Nebuchadnezzar who betrayed the last human city, Zion, by helping Agent Smith hack into its' mainframe. In return, Cypher wanted to go back to the Matrix ⓒ with his memory wiped of the 'real world'. In one of the film's most important scenes, Cypher meets with Agent Smith over a steak dinner. Cypher says, "You know, I know this steak doesn't exist. I know that when I put it in my mouth, the Matrix is telling my brain that it is juicy and delicious. After nine years, you know what I realize? Ignorance is bliss." This line not only calls into question how we experience 'reality' and 'existence' but also the value we attach to it. For Cypher, the Matrix and its blissful ignorance are ⓔmore valuable than the 'real world'. To understand the ideology behind Cypher's thinking, one need only look to the very art form that most resembles the Matrix — film, itself.

Pioneering film philosopher Stanley Cavell discusses the ontology of the cinematic image in his essay "What Becomes of Things on Film." For Cavell, the cinematic image (the projections of people, places, and objects on film) are not only reflections of the "real world" but the mere fact of their filming brings life into those projections themselves. When a person is filmed, their essence is radically changed by their on-film representation. Cavell would argue that a popular actor, Jimmy Stewart for instance, is ⓓbut an amalgam of his various on-screen appearances as L.B. Jefferies, Rans Stoddard, John Ferguson, etc.

As humans, we attach value to what and who is seen or perceived. Philosopher George Berkeley argued that in fact, "To be is to be perceived." Film is perceived and thus, is. When Cypher is requesting to be put back into the Matrix, he adds, "And I want to be someone important, like an actor." As an audience, this line makes us aware of our own gaze; we watch the projection of an actor playing a character who exists in a fictional cinematic world who wishes to be placed in a simulation of that fictional world where he wants to make a living as an actor. In other words, we watch a projection seeking to go back into a world of projections so that he can be a projection. For Cypher, like Berkeley and Cavell, _____.

15 Among ㉠~㉤, which of the following <u>INTERFERES WITH</u> the flow of the passage?

① ㉠

② ㉡

③ ㉢

④ ㉣

⑤ ㉤

16 Which of the following best fills in the blank in the passage?

① reality comes to be perceived as of value when accepted as it is.

② reality is dependent upon our perception of it to which we attach its value.

③ ironically, the very act of distorting reality adds to the truthfulness of reality.

④ reality and illusion are just two sides of the same coin.

⑤ distinguishing between reality and illusion is a meaningless act.

UNIT

8

[외부지문]

17 아래 지문은 Film and Skepticism: Stanley Cavell on the Ontology of Film에서 발췌한 내용이다. 영화에 내재된 skepticism에 대한 Stanley Cavell의 관점에 대한 기술이다. 글의 흐름을 방해하는 내용을 담고 있는 것은?

 NOTE

"For Cavell, skepticism is inherent in the ontology of the film image, which reveals things as always already displaced from us and us as always already displaced from them. In silent film comedy (e.g. Chaplin and Keaton) – but also in cinema in general – our relationship to objects is that of "seeing as". ①It is precisely this capacity for seeing something as something (e.g. Chaplin treats a shoe as if it were a piece of steak, and bread rolls as if they were a pair of shoes) that demonstrates the fundamental skepticism underlying human existence. However, although Chaplin's charming playfulness with things reveals a profound skepticism concerning our relationship to the world of things, ②this is not a negative skepticism expressing an anxiety over our inability to penetrate appearances and know things in their essence, but rather a positive skepticism that takes pleasure in the unstable nature of things and in our inability to reduce them to specific, humanly defined functions: this type of skepticism celebrates the acceptance of things to our attempts at conceptualizing i.e., using them. When Chaplin and Keaton attribute different functions to the same object, or the same function to different objects, ③they do not demonstrate our control over things but precisely the failure of our concepts to capture the things they supposedly refer to in all their multiplicity and complexity i.e., in their essential inhumanity. ④There is always something in things that does not belong to us, that we do not recognize and cannot assimilate, just as there is always something in the film image that, despite its strong indexical relationship to reality, withdraws from us and from the real into that realm we clumsily call "the unreal", "absence", or "nothingness". ⑤Cavell concludes that, paradoxically, rather than a threat to reality cinema is its best guarantee precisely insofar as cinema chips away at the real, keeping skepticism alive."

From *Film and Skepticism: Stanley Cavell on the Ontology of Film by Temenuga Trifonova*

PART

5 Sentence Completion

1 These bulbs remain _____ for a period of time, before becoming active again under the earth during winter.

① dormant   ② dominant   ③ extinct

④ lively   ⑤ lightened

어휘

bulb 전구, (꽃의) 구근 **dormant** 잠을 자는, 휴면의 **extinct** 멸종의, 멸종된 **lively** 왕성한 **lightened** 완화된, 가벼워진

2 Nearly all mothers nowadays deliver their babies while lying on their backs. This is not necessarily for the mother's convenience; rather, it is easier for the obstetrician to listen to the infant heartbeat with a _____.

① stethoscope   ② sonar

③ sonograph   ④ hearing aid

어휘

deliver 분만하다 **obstetrician** 산부인과 의사 **stethoscope** 청진기 **sonar** 수중 음파 탐지기 **sonograph** 소노그라프(음향, 진동을 음성기호로 바꿈)

3 The _____ speech, given on the spur of the moment, received as much publicity as a carefully planned announcement.

① resilient   ② impromptu

③ well-prepared   ④ monotonous

어휘

speech 연설 **spur** 충동 **on the spur of the moment** 충동적으로, 즉흥적으로, 즉석에서 **receive** ~을 받다 **as ~ as -** -만큼 ~한 **publicity** 명성, 평판, 대중성 **careful** 신중한, 주의 깊은 **plan** ~을 계획하다 **announcement** 발표, 알림 **carefully planned** 신중하게 계획된 **resilient** 복원력이 있는, (불운·병으로부터) 회복이 빠른 **impromptu** 즉석의 **well-prepared** 잘 준비된 **monotonous** 단조로운, 지루한

4 The environmental _____ created in economically poor countries includes destruction of forests and other habitats, erosion, and extinction of species.

① filth   ② havoc

③ rapture   ④ entreaty

> **어휘**
> environmental 주위의, 환경의 create ~을 창조하다, 만들다 (= concoct) economically 경제적으로 include ~을 포함하다 destruction 파괴, 파멸 forest 숲, 삼림 habitat 서식지 erosion 침식 extinction 멸종, 절멸 species 종, 종류 filth 오물, 불결한 것, 더러움 havoc 파괴, 황폐 wreak havoc on ~에 심각한 피해를 입히다 rapture 큰 기쁨, 황홀, 환희 entreaty 탄원, 간청, 애원

5 You'd better write a short _____ paragraph telling who you are and what you have done in the past two years.

① prolonged   ② declamatory

③ autobiographical   ④ interrogative

> **어휘**
> had better ~하는 편이 좋다, ~해야 한다 write ~을 쓰다, 기록하다 short 짧은, 모자라는 paragraph 단락, 절 tell ~을 말하다; 명령하다; 구별하다 (= distinguish) who you are 당신이 누구인지 what you have done 당신이 해온 것이 무엇인지 past 지난, 과거의 in the past two years 지난 2년 동안 prolonged 연장한, 장기의 declamatory 비난적인, 연설조의 autobiographical 자서전적인 interrogative 질문의, 미심쩍은 듯한

6 When used in its intended form, "crazy like a fox" is an _____ meaning seemingly foolish but in fact extremely cunning. If you call someone "crazy like a fox" you are saying that person is sly and capable of outwitting others.

① euphemism   ② homonym

③ oxymoron   ④ phraseology

> **어휘**
> use ~을 사용(이용)하다 intended 의도된, 고의의 form 모양, 형태 crazy 미친, 열중한, 최고의 fox 여우, 교활한 사람 meaning 의미 seemingly 겉보기에, 표면적으로는(실제로 내면은 다르지만) foolish 어리석은, 바보 같은 extremely 극도로, 대단히 cunning 교활한, 약삭빠른 if 만약 ~라면 call A B A를 B라고 부르다 sly 교활한; 은밀한 be capable of ~ing ~할 능력이 있다 outwit ~의 의표(허)를 찌르다, 속이다 euphemism 완곡어법(die 대신에 pass away 라고 하는 것) homonym 동음이의어(meet와 meat, fan(팬)과 fan(부채)등) oxymoron 모순 어법(crowded solitude, cruel kindness 등) phraseology 말씨, 어법

7 How could words, confined as they individually are to certain _____ meanings specified in a dictionary, eventually come, when combined in groups, to create obscurity and actually to prevent thought from being _____?

① indefinite – articulated

② conventional – conceivable

③ unlikely – classified

④ archaic – expressed

⑤ precise – communicable

8 A reasonable proficiency in English is a _____ for joining this advanced course.

① prerequisite   ② credit

③ repentance   ④ communication

9 Such arrant hypocrisy is indicative of a thoroughly _____ approach to running for office.

① opportunistic   ② benevolent

③ inhuman   ④ callous

10 _____ of refuse and garbage at open dumps long remained a major _____ of air pollution in many of our cities.

① Purchasing – result

② Burning – cause

③ Consideration – concern

④ Collection – benefit

⑤ Rejection – reason

어휘 refuse 쓰레기, 폐물 garbage 쓰레기, 음식 찌꺼기 dump 쓰레기 버리는 곳, (석탄·쓰레기 따위의) 더미 remain 남아있다, 여전히 ~이다 major 주요한, 주된 air pollution 공해 in many of our cities 우리 도시들 대부분에서 purchase ~을 구입하다, 획득하다 result 결과 burn ~을 태우다 cause 원인, 이유 consideration 고려 concern 관계, 관심 collection 수집, 소장품 benefit 이익, 이득 rejection 거절 reason 이유, 이성

UNIT 9

문학_단편소설

The Story of An Hour

by Kate Chopin

AI그림 달의이성

Voca Master

☐ **be afflicted with** — To suffer from a particular condition or illness

- Many people in the region <u>were afflicted with</u> the flu during the winter months.

☐ **in broken sentences** — To speak or communicate in an incomplete or disjointed manner

- The witness testified <u>in broken sentences</u>, making it difficult to understand the sequence of events.

☐ **in half concealing** — Partially hiding or concealing something

- The artist painted the subject <u>in half concealing</u> light to create a sense of mystery.

☐ **intelligence** — **n** Information, news, or knowledge

- He quickly gathered <u>intelligence</u> about the upcoming product launch.

☐ **hasten to** — To do something quickly or without delay

- She <u>hastened to</u> apologize for her mistake.

☐ **forestall** — **v** To prevent or obstruct something from happening, often by taking action in advance

- She wanted to <u>forestall</u> any misunderstandings by addressing the issue immediately.

☐ **bear** — **v** To carry or transport something, especially a heavy load

- The donkey was used to <u>bear</u> supplies up the steep mountain path.

with sudden, wild abandonment

In a manner that is spontaneous and unrestrained

- The children played <u>with sudden, wild abandonment</u> in the park, running and laughing freely.

roomy

a Having a lot of space; spacious

- The SUV was <u>roomy</u> enough to comfortably fit a large family.

physical exhaustion

Extreme fatigue or tiredness resulting from physical activity or exertion

- The demanding hike left them with a feeling of <u>physical exhaustion</u>.

haunt

v To persistently or recurrently occupy one's thoughts or emotions; to trouble or disturb

- The ghost stories told around the campfire would <u>haunt</u> the children's dreams.

the open square

A public space or area that is open and not enclosed, often used for gatherings or events

- People gathered in <u>the open square</u> to celebrate the holiday with music and dance.

aquiver

a Trembling or shaking, often due to excitement or anticipation

- The crowd was <u>aquiver</u> with anticipation as the performers took the stage.

in the eaves

In the area near the overhanging edges of a roof

- The cat was hiding <u>in the eaves</u> to escape the rain.

except when S V

With the exception of occasions when a specific condition is met

- He was generally quiet, <u>except when</u> he watched his favorite sports team play.

☐ **sob**	**v** To cry with convulsive gasps; to weep uncontrollably
	• He would often <u>sob</u> himself to sleep after a particularly difficult day.
☐ **cry oneself to sleep**	To cry until one falls asleep, often due to emotional distress
	• The child missed her parents and would <u>cry herself to sleep</u> every night at the sleepaway camp.
☐ **fair**	**a** Having light skin color; pale
	• <u>Fair</u> skin is more susceptible to damage from UV rays.
☐ **bespeak**	**v** To indicate, show, or give evidence of; to suggest or demonstrate
	• His actions <u>bespeak</u> a deep commitment to the cause he supports.
☐ **dull**	**a** Lacking interest, excitement, or brightness; boring
	• He found the movie to be quite <u>dull</u>, with a slow-moving plot.
☐ **yonder**	**ad** In a distance, far away; over there
	• She pointed to a house <u>yonder</u> and told us it was her childhood home.
☐ **a suspension of intelligent thought**	A temporary state of not thinking rationally or logically
	• The excitement of the concert led to <u>a suspension of intelligent thought</u>, and people rushed toward the stage.
☐ **too subtle and elusive to name**	Something that is so delicate and difficult to describe that it cannot be given a specific name
	• Her feelings for him were <u>too subtle and elusive to name</u>, a complex mix of emotions.
☐ **scent**	**n** A pleasant or distinctive smell; fragrance
	• She followed the <u>scent</u> of freshly baked bread to the bakery.

bosom　　　**n** The chest, especially as considered the seat of emotions or feelings

- She held the secret close to her <u>bosom</u> for many years.
- He found comfort in her warm <u>bosom</u> during difficult times.

tumultuous　　**a** Marked by chaos, noise, and disorder; characterized by uproar or commotion

- The <u>tumultuous</u> protest continued into the night, with people chanting slogans and waving banners.

possess　　　**v** To have or own something; to have control or mastery over something

- She <u>possessed</u> a rare collection of vintage books.
- He was determined to <u>possess</u> the skills needed to succeed in his career.

strive to　　To make great efforts or work hard to achieve a particular goal or result

- She <u>strived to</u> excel in her studies and become a top.

with her will　　By her own determination or resolve

- <u>With her will</u> power, she managed to complete the challenging marathon.

slender　　**a** Thin in an attractive or graceful way; not thick or bulky

- The tree had <u>slender</u> branches that swayed in the breeze.

abandon　　**v** To give up or stop doing something, often suddenly and completely

- The explorers had to <u>abandon</u> their expedition due to harsh weather conditions.

under one's breath　　In a quiet and almost inaudible manner

- He criticized the decision <u>under his breath</u> during the meeting.

☐ **keen**

a Having a sharp or strong perception; eager or enthusiastic

- His <u>keen</u> interest in art led him to visit museums regularly.

☐ **monstrous**

a Extremely large, ugly, or wicked; resembling a monster

- The dictator's actions were considered <u>monstrous</u> by the international community.

☐ **dismiss A as B**

To regard or treat something or someone as being of little importance or significance

- He <u>dismissed</u> the criticism <u>as</u> jealousy from his competitors.

☐ **exalted**

a Raised in status or rank; held in high regard or praise

- The poem received <u>exalted</u> reviews from literary critics.

☐ **save**

Except for; with the exception of

- The whole team was in good spirits, <u>save</u> for the team captain who seemed upset.

☐ **procession**

n A group of people or vehicles moving in an orderly and formal manner, especially as part of a ceremony

- The wedding <u>procession</u> included the bride and groom, followed by their families and friends.

☐ **live for**

To have a strong passion or desire for something and make it the central focus of one's life

- His dream was to <u>live for</u> adventure and travel to new and exciting places.

☐ **will**

n Determination, resolve, or the mental strength to carry out one's intentions or goals

- Her unwavering <u>will</u> to help others inspired those around her.

☐ **persistence**　**n** The quality of continuing to do something despite obstacles or opposition; determination

- The persistence of the volunteers made the community project a success.

☐ **in that blind persistence**　Referring to the unwavering determination and effort put into something, often without clear direction or understanding

- In that blind persistence, she continued to pursue her dream, not knowing where it would lead.

☐ **impose A on B**　To force or place a burden, responsibility, or requirement on someone or something

- She didn't want to impose her opinions on others and encouraged open discussion.

☐ **illumination**　**n** The act of providing light or the state of being lit; also, a source of light

- The illumination of the city streets at night was breathtaking.

☐ **no less**　Used to emphasize that something is just as significant or important as mentioned

- Her accomplishments in the field of medicine were no less remarkable than her humanitarian work.

☐ **impulse**　**n** A sudden and strong desire or urge to do something without much thought or consideration

- His impulse purchase at the store left him with regret when he got home.

☐ **implore**　**v** To beg or plead earnestly and desperately

- The child implored for a second chance and promised to behave better.

☐ **for heaven's sake**　An exclamation used to emphasize a request or plea

- For heaven's sake, could you stop making so much noise?

☐ **elixir**　　**n** A magical or medicinal potion believed to have the power to cure or improve health and well-being

- The herbalist claimed that her special <u>elixir</u> could cure any ailment.

☐ **fancy**　　**n** A passing or transient thought, idea, or inclination

- Her <u>fancy</u> for travel led her to explore various countries.

☐ **run riot**　　To behave in a wild, unrestrained, or undisciplined manner

- Without proper supervision, the party guests began to <u>run riot</u>, causing a mess in the house.

☐ **breathe**　　**v** To speak quietly, often in a hushed or confidential manner

- He couldn't help but <u>breathe</u> a sigh of relief after passing the challenging exam.

☐ **at length**　　After a long period of time or discussion; eventually

- After <u>at length</u> negotiations, the two companies finally agreed to a merger.

☐ **importunity**　　**n** The persistent and insistent request or demand for something

- He gave in to the <u>importunity</u> of his friends and joined them on the road trip.

☐ **feverish**　　**a** Marked by intense excitement, activity, or restlessness; having a high body temperature

- The <u>feverish</u> pace of life today gives little time for relaxation and quiet rest for those who seek it.

☐ **unwittingly**　　**ad** Without awareness or intention; unknowingly

- She <u>unwittingly</u> made a mistake in her report, not realizing the error until later.

descend
v To move or go downward from a higher place to a lower one

- The elevator slowly started to <u>descend</u> to the ground floor.

latchkey
n A key to an outer door, typically used for access when the door is locked

- After school, the children used their <u>latchkey</u> to enter the house since their parents were still at work.

travel-stained
a Marked or stained from travel; showing the effects of a journey

- The <u>travel-stained</u> backpack had been on many adventures around the world.

composedly
ad In a calm, serene, and self-possessed manner; without agitation or nervousness

- He delivered his speech <u>composedly</u>, even though the audience was large and intimidating.

grip-sack
n A small bag or suitcase with handles, typically used for carrying personal belongings during travel

- The <u>grip-sack</u> contained his clothes and toiletries for the short trip.

piercing
a Having a sharp or penetrating quality, such as a sound or gaze

- Her <u>piercing</u> eyes seemed to see right through people, making them uneasy.

2 Text Reading

: The Story of An Hour by Kate Chopin

Text 1

Knowing that Mrs. Mallard was afflicted with a heart trouble, great care was taken to break to her as gently as possible the news of her husband's death.

It was her sister Josephine who told her, (가)in broken sentences; veiled hints that revealed in half concealing. Her husband's friend Richards was there, too, near her. It was he who had been in the newspaper office when intelligence of the railroad disaster was received, with Brently Mallard's name leading the list of "killed." He had only taken the time to assure himself of its truth by a second telegram, and had hastened to forestall any less careful, less tender friend in bearing the sad message.

(나)She did not hear the story as many women have heard the same, with a paralyzed inability to accept its significance. She wept at once, with sudden, wild abandonment, in her sister's arms. When the storm of grief had spent itself she went away to her room alone. She would have no one follow her.

There stood, facing the open window, a comfortable, roomy armchair. Into this she sank, pressed down by a physical exhaustion that haunted her body and seemed to reach into her soul.

1   Which of the following best describes the purpose of Josephine saying "in broken sentences; veiled hints that revealed in half concealing" in (가)?

① To deliver the news of her husband's death directly and bluntly
② To make the news of her husband's death less painful by using euphemisms
③ To keep Mrs. Mallard in suspense by not revealing the truth immediately
④ To confuse Mrs. Mallard with cryptic messages
⑤ To prepare Mrs. Mallard emotionally for the shocking news in a gentle manner

2   What can be inferred from the phrase "She did not hear the story as many women have heard the same, with a paralyzed inability to accept its significance" in (나)?

① She was indifferent to the story and didn't pay attention to its details.
② She reacted with immediate shock and disbelief upon hearing the story.
③ She listened attentively to the story, trying to understand its deeper meaning.
④ She pretended to be unaffected by the story despite feeling emotional.
⑤ She reacted to the story differently than most women, rather experiencing a different emotional reaction.

어구 및 표현 연구

 핵심 PLUS!

1 Knowing that Mrs. Mallard was afflicted with a heart trouble, <u>great care was taken to break</u> (to her) (as gently as possible) <u>the news of her husband's death</u>.

- take care to의 수동태 표현
  Care is taken to V: 조심스럽게 ~하다
- 타동사 break의 목적어는 the news of her husband's death임.

2 <u>It</u> was [her sister Josephine] <u>who</u> told her, in broken sentences; veiled hints (<u>that</u> revealed in half concealing).

- It ~ that(who) 강조구문과 주격 관계대명사 that

3 <u>It</u> was he <u>who</u> had been in the newspaper office, <u>when</u> intelligence of the railroad disaster was received, (<u>with</u> Brently Mallard's name <u>leading</u> the list of "killed)."

- It ~ that(who) 강조구문
- when은 앞에 코마를 붙여 계속적 용법의 관계부사로 파악할 것.
- 부대구문 with N v-ing
  괄호는 내용상 intelligence 수식

4 He had only taken the time to <u>assure</u> himself <u>of</u> its truth by a second telegram, and had hastened to forestall any less careful, less tender friend (<u>in bearing</u> the sad message).

- assure A of B: A에게 B를 확신시키다
- in V-ing: ~하는데 있어, ~할 때

5 She did not hear the story <u>as</u> many women have heard the same, with a paralyzed inability to accept <u>its</u> significance.

- 부사절 접속사 as: ~처럼
- its = the story = her husband's death

6 When <u>the storm of grief</u> had spent itself she went away to her room alone. She would <u>have</u> / no one / follow her.

- [a(the) + N + of]의 비유적 표현
  the storm of grief: 폭풍 같은 슬픔
- 5형식 사역동사 have

7 There stood, (facing the open window), a comfortable, roomy <u>armchair</u>.

- there 구문의 주어는 armchair

[A] She could see in the open square before her house the tops of trees that were all aquiver with the new spring life. The delicious breath of rain was in the air. In the street below a peddler was crying his wares. The notes of a distant song which some one was singing reached her faintly, and countless sparrows were twittering in the eaves. There were patches of blue sky showing here and there through the clouds that had met and piled one above the other in the west facing her window.

[B] She sat with her head thrown back upon the cushion of the chair, quite motionless, except when a sob came up into her throat and shook her, as a child who has cried itself to sleep continues to sob in its dreams. She was young, with a fair, calm face, whose lines bespoke repression and even a certain strength. But now there was a dull stare in her eyes, whose gaze was fixed away off yonder on one of those patches of blue sky. It was not a glance of reflection, but rather indicated a suspension of intelligent thought.

3   The underlined phrases in paragraph [A], "the tops of trees that were all aquiver with the new spring life", "breath of rain", "crying" all symbolize a common meaning. Which of the following best represents that meaning?

① Renewal and freshness
② Sadness and grief
③ Silence and solitude
④ Chaos and commotion
⑤ Nostalgia and longing

4   다음은 문단 [B]의 밑줄 친 내용에 대한 분석이다. 밑줄 친 표현 중 문맥상 어색한 것은?

> The comparison to a child sobbing in its dreams suggests that the sorrow of the protagonist is ①persistent and continues even in her moments of apparent ② stillness. The description of the protagonist's face and lines suggests that she may have experienced ③challenges or ④emotional suppression in the past, which may have given her a sense of ⑤inner weakness.

어구 및 표현 연구

 핵심 PLUS!

1 She could <u>see</u> (in the open square) (before her house) <u>the tops of trees</u> (<u>that</u> were all <u>aquiver</u> with the new spring life).

- 타동사 see의 목적어는 **the tops of trees**.
- 주격 관계대명사 that
- aquiver는 형용사로 "떨면서"의 의미

2 [The notes of a distant song **which** some one was singing] reached her faintly, and countless sparrows were twittering in the eaves.

- 주격 관계대명사 which의 수식을 받는 긴 주어

3 There were [patches of blue sky] **showing** here and there through the clouds (<u>that</u> had met and piled one above the other in the west) (<u>facing</u> her window).

- There구문의 주어는 현재분사 showing의 수식을 받는 patches of blue sky
- the clouds는 선행사로 주격 관계대명사 that의 수식을 받는 동시에 현재분사 facing의 수식을 받고 있음.

4 She sat (<u>with</u> her head **thrown** back upon the cushion of the chair), quite <u>motionless</u>, [except when a sob came up into her throat and shook her, (as a child **who** has cried itself to sleep / continues to sob in its dreams)].

- 부대구문: with N V-ed "N가 ~한 채"
- motionless는 완전자동사 sit에 걸리는 유사보어로 파악.
- 접속사 as의 주어인 a child는 주격 관계대명사의 수식을 받아 길어진 경우.

5 She was young, with a fair, calm face, (**whose** lines bespoke repression and even a certain strength).

- 선행사 face를 수식하는 소유격 관계대명사 whose

6 But now there was a dull stare in her eyes, [**whose** gaze was fixed away off yonder on one of those patches of blue sky].

- 선행사 her eyes를 수식하는 소유격 관계대명사 whose

There was something coming to her and she was waiting for it, fearfully. What was it? She did not know; it was too subtle and elusive to name. But she felt it, creeping out of the sky, reaching toward her through the sounds, the scents, the color that filled the air.

Now her bosom rose and fell tumultuously. She was beginning to recognize this thing that was approaching to possess her, and she was striving to beat it back with her will—as powerless as her two white slender hands would have been. When she abandoned herself, a little whispered word escaped her slightly parted lips. She said it over and over under her breath: "free, free, free!" The vacant stare and the look of terror that had followed it went from her eyes. They stayed keen and bright. Her pulses beat fast, and the coursing blood warmed and relaxed every inch of her body.

She did not stop to ask if it were or were not a monstrous joy that held her. A clear and exalted perception enabled her to dismiss the suggestion as trivial. She knew that she would weep again when she saw the kind, tender hands folded in death; the face that had never looked save with love upon her, fixed and gray and dead. But she saw beyond that bitter moment a long procession of years to come that would belong to her absolutely. And she opened and spread her arms out to them in welcome.

5 다음은 본문에 드러난 남편의 죽음 이후 Mrs. Mallard 부인이 겪는 내용을 분석한 내용이다. 밑줄 친 문장 중 글의 흐름을 방해하는 내용을 포함하고 있는 것은?

The moment of revelation comes when Mrs. Mallard whispers "free, free, free" to herself repeatedly. ①This word represents her realization that her husband's death has unexpectedly granted her freedom from the constraints of her marriage. Her fear and vacant stare are replaced by a keen and bright look. ②Her physical sensations intensify as her body responds to this newfound liberation. ③The passage suggests that Mrs. Mallard is more than ready to acknowledge her feelings as joy because of the recent death of her husband. ④However, she is acutely aware of the opportunities and possibilities that lie ahead in her life as a free and independent woman. ⑤She envisions a future where she will have control over her own destiny, and she welcomes it with open arms.

1 She did not know; it was **too** subtle and elusive **to** name. But she felt it, |creeping| out of the sky, |reaching| toward her through [the sounds, the scents, the color **that** filled the air].

- too ~ to용법과 분사구문의 병치: creeping ~, reaching ~
- 주격 관계대명사 that

2 She was beginning to recognize this thing (**that** was approaching to possess her), and she was striving to beat it back with her will - <u>as powerless as her two white slender hands would have been</u>.

- 주격 관계대명사 that
- 양보구문의 도치와 강조. "비록 ~이지만" <u>although</u> her two white slender hands would have been **powerless**
  = **powerless** as her two white slender hands would have been (도치)
  = **as** powerless as her two white slender hands would have been (강조)

3 The vacant stare and the look of terror (**that** had followed <u>it</u> <u>went</u> from her eyes).

- 주격 관계대명사 that
- it = the vacant stare
- 해당 문장에서 go는 "사라지다"라는 의미.

4 She did not stop to ask [if it were or were not a monstrous joy **that** held her].

- 주격 관계대명사 that

5 She knew that she would weep again when she saw the kind, tender hands **folded** in death; |the face| (**that** had never looked save with love upon her), (which was) (fixed and gray and dead).

- hands를 수식하는 과거분사 folded
- the face는 주격 관계대명사와 형용사구 fixed and gray and dead에 이중 수식을 받음.

6 But she <u>saw</u> (beyond that bitter moment) [a long procession of years (to come) (**that** would belong to her absolutely)].

- 타동사 saw의 목적어 **a long procession of years**는 구와 절의 이중 수식을 받고 있음.

There would be no one to live for during those coming years; she would live for herself. There would be no powerful will bending hers in that blind persistence with which men and women believe they have a right to impose a private will upon a fellow-creature. A kind intention or a cruel intention made the act seem no less a crime as she looked upon it in that brief moment of illumination.

And yet she had loved him—sometimes. Often she had not. What did it matter! What could love, the unsolved mystery, count for in the face of this possession of self-assertion which she suddenly recognized as the strongest impulse of her being!

"Free! Body and soul free!" she kept whispering.

Josephine was kneeling before the closed door with her lips to the keyhole, imploring for admission. "Louise, open the door! I beg; open the door—you will make yourself ill. What are you doing, Louise? For heaven's sake open the door."

"Go away. I am not making myself ill." No; she was drinking in a very elixir of life through that open window.

6 What does the phrase "A kind intention or a cruel intention made the act seem no less a crime" suggest about the protagonist's perspective on love and her husband's death?

① She believes that love justifies any action.
② She considers love and crime to be unrelated.
③ She sees that even well-intentioned actions can be seen as wrong.
④ She thinks her husband's death was entirely a result of a cruel intention.
⑤ She views love as an insignificant emotion in the face of a crime.

7 Which word best describes the protagonist's emotional state as reflected in the phrase "Free! Body and soul free!"?

① Content   ② Depressed
③ Jubilant   ④ Anxious
⑤ Vengeful

 핵심 PLUS!

1 There would be no powerful will **bending** hers (in that blind persistence) [**with which** men and women believe (**that**) they have a right to impose a private will upon a fellow-creature].

- 선행사 will을 수식하는 현재분사 bending.
- hers = her will
- [전치사 + 관계대명사 + S V] 구조에서 which = that blind persistence

2 S [A kind intention or a cruel intention] made / the act / seem no less a crime (as she looked upon it in that brief moment of illumination).

- 5형식 사역동사 make
- the act = to impose a private will upon a fellow-creature
- no less = as much as
- it = the act

3 What could love, the unsolved mystery, count for in the face of this possession of self-assertion **which** she suddenly recognized as the strongest impulse of her being!

- 목적격 관계대명사 which

4 Josephine was kneeling before the closed door (**with** her lips **to the keyhole**, imploring for admission).

- [with + N + 전치사구]: N을 ~한 채

Her fancy was running riot along those days ahead of her. Spring days, and summer days, and all sorts of days that would be her own. She breathed a quick prayer that life might be long. It was only yesterday she had thought with a shudder that life might be long.

She arose at length and opened the door to her sister's importunities. There was a feverish triumph in her eyes, and she carried herself unwittingly like a goddess of Victory. She clasped her sister's waist, and together they descended the stairs. Richards stood waiting for them at the bottom.

Someone was opening the front door with a latchkey. It was Brently Mallard who entered, a little travel-stained, composedly carrying his grip-sack and umbrella. He had been far from the scene of the accident, and did not even know there had been one. He stood amazed at Josephine's piercing cry; at Richards' quick motion to screen him from the view of his wife.

When the doctors came they said she had died of heart disease—of the joy that kills.

8 다음은 남편이 살아 돌아온 점과 밑줄 친 주인공의 죽음과 관련된 분석이다. 밑줄 친 표현 중 어색한 것은?

The unexpected return of her husband, Brently Mallard, turns the story on its head. He appears unharmed, having been far from the reported accident scene, and is ①unaware of the tragedy. Mrs. Mallard's reaction to this shock is where the story takes ②a poignant twist. Instead of a joyful reunion, her heart gives out, and she dies. The final line, "When the doctors came they said she had died of heart disease—of the joy that kills," is a powerful and ③ironic ending. It suggests that her heart couldn't bear the sudden surge of joy followed by the despair of realizing her newfound freedom was ④enduring. The story ultimately reveals the ⑤suffocating effects of societal norms and expectations on women of that era and the unexpected consequences of freedom.

UNIT

9

 핵심 PLUS!

1 Spring days, and summer days, and all sorts of days **that** would be her own. She breathed a quick prayer **that** life might be long.

- 주격 관계대명사 that과 동격의 that

2 **It** was only yesterday (**that**) she had thought (with a shudder) **that** life might be long.

- It ~ that 강조 용법에서 that 생략
- 두 번째 that은 타동사 thought의 목적어 자리의 명사절 that

3 **It** was Brently Mallard **who** entered, (a little) **travel-stained**, (composedly) **carrying** his grip-sack and umbrella.

- It ~ that 강조 용법에서 사람을 강조하는 who 대체
- 완전자동사 enter에 걸리는 유사보어 travel-stained와 분사구문 carrying

4 He stood amazed **at** Josephine's piercing cry; **at** Richards' quick motion to screen him from the view of his wife.

- 전치사 at의 병치
  첫 번째 at은 "~을 듣고," 두 번째 at은 "~을 보고"로 해석
- screen A from B: A가 B 못하도록 가로 막다

3 Voca Check

* 빈칸에 들어갈 적절한 단어를 박스에서 찾아 넣으시오.

1

conceal / exhausted / possessed / tumultuous / elusive / stifle / bespeak / forestall / roomy / hasten / dull / strive / haunt

1   She tried to _____ her tears, but a few quiet sobs escaped.

2   The eerie tales of the haunted house continue to _____ the townspeople's dreams.

3   He decided to _____ his productivity by setting clear goals and priorities.

4   The detective pursued the _____ criminal for years but couldn't capture him.

5   The _____ meeting left everyone in the office feeling drained and overwhelmed.

6   The teacher urged the students to _____ for excellence in their studies.

7   The _____ forest was home to a variety of wildlife.

8   The spacious, _____ living room was perfect for hosting gatherings and events.

9   The elegant attire and refined manners _____ her upbringing in a cultured household.

10 The _____ doll seemed to move on its own, sending shivers down their spines.

11 He tried to _____ his concern for his friend's safety.

12 The athlete's _____ legs were a testament to his dedication to training.

13 She wanted to _____ the news of her promotion until her family gathered to celebrate.

UNIT

9

2

slender / piercing / persistent / feverish / riot / implored / composedly / descended / procession / elixir / importunity / monstrous / run / keen / unwittingly

1 The _____ rays of the morning sun lit up the entire valley.

2 The beggar _____ on the street corner, pleading for some spare change.

3 Despite the _____ storm, the ship continued its voyage.

4 The children were allowed to _____ in the park, but they had to return home by sunset.

5 The _____ of the royal family through the city was a grand spectacle.

6 She had a _____ interest in astronomy and spent many nights stargazing with her telescope.

7 She spoke _____ during the interview, answering each question with confidence and clarity.

8 The explorer _____ deep into the cave to uncover its hidden secrets.

9 The scientist believed he had discovered the _____ to eternal life.

10 Her _____ attitude and determination led her to achieve her goals.

11 His _____ act of kindness towards a stranger made a profound impact.

12 The _____ music echoed through the concert hall, captivating the audience.

13 Despite her repeated refusals, he persisted in his _____, asking her out on a date every time they met.

14 The _____ creature emerged from the depths of the forest, casting a shadow over everything in its path.

15 The _____ students stumbled upon a hidden treasure during their adventure.

Reading Comprehension

[1-2] Read the passage and answer each question.

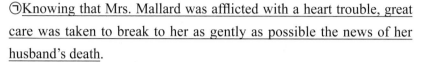

⑦Knowing that Mrs. Mallard was afflicted with a heart trouble, great care was taken to break to her as gently as possible the news of her husband's death.

It was her sister Josephine who told her, in broken sentences; veiled hints that revealed in half concealing. Her husband's friend Richards was there, too, near her. It was he who had been in the newspaper office when intelligence of the railroad disaster was received, with Brently Mallard's name leading the list of "killed." He had only taken the time to assure himself of its truth by a second telegram, and had hastened to forestall any less careful, less tender friend in bearing the sad message.

She did not hear the story as many women have heard the same, with a paralyzed inability to accept its significance. She wept at once, with sudden, wild abandonment, in her sister's arms. When the storm of grief had spent itself she went away to her room alone. She would have no one follow her.

There stood, facing the open window, a comfortable, roomy armchair. Into this she sank, pressed down by a physical exhaustion that haunted her body and seemed to reach into her soul.

She could see in the open square before her house the tops of trees that were all aquiver with the new spring life. The delicious breath of rain was in the air. In the street below a peddler was crying his wares. The notes of a distant song which some one was singing reached her faintly, and countless sparrows were twittering in the eaves.

There were patches of blue sky showing here and there through the clouds that had met and piled one above the other in the west facing her window.

She sat with her head thrown back upon the cushion of the chair, quite motionless, except when a sob came up into her throat and shook her,

NOTE

UNIT

9

as a child who has cried itself to sleep continues to sob in its dreams.

She was young, with a fair, calm face, whose lines bespoke repression and even a certain strength. But now there was a dull stare in her eyes, whose gaze was fixed away off yonder on one of those patches of blue sky. It was not a glance of reflection, but rather indicated a suspension of intelligent thought.

ⓛThere was something coming to her and she was waiting for it, fearfully. What was it? She did not know; it was too subtle and elusive to name. But she felt it, creeping out of the sky, reaching toward her through the sounds, the scents, the color that filled the air.

Now her bosom rose and fell tumultuously. She was beginning to recognize this thing that was approaching to possess her, and she was striving to beat it back with her will—as powerless as her two white slender hands would have been. When she abandoned herself, a little whispered word escaped her slightly parted lips. She said it over and over under her breath: "free, free, free!" The vacant stare and the look of terror that had followed it went from her eyes. They stayed keen and bright. Her pulses beat fast, and the coursing blood warmed and relaxed every inch of her body.

She did not stop to ask if it were or were not a monstrous joy that held her. A clear and exalted perception enabled her to dismiss the suggestion as trivial. She knew that she would weep again when she saw the kind, tender hands folded in death; the face that had never looked save with love upon her, fixed and gray and dead. But she saw beyond that bitter moment a long procession of years to come that would belong to her absolutely. And she opened and spread her arms out to them in welcome.

ⓒThere would be no one to live for during those coming years; she would live for herself. There would be no powerful will bending hers in that blind persistence with which men and women believe they have a right to impose a private will upon a fellow-creature. A kind intention or a cruel intention made the act seem no less a crime as she looked upon it in that brief moment of illumination.

And yet she had loved him—sometimes. Often she had not. What did it matter! What could love, the unsolved mystery, count for in the face of this possession of self-assertion which she suddenly recognized as the strongest impulse of her being!

"Free! Body and soul free!" she kept whispering.

ⓔJosephine was kneeling before the closed door with her lips to the keyhole, imploring for admission. "Louise, open the door! I beg; open the door—you will make yourself ill. What are you doing, Louise? For heaven's sake open the door."

"Go away. I am not making myself ill." No; she was drinking in a very elixir of life through that open window.

Her fancy was running riot along those days ahead of her. Spring days, and summer days, and all sorts of days that would be her own. She breathed a quick prayer that life might be long. It was only yesterday she had thought with a shudder that life might be long.

She arose at length and opened the door to her sister's importunities. There was a feverish triumph in her eyes, and she carried herself unwittingly like a goddess of Victory. She clasped her sister's waist, and together they descended the stairs. Richards stood waiting for them at the bottom.

Someone was opening the front door with a latchkey. ⓓIt was Brently Mallard who entered, a little travel-stained, composedly carrying his grip-sack and umbrella. He had been far from the scene of the accident, and did not even know there had been one. He stood amazed at Josephine's piercing cry; at Richards' quick motion to screen him from the view of his wife.

When the doctors came they said she had died of heart disease—of the joy that kills.

1 Among ㉠ ~ ㉤, which statement from the excerpt most strongly supports the following sentence: "A woman discovers she had felt burdened by her marriage and looks forward to living independently of her husband"?

① ㉠ "Knowing that Mrs. Mallard was afflicted with a heart trouble, great care was taken to break to her as gently as possible the news of her husband's death."

② ㉡ "There was something coming to her and she was waiting for it, fearfully. What was it? She did not know; it was too subtle and elusive to name."

③ ㉢ "There would be no one to live for during those coming years; she would live for herself. There would be no powerful will bending hers in that blind persistence with which men and women believe they have a right to impose a private will upon a fellow-creature."

④ ㉣ "Josephine was kneeling before the closed door with her lips to the keyhole, imploring for admission."

⑤ ㉤ "It was Brently Mallard who entered, a little travel-stained, composedly carrying his grip-sack and umbrella."

2 Whose reaction to the last sentence is most AWKWARD?

① 수진: What is ironic is that the story ends with an event the characters tried to avoid in that Mrs. Mallard's life, which her friends and family tried so hard to protect at the beginning, is lost at the end.

② 혜령: I think that in a way, Mrs. Mallard's death is the only way for her to gain independence, in light of the fact that her husband is still alive.

③ 지석: Mrs. Mallard dies not because she regains joy, but because she suddenly loses it after having only briefly tasted it.

④ 정우: The expression 'the joy that kills' clearly tells that Mrs. Mallard's happiness killed her. That would prove just how much she disliked her husband.

⑤ 몽크: The story has an ironic ending: Mrs. Mallard dies just when she is beginning to live.

[3-4] Read the passage and answer each question.

[A] Knowing that Mrs. Mallard was afflicted with a heart trouble, great care was taken to break to her as gently as possible the news of her husband's death. It was her sister Josephine who told her, in broken sentences; veiled hints that revealed in half concealing. Her husband's friend Richards was there, too, near her. It was he who had been in the newspaper office when intelligence of the railroad disaster was received, with Brently Mallard's name leading the list of "killed." He had only taken the time to assure himself of its truth by a second telegram, and had hastened to forestall any less careful, less tender friend in bearing the sad message.

[B] She did not hear the story as many women have heard the same, with a paralyzed inability to accept its significance. She wept at once, with sudden, wild abandonment, in her sister's arms. ㉠When the storm of grief had spent itself she went away to her room alone. She would have no one follow her. There stood, facing the open window, a comfortable, roomy armchair. Into this she sank, pressed down by a physical exhaustion that haunted her body and seemed to reach into her soul.

[C] ㉡She could see in the open square before her house the tops of trees that were all aquiver with the new spring life. The delicious breath of rain was in the air. In the street below a peddler was crying his wares. The notes of a distant song which some one was singing reached her faintly, and countless sparrows were twittering in the eaves.

[D] There were patches of blue sky showing here and there through the clouds that had met and piled one above the other in the west facing her window. She sat with her head thrown back upon the cushion of the chair, quite motionless, except when a sob came up into her throat and shook her, as a child who has cried itself to sleep continues to sob in its dreams.

[E] She was young, with a fair, calm face, whose lines bespoke repression and even a certain strength. But now there was a dull stare in her eyes, whose gaze was fixed away off yonder on one of

UNIT

9

Reading Comprehension | 275

those patches of blue sky. It was not a glance of reflection, but rather indicated a suspension of intelligent thought. There was something coming to her and she was waiting for it, fearfully. What was it? She did not know; it was too subtle and elusive to name. But she felt it, creeping out of the sky, reaching toward her through the sounds, the scents, the color that filled the air.

[F] Now her bosom rose and fell tumultuously. She was beginning to recognize this thing that was approaching to possess her, and she was striving to beat it back with her will—as powerless as her two white slender hands would have been. When she abandoned herself, a little whispered word escaped her slightly parted lips. She said it over and over under her breath: "free, free, free!" The vacant stare and the look of terror that had followed it went from her eyes. ©They stayed keen and bright. Her pulses beat fast, and the coursing blood warmed and relaxed every inch of her body.

[G] She did not stop to ask if it were or were not a monstrous joy that held her. A clear and exalted perception enabled her to dismiss the suggestion as trivial. ㉣She knew that she would weep again when she saw the kind, tender hands folded in death; the face that had never looked save with love upon her, fixed and gray and dead. But she saw beyond that bitter moment a long procession of years to come that would belong to her absolutely. And she opened and spread her arms out to them in welcome.

[H] There would be no one to live for during those coming years; she would live for herself. There would be no powerful will bending hers in that blind persistence with which men and women believe they have a right to impose a private will upon a fellow-creature. A kind intention or a cruel intention made the act seem no less a crime as she looked upon it in that brief moment of illumination. And yet she had loved him—sometimes. Often she had not. What did it matter! ㉤What could love, the unsolved mystery, count for in the face of this possession of self-assertion which she suddenly recognized as the strongest impulse of her being! "Free! Body and soul free!" she kept whispering.

3 The historical background of the work was the 19th century, and women were expected to be passive and delicate. From the first paragraph of [A], Mrs. Mallard's physical weakness _____

    ① encourages her to go against society's sexist expectations.

    ② forces her to gain financial independence from her husband.

    ③ further encourages the people around her to stifle her emotions and overprotect her.

    ④ ironically allows her to experience the kind of physical and emotional excitement that she is supposed to avoid.

    ⑤ makes it impossible for her to recognize the meaning of her husband's death.

4 Which of the following is the most <u>AWKWARD</u> analysis of the underlined ㉠~㉤?

    ① ㉠ Louise's desire to be alone with her grief is the first indication of her inclination toward freedom and independence.

    ② ㉡ The elements of spring embody an approaching revelation.

    ③ ㉢ Louise's transition from physical exhaustion to physical excitement is an indication of her happiness regarding her new independent life.

    ④ ㉣ That Louise will not regret seeing her husband's dead body emphasizes the fact that she held grudge against him.

    ⑤ ㉤ Louise's self-assertion renders her both physically and emotionally free, as evidenced by her exclamation, "Body and soul free!"

Sentence Completion

1 The judge ordered that the prosecution stop badgering the elderly witness, and he exclaimed that the prosecution's attempts to frighten the old lady were a terrible example of _____, and that such behavior would not be allowed in his court.

① support   ② neglect

③ defiance   ④ intimidation

⑤ economy

> **어휘** judge 판사 order ~라고 명령하다; 주문하다 prosecution 기소 stop ~ing ~하는 것을 멈추다, 그만두다 badger ~을 괴롭히다 elderly 나이가 지긋한 witness 목격자, 증언, 증거 exclaim 외치다, 큰 소리로 주장하다 attempt 시도 frighten ~을 두려워하게 하다, 무섭게 하다 terrible 끔찍한, 터무니없는, 무서운 example 예 behavior 행동, 행위 allow ~을 허락하다 court 법원; 궁전; 뜰 support 지지, 지원, 원조 neglect 태만, 부주의, 무시 defiance 도전, 반항 intimidation 협박, 위협 economy 경제, 절약

2 Moving about in an unfamiliar environment, at home or abroad, is often not unlike a _____ into the unknown, the uncharted, and, alas, the incomprehensible.

① shift   ② sojourn

③ pass   ④ voyage

> **어휘** unfamiliar 익숙지 않은, 낯선 environment 환경, 주위 at home 집에서; 본국에, 고향에; 마음 편히 abroad 해외에, 외국으로 often 종종, 자주 *is not unlike = is like the unknown 미지 uncharted 지도에 실려 있지 않은, 미지의 alas 참으로, 아아(슬픔·근심 등을 나타냄) incomprehensible 이해할 수 없는, 불가해한 shift 변화, 변천, 교체 sojourn 머무름, 체재 pass 통행, 통과 voyage 여행, 항해, (특히) 긴 배 여행

3 To be _____ is to be _____ restrained.

① wanton – emotionally   ② placid – morally

③ continent – morally   ④ succinct – thoroughly

> **어휘** restrained 삼가는, 자제하는, 억제하는 wanton 무자비한, 음탕한 emotionally 감정적으로 placid 평온한 morally 도덕적으로 continent 자제하는, 금욕적인 succinct 간결한, 간명한 thoroughly 철저하게, 완전히

4 If someone is caught _____, they are caught while they are in the act of doing something wrong.

① red-handed   ② empty-handed

③ left-handed   ④ right-handed

어휘   someone 누군가 caught [catch의 과거·과거분사] be caught 잡히다 while ~하는 동안에; ~하는 반면에 something 무언가, 어떤 것 wrong 잘못된, 틀린, 그릇된 red-handed 현행범으로 empty-handed 빈손의 left-handed 왼손잡이의, 서투른, 솜씨 없는, right-handed 오른손잡이의

5 When someone gets rich very quickly, we say that the person went _____.

① into the jackpot   ② bankrupt

③ barefoot   ④ from rags to riches

⑤ over the top

어휘   get +ⓐ ~이 되다 get rich 부자가 되다, 부유해지다 quickly 빨리 go into the jackpot 대성공하다 go bankrupt 파산하다 go barefoot 맨발로 가다 go from rags to riches 가난뱅이에서 부자가 되다 go over the top 대담한 일을 하다, 목표 이상의 성과를 올리다

6 _____ is the mark of _____.

① Timorousness – hero   ② Thrift – impoverished

③ Avarice – philanthropist   ④ Trepidation – coward

⑤ Vanity – obsequious

어휘   mark 표시, 특징, 기호 timorousness 소심함, 겁이 많음 hero 영웅 thrift 검약, 검소 impoverished 가난한, 결핍한 avarice 탐욕, 욕심 philanthropist 박애주의자 trepidation 소심함, 겁이 많음 coward 겁쟁이 vanity 허영심, 허식; 무익, 헛됨 obsequious 아첨(아부)하는, 비굴한

7 Because _____ is such an unsightly disease, its victims have frequently been shunned.

① leprosy   ② cancer

③ halitosis   ④ poverty

⑤ tuberculosis

어휘   unsightly 추한, 꼴사나운 disease 병, 질병 victim 희생자 frequently 자주, 빈번히 shun ~을 피하다 have been shunned 피해져 왔다, 무시되어 왔다, 경멸당해 왔다 leprosy 나병(Hansen's disease), 문둥병; (사상·도덕적인) 부패 cancer 암 halitosis 구취 poverty 가난, 결핍

8 _____ people are not apt to engage in small talk.

① molest   ② taciturn

③ tolerate   ④ feline

어휘

be apt to ® ~하기 쉽다, ~하는 경향이 있다 engage in ~에 종사하다, 참여하다 small talk 잡담 molest ~을 괴롭히다 taciturn 말없는, 과묵한 tolerate ~을 관대히 다루다, 참다, 견디다 feline 고양잇과의, 고양이의

9 _____ means a serious case of lawbreaking.

① larceny   ② robbery

③ transgression   ④ felony

어휘

mean ~을 의미하다; ~을 의도하다; 비열한, 인색한; 보통의, 평균의; 훌륭한, 대단한 serious 진지한, 중대한, 심각한 case 경우, 사건; 상자 lawbreaking 법률위반 larceny 절도죄 robbery 강도죄 transgression 위반 felony 중범죄 cf) misdemeanor 경범죄

10 A person who runs away from military duty is a(n) _____.

① runaway   ② eloper

③ deserter   ④ dropout

어휘

run away 달아나다, 도망치다 military duty 병역의무 runaway 도망자, 탈주자 elope (남녀가) 눈이 맞아 달아나다 deserter 유기자, 탈영자, 탈주자 dropout 낙오자, 탈락자

MAGNUS 리딩 에이 원 프리미엄 독해 시리즈: 문학/비문학편

Reading A one

1

박지성 저

Start-up

정답/해설

중학 고급 영문 독해

특목고(외고/국제고), 자사고 대비
문학·비문학 고급 영문 독해 수험서

- PART 1 ┃ Voca Master
- PART 2 ┃ Text Reading
- PART 3 ┃ Voca Check
- PART 4 ┃ Reading Comprehension
- PART 5 ┃ Sentence Completion

반석출판사

정답/해설

Part 2 Text Reading

Text 1

1 ②

해설 The passage states that the narrator had to sack Tayloe because he tried to poison Barney.

2 ①

해설 The passage mentions that the poison container was overturned and a trail of powder led to Barney's dish, indicating that the attempt to poison Barney was clumsy.

3 ①

해설 The passage mentions that the narrator could have forgiven Tayloe's petty vandalisms, suggesting that they did not cause harm to Barney.

Text 2

4 ③

해설 The passage states that Tayloe had a "violent antagonism" towards Barney and that the author can "only ascribe" this behavior to jealousy. This suggests that Tayloe was jealous of Barney.

5 ③

해설 The passage states that Tayloe had abandoned his guinea pigs, suggesting that they are no longer in his possession.

6 ②

해설 The passage describes Barney's "newly awakened intellectual curiosity" and the author's observation of how Barney "carries himself about." This suggests that the author is pleased with Barney's behavior. The passage also mentions that the author is "certain" that Barney knows there is knowledge to be gained from the books, further indicating the author's approval of Barney's behavior.

Text 3

7 ⑤

해설 The passage mentions that the speaker has to confine Barney because they are afraid that Barney might be able to communicate his intelligence to others. Therefore, Barney needs to be kept away from the experiments to avoid any risks.

8 ①

해설 The passage suggests that there is a small chance Barney might be able to communicate his intelligence to others. The speaker considers this a risk that cannot be ignored, implying that Barney's intelligence could potentially be a threat.

9 ①

(해설) The passage states that there is a vault in the basement built to keep vermin out, and the speaker mentions that it will serve equally well to keep Barney in. This indicates that Barney is confined in the basement vault.

Text 4

10 ①

(해설) The passage mentions that the speaker let Barney out to frisk around before starting new tests.

11 ②

(해설) The passage states that the speaker spotted Barney on the coping of the well after reaching the yard.

12 ②

(해설) The passage describes how the key was removed by Barney, and the speaker arrived just in time to hear it splash into the water below the well.

Text 5

13 ③

(해설) The passage mentions that the speaker knotted a length of rope at intervals to create a ladder to facilitate their descent into the well.

14 ①

(해설) He was excited about the condition of the rope ladder. Barney made excited squeaks near the top to alert the speaker about the precarious condition of the rope ladder, which was almost completely severed due to chafing against the edge of the masonry.

15 ②

(해설) The passage indicates that the speaker replaced the damaged section of rope and arranged old sacking beneath it to prevent a recurrence of the accident.

Text 6

16 Barney

17 He sprained his wrist.

18 ③

Part 3 Voca Check

1   1 under the influence of alcohol   2 stand in the way of   3 jolt   4 vandalism
    5 flimsy   6 malice   7 petty   8 sack   9 clumsy

2 1 abandonment 　 2 become too much for 　 3 guinea pig 　 4 affair
5 glutamic acid 　 6 mute 　 7 reproach 　 8 spell 　 9 ascribe 　 10 to the last
11 sport 　 12 drag 　 13 take off

3 1 confined 　 2 vermin 　 3 do away with 　 4 go over 　 5 too great to ignore
6 frisked 　 7 vault 　 8 coping 　 9 retrieving 　 10 commence
11 insurmountable 　 12 own

4 1 sacking 　 2 chafed 　 3 bring up to date 　 4 came off 　 5 facilitate
6 at intervals 　 7 gave out 　 8 sever 　 9 groped 　 10 rude 　 11 fixed
12 masonry 　 13 squeaked 　 14 plight

Part 4 Reading Comprehension

1 ③
해설 Barney가 인간 수준의 글쓰기 능력을 성취하지 못했다고 해서 주인공 과학자의 실험이 실패했다고 보는 내용은 옳지 않다. 오히려, 과학자를 죽이려는 일련의 과정을 보면 Barney가 "지나치게" 성공했다고 보는 것이 옳다.

2 ⑤
해설 Barney는 의도적으로 우물에 열쇠를 떨어뜨림 → 과학자를 우물 속에 유인해 죽이려 하려는 의도임.

3 ④
해설 근거문장: Apparently I have spoken too soon.
해당 문장은 9월 9일자 일기에서 드러나듯이 과학자가 Barney를 "너무 얕잡아 봤다"는 의미로 쓰이고 있다.

4 ③
해설 precious guinea pigs = possibly males
Taylor가 데리고 있던 "precious guinea pigs"가 모두 female이란 내용은 없다. 오히려, 내용 전개상 males일 가능성이 높다.

Part 5 Sentence Completion

1 ①
해설 빈칸에 영향을 미치는 요소는 관계대명사 'that'에 걸리는 내용이다.

> that <u>distinguishes</u> human beings from the other animals → an <u>unique</u> quality
> 다른 동물과 인간을 구별 짓는 → 독특한 특성

해석 말할 수 있는 능력은 다른 모든 동물과 인간을 구별하는 독특한 특성이다.

아래 공식을 반드시 기억하도록 한다.

$$\underline{N(A)\ \ that\ \ S\ \ V(B)}$$
$$A\ \ =\ \ B$$

2 ②

해설 빈칸에 직접적으로 영향을 미치는 요소는 of the blizzard이다.

many people were unprepared for the _____ ⊖ _____ of the blizzard of 1888

강한 눈보라의 _____ ⊖ _____ 에 대한 대비가 부족했다

그러므로, 빈칸에 들어갈 단어는 부정의 의미를 내포하는 단어이어야 한다. 보기 항의 단어를 긍정, 부정 또는 중립적인 단어로 구분해 보면 다음과 같다.

① inevitability 부정   ② ferocity 부정   ③ importance 긍정
④ probability 중립   ⑤ mildness 긍정

이 경우 보기 항 ③과 ⑤는 먼저 소거하고, ①과 ②를 각각 문맥에 대입하여 가장 적절한 것을 고르면 된다. ④의 경우 앞의 두 표현이 적절하지 않을 경우 가장 마지막에 넣어보면 된다.

해석 비록 다코타에서는 가공할 만한 추위의 겨울이 일반적이었지만, 많은 사람들은 1888년의 강한 눈보라의 사나움에 대한 대비가 부족했다.

3 ①

해설 첫 번째 빈칸에 들어갈 단어의 긍정/부정의 성격을 먼저 파악해 보자.

As <u>first</u> streamlined car, Airflow represented _____ ⊕ _____ in automotive development

긍정   =   긍정

동격의 코마를 활용하면, 'first(최초의) streamlined car = Airflow'가 되므로 주어인 Airflow는 'in automotive development' 표현과 함께 긍정적인 의미를 전달한다. A represents B는 A=B이므로 B에 들어가는 단어도 긍정이 된다. 그러므로 첫 번째 빈칸은 긍정의 단어가 들어가야 한다. 두 번째 빈칸의 내용은 양보구문의 although를 활용한다.

although its sales _____ ⊖ _____ , it had an <u>immense</u> influence on automobile design.

부정 ←——→ 긍정

고로, 보기 항은 긍정과 부정의 표현으로 구성되어야 한다.

① milestone - disappointing   긍정 - 부정
② breakthrough - significant   긍정 - 긍정
③ regression - unimportant   부정 - 부정

④ misjudgment - calculable 부정 - 긍정
⑤ revolution - tolerable 긍정 - 긍정

보기 항 ①만이 긍정-부정으로 이루어져 있다.

[해석] 최초의 현대적인 자동차로서 Airflow는 자동차의 발전에서 획기적인 사건에 해당한다. 그리고 비록 그것의 판매는 실망스러웠지만, 자동차 디자인에 엄청난 영향력을 끼쳤다.

4 ①
[해설] 빈칸에 들어갈 단어의 성격을 두 대상의 대조구가 설정되는 역접의 while을 이용해 정한다.

nurturing parents	While	**cold or inconsistent** parents
compensate for adversity	↔	_____ ⊖ it

① exacerbate 부정   ② neutralize 중립
③ eradicate   긍정(부정적인 요소를 제거하다)
④ ameliorate   긍정(부정적인 상황/현 상황을 향상시키다)   ⑤ relieve 긍정

보기 항 ①만이 부정적 어감을 드러내는 단어이다.

[해석] 좋은 부모는 역경에 대해 보상을 받을 수 있지만 냉정하고, 일관되지 않은 부모는 고난을 더 심화시킬 수 있다.

5 ④
[해설] 두 빈칸을 수식하는 표현이 모두 긍정이다. 빈칸에 들어갈 표현도 긍정이 된다. 즉, 보기 항이 긍정-긍정으로 구성된 짝을 골라야 한다. politics는 앞에서 언급된 사회적 긴장감을 완화시키는 역할을 하는 것을 and 이후 'resolving their conflict'에서 확인할 수 있다.

adult factions		children
Social tensions be ___ ⊕ ___ by politics	but	no such _____ for resolving conflict
→ politics가 긍정의 수단이므로 사회적 긴장감이 해결되는 쪽의 긍정의 단어가 들어간다.		→ 빈칸은 politics와 같은 기능인 동시에 긍정의 의미를 전달하는 단어가 들어간다.

고로 보기 항은 긍정-긍정의 단어로 연결된 짝이다.

① intensified - attitude   부정 - 부적절한 단어
② complicated - relief   부정 - 긍정
③ frustrated - justification   부적절인 동시에 부정 - 부적절한 단어
④ adjusted - mechanism   긍정 - 긍정인 동시에 politics와 같은 기능 수행을 나타내는 단어
⑤ revealed - opportunity   부정 - 긍정

보다시피, 긍정-긍정으로 이루어진 보기 항은 ④ 밖에 없다. 이런 경우 첫 번째 단어가 긍정의 표현이라는 것을 알 경우 첫 번째 빈칸에 들어갈 단어에 해당하는 보기 항을 먼저 살펴보면 답 접근이 용이해 진다.

[해석] 어른들로 구성된 당파에서 사회적 긴장감은 정치에 의해 조정된다. 그러나 청소년과 아이들은 어른들

의 배타적인 세계와의 갈등을 해결하기 위한 해결책으로서의 어떠한 그러한 도구를 가지지 못한다.

6 ①

해설 대조의 while을 활용한다. 일반적으로 while에 걸리는 내용과 주절의 내용이 반대로 전개된다. 주절의 내용이 'the plans'에 대해서 부정적인 관점을 드러내는 내용이다. 고로 부사절 while에 걸리는 내용은 긍정일 가능성이 높다. 보기 항을 먼저 보고 분석을 살펴보자.

① feasible 긍정   ② crippling 부정
③ flimsy 부정   ④ unrealizable 부정

	the plans to stimulate the flagging economy
to government economists	feasible on paper
ministry spokesmen	strong doubts about their practicability

해석 정부의 경제학자들에게는 침체된 경제를 자극하기 위한 계획이 이론상으로는 실현 가능해 보이지만, 관계부처 대변인은 그 실행가능성에 대해 강한 의혹을 표명했다.

7 ①

해설 순접부연의 세미콜론을 먼저 활용한다. 'A; B'는 'A = B'이다. 세미콜론 이후의 내용을 보면, '나는 다시는 음주운전을 하지 않을 것이다'라는 긍정적인 태도의 내용이므로 앞 문장 전체의 내용도 긍정이 됨을 알 수 있다. 다음과 같이 볼 수 있다.

> The accident was a _____⊕_____ lesson.

보기 항을 하나씩 살펴보자.

① salutary 긍정   ② skeptical 부정   ③ mournful 부정   ④ polemic 부정

보기 항 중 긍정인 것은 ① 밖에 없다.

해석 그 사고는 유익한 교훈이었다. 나는 다시는 절대 음주운전을 하지 않을 것이다.

8 ③

해설 관계대명사 'that' 이하의 내용을 가장 잘 반영하는 단어를 문맥에 맞게 파악해야 한다.

> that are passed on from one generation to the next → certain attributes
> 한 세대에서 다음 세대로 전해지는 → 일정한 속성

피수식어구의 의미상 성격은 수식어구의 내용에 영향을 받는다. 즉, 피수식어구가 긍정이면, 수식어구도 긍정이며, 피수식어구가 부정이면, 수식어구도 부정의 어감을 지니게 된다.

해석 모든 유기체는 한 세대에서 다음 세대로 전해지는 일정한 속성(특성)을 지니고 있다.

9 ①

해설 제시된 문장은 다음과 같이 변형시킬 수 있다.

> The acclaimed author (who is) lauded by all for his brilliant insights and helpful advice.

관계대명사 'who' 이하에 걸리는 내용의 수식을 받는 선행사 자리에 빈칸이 있으므로, 관계대명사의 내용이 빈칸의 의미를 한정한다.

> lauded by all for his brilliant insights and helpful advice (긍정) → acclaimed (긍정)
> 그의 뛰어난 통찰력과 유용한 충고로 인해 모든 이가 칭송하는 → 환호 받는

해석 그 환호 받는 작가는 그의 뛰어난 통찰력과 유용한 충고로 인해 모든 이가 칭송한다.

10 ①

해설 역접의 'but'을 이용하여, 'exceptionally clear'와 대조되는 단어를 선정할 수도 있지만, 빈칸이 관계대명사 'that' 이하의 내용에 수식을 받고 있다는 점을 활용해 보자.

> an obscure significance that they did not at all possess in fact
> 실질적으로 전혀 소유하고 있지 않은 (부정) → 불분명한 중요성 (부정)

문장완성을 푸는 방법론은 여러 가지 될 수 있다는 점을 기억하고, 다양한 시각에서 나만은 접근 방법을 만들어 내도록 한다.

해석 그녀의 마음을 아주 분명했지만, 이 마음은 실제 소유하고 있지 않은 이러한 불분명한 중요성으로 둘러싸인 아주 사소한 사실들에만 초점이 맞추어 있었다.

Unit 2 The Road Not Taken by ROBERT FROST

Part 3 Voca Check

1
1 diverge　2 bend　3 undergrowth　4 fair　5 claim　6 grassy　7 want
8 wear　9 lie　10 tread　11 rhyme scheme　12 repeat　13 line　14 stanza
15 face　16 bend

2
1 suppose　2 subtle　3 fork　4 dense　5 worn-in　6 reinforce　7 statement
8 exclaim　9 save　10 contradict　11 acknowledgement　12 recount

Part 4 Reading Comprehension

1 four / five / ABAAB

2 ②, ③, ⑤

해설 ① ㉠ 본문에서 언급된 "두 길"은 인생의 많은 필연적 선택을 나타내는 표현이다. 삶의 후반기에 접하는 "두 가지 중요한 선택"을 나타낸다는 내용은 없다. 인생 전반 또는 삶의 초기에 접하는 선택이라 보는 것이 옳다.

④ ㉢

Then took the other, as just as fair,
And having perhaps the better claim,
Because it was grassy and wanted wear;
Though as for that the passing there
Had worn them really about the same,

And both that morning equally lay
In leaves no step had trodden black.

위 내용을 보면, 보기에 "덜 밟아" 보여 첫 번째가 아니라 두 번째를 선택하지만, 결국에는 어느 쪽이 덜 밟힌 것인지 알지 못한다고 말하고 있고, 선택한 길이 결론적으로 "바르다 (right)"고 판단할 근거는 없다. 이는, 인생의 선택이 그 당시에는 바른 판단일지 모르지만, 그것이 좋은 결과든 그렇지 않은 결과든 "더 나은" 선택이 아닐 수 있다는 의미로도 볼 수 있다.

3 ④

해설 I. The title "The Road Not Taken" refers to the less-chosen path ~~that the speaker ultimately selected~~.

→ "The Road Not Taken" refers to the path that the speaker (who represents us) don't choose in his life.

II. The speaker convinces himself that he can ~~backtrack the road if efforts are made~~.

9

→ The speaker acknowledges the uncertainty of ever returning to the other road: "Yet knowing how way leads on to way, I doubted if I should ever come back."

III. In the 1st stanza, the speaker is deliberating his future between two reasonable choices. (○)

→ The speaker stands at a crossroads, contemplating which road to take.

IV. In the 4st stanza, the speaker ~~regrets~~ his choice, because it is proven to be ~~unreasonable~~, compared to the other. → The speaker reflects on the choice he made with a sense of sigh, indicating a wistful acceptance rather than outright ~~regret~~, and there is not sign of the choice chosen being "unreasonable."

V. The main theme of the poem is ~~pioneering uncultivated future and making new attempts~~.

→ While the poem does touch upon themes of choice and individuality, it's more about reflecting on the nature of choices rather than specifically pioneering into an uncultivated future.

4 ③

해설 ~~Hyperbole~~(과장법) → Irony

The speaker says that he took the road less traveled by, but earlier in the poem, he admits that both roads were equally worn.

근거: Though as for that the passing there
        Had worn them really about the same

Part 5 Sentence Completion

1 ①

해설 조건부의 unless를 활용한다. 법원은 환경주의자들이 어떤 제안을 하면, 인가를 하지 않을지 생각하면 된다. 결국 조건부의 unless는 인과로 파악할 수 있다. 주절의 주어는 법원인 the courts이다.

결론	: the courts will disallow their proposition as too vague
판단의 근거	: **unless** the environmentalists can draft a more specific proposal

환경주의자들의 제안이 더욱 구체적이지 않은 이상 법원은 이들이 제안을 너무 애매한 것으로 치부해 이들의 제안을 받아들이지 않는다는 내용이다. 빈칸에 들어갈 단어는 법원의 입장에서 긍정의 단어가 들어가야 한다. 보기 항을 살펴보자.

① specific   긍정 (어떤 제안이 구체적이면, 긍정적인 의미로 해석된다)
② ambiguous = ③ obscure 부정
④ dubious   부정

보기 항 ②와 ③은 동의어 관계로 정답에서 제외될 가능성이 아주 높다. 또한 ①번 보기 항 외에 나머지가 모두 부정으로 파악되기에, 이런 경우 보기 항만으로도 답이 ①이 아닐까 먼저 빈칸에 넣어보고 접근한다.

해석 환경보호론자들이 보다 더 명확한 내용의 제안서를 작성하지 않으면 법원은 그들의 제안을 너무 모호한 것으로 보아 받아들이지 않을 것이다.

2 ③

해설 아래와 같이 주부와 서술부의 관계를 바탕으로 접근해 보자.

주부 + 서술부

주부의 내용이 서술부의 내용에 영향을 미치는 관계로 주부의 성격을 파악할 경우
서술부의 내용이 파악이 된다. 예문을 통해 조금 자세히 살펴보자.

예) People with two different ideas / usually come to a disagreement.
서로 다른 생각을 가진 사람(주부) → 일반적으로 불일치에 이른다(서술부)

해석 거의 혹은 아무것도 받지 못하는 친척들은 고인이 그 서류(유언장)에 서명할 때 정상적인 상태가 아니었다고 주장함으로서 유언장의 법적 효력을 없애려 했다.

3 ②

해설 부연진술의 콜론과 in fact와 인과의 so ~ that을 활용한다. their viewpoints가 주어이다.

---

so polarized that no chance at all to reach an agreement of any kind
너무 달라(원인) ──────→ 어떠한 동의에도 다다르지 못하다(결과)

보기 항을 볼 경우 ②와 ④가 반의어의 관계이다. 일반적으로 빈칸에 들어가는 단어와 반의어를 보기 항에 하나 이상 제시하는 경우가 많으므로 이러한 점을 잘 활용하면 보기 항 중 어느 것을 먼저 빈칸에 넣고 생각할지 판단이 쉬워진다. 보기 항에 반의어 관계가 있는 단어가 있으면, 그 단어 중 하나가 답일 가능성이 높다.

해석 두 그룹은 전혀 의견이 일치하지 않았다: 사실 그들의 관점은 너무나 대립되어서 협의에 도달할 가능성은 전혀 없어 보였다.

4 ②

해설 비유를 드러내는 특수구문인 A is to B what C is to D (A가 B에 대한 관계는 C가 D에 관한 관계와 같다; A = C이고 B = D이다)를 활용한 지문이지만, 빈칸이 들어간 문장의 요소를 긍정과 부정 그리고 무엇이 어디에 영향을 미치는지를 파악하면 좀 더 쉽게 접근이 가능하다.

1) 빈칸이 들어간 문장 주어 성격 파악

The man(⊖) who can not be trusted

부정의 의미가 들어간 관계대명사 who의 수식을 받는 man은 부정적인 인물이다.

2) 앞에서 설명한 비유구문을 활용하면 다음과 같다.

The man(⊖) = a bit of <u>rotten timber</u>
society = a house

The man의 성격이 부정이기에 빈칸의 단어도 부정이라 보기 항 ② 또는 ④가 된다. 본문의 문맥에서 앞에 집과 목재의 관계를 드러내는 내용과 통일성을 갖추기 위해선 보기 항 ②가 가장 적절하다.

해석 사회는 건물과 비유되는데, 그 기반이 튼튼하고 목재가 견실하면 건물이 확고하게 선다. 미덥지 못한 사람과 사회의 관계는 마치 썩은 목재와 집에 대한 관계와 같다.

5 ①

해설 accuse라는 단어는 'accuse A of B'라는 숙어를 가진다. 이때, 주의할 것은 'accuse'라는 단어의 성격이 내재적으로 A라는 대상의 잘못된 행위(B)에 대한 비난을 드러내므로, B의 내용은 부정적인 어감의 단어가 와야 한다. 이를 활용하여, 문맥상 '책임감의 회피'라는 답안을 고를 수 있다. 우리말에 '책임감에서 빠져나오다'라는 표현을 적용해 선택지 ③을 골라선 안 된다. 영어에서 책임감 회피라는 표현은 'evasion of responsibility'로 표현한다.

accuse A of B(⊖)
B는 항상 부정적 의미를 전달하는 단어이다.

참고 **accuse A of B와 함께 외워둘 표현**

① blame A for B = blame B on A

예) She blamed herself for having been a dull company.
그녀는 재미있게 상대해 주지 못한 것을 후회했다.

② condemn A for B

예) The boss condemned him for his idleness
아무의 나태를 꾸짖다

③ censure A for B

예) My teacher censured me for being late for school.
선생님은 학교에 늦은 걸로 나를 나무랬다.

④ castigate A for B

예) He castigated himself for being so stupid.
그는 그처럼 어리석었던 것을 크게 자책했다.

⑤ rebuke A for B

예) The company was publicly rebuked for having neglected safety procedures.
그 회사는 안전 규정 소홀로 공개적인 질책을 받았다.

해석 야당은 정부의 책임감 회피를 비난했다.

6 ②

해설 부정적 주어의 행위는 부정적 행위를 이끌어 낸다.

> His overly saccharine demeanor = the voters' decision to cast a vote against him
>
> 그의 과도한 설탕발림 태도 → 부정적 결과

본문에서 'overly saccharine'은 'not genuine'과 같은 개념으로 쓰이고 있다.

해석 그의 과도한 사탕발림적인 태도는 대부분의 유권자들로 하여금 반대표를 던지는 것을 결정하도록 만들었다. 왜냐하면 그들은 그가 진실하지 못하고, 사실 너무 정치꾼의 성격이라고 생각했기 때문이다.

7 ④

해설 빈칸의 내용은 관계대명사 'that'의 수식을 받고 있다. 그 의미가 관계대명사에 한정된다는 점을 활용한다.

> competing nation-states that scramble for markets, power and resource
>
> 시장, 권력 그리고 자원을 위해 싸우는 → 경쟁적

해석 지속가능한 개발이 직면한 도전은 시장, 권력 그리고 자원을 위해 다투는 경제적 국가라는 바로 그 사상을 과거의 산물로 만들 것이다.

8 ②

해설 첫 번째 빈칸에 들어갈 단어는 'He'의 성격을 규정하는 형용사이다.

> a _____ man(=he) who _____ considers the consequences before he acts
>
> A   =   B

첫 번째 빈자리는 관계대명사 'who'이하의 내용에 그 성격이 결정되고, 이후 두 번째 빈칸은 문맥에 가장 적절한 단어를 고르면 된다.

> who alway considers the consequences before he acts → a wary man
>
> 항상 행동하기 전 결과를 고려하는 → 조심성 있는 사람
>
> A   =   B

해석 그는 일반적으로 행동하기 전에 결과를 고려하는 조심성 있는 사람으로 여겨진다.

9 ①

해설 빈칸의 내용에 영향을 미치는 요소는 관계부사 when에 걸리는 절이다. 주어가 심장마비환자라는 점을 감안하여, 주절의 내용을 한정하는 관계부사에 주목하며 접근하면 된다.

> 부정적 원인 : <u>more likely to miss</u> or <u>wait longer</u> for crucial treatments
>
> 부정적 결과 : a <u>slightly higher</u> risk of death

해석 심장마비 환자는 중요한 치료를 놓치거나 더 오래 기다릴 가능성이 높은 주말에 병원에 가면 사망 위험이 약간 더 높습니다.

10 ③

해설 선행사의 의미를 한정하는 관계대명사 that과 역접의 but을 활용한다.

1) 관계대명사 that을 활용한다. 주어가 사회학자임을 감안하면서 다음과 같은 수식관계를 파악할 수 있다.

> <u>norms/regulations</u> **that describe the appropriate behavior of children and adults**
>
> 아이와 어른의 적절한 행동을 설명하는 분명한 (규범/규칙) 세웠다

2) 역접의 but을 활용한다.

> <u>fairly clear-cut</u> norms that describe the appropriate behavior of children and adults, but <u>confusion</u> about what constitutes appropriate behavior for adolescents

해석 사회과학자들은 아이와 어른의 적절한 행동을 설명하는 분명한 규범을 세웠다. 그러나 무엇이 청소년기에 적절한 행동을 구성하는가에 관해서는 혼란이 존재하는 것으로 여겨진다.

Unit 3 The Scientific Revolution in the 17th Century

Part 2 Text Reading

1 ④

해설 I. The 1600s were characterized by a prevailing belief in God and the attribution of natural phenomena to divine will. (O)

→ The passage mentions that it was a world where everyone was God-fearing and attributed natural events to the inscrutable will of a stern deity.

II. Isaac Newton's pursuits in alchemy and numerological codes in the Bible were ~~entirely unrelated~~ to modern materialism and rationality.

→ While Newton did engage in pursuits such as alchemy and numerology, these were not entirely unrelated to modern materialism and rationality. The passage mentions that Newton's work was a mix of science and older, arcane disciplines.

III. The scientific revolution of the 1600s ~~finally eliminated the need for divine intervention in understanding the cosmos~~.

→ While the scientific revolution introduced new ways of understanding the cosmos, it did not completely eliminate the need for divine intervention, as evidenced by Newton's dismay when others suggested so.

IV. Isaac Newton's Principia Mathematica is considered one of the most influential books ever written and contains equations still used in practical applications today. (O)

→ The passage mentions that Newton's Principia Mathematica is among the most influential books ever written, and its equations are still used in practical applications today.

V. The scientific revolution of the 1600s, led by figures like Newton and Kepler, introduced the idea that the universe operates according to regular, ordered principles that can be described with simple equations. (O)

→ The passage discusses how figures like Newton and Kepler introduced the idea that the universe operates according to regular, ordered principles describable by simple equations.

Part 3 Voca Check

1   1 candidate   2 inscrutable   3 deity   4 unpromising   5 crowning
    6 fortitude   7 deliberately   8 struck dumb   9 eccentric   10 stranglehold
    11 exclusive   12 pagan

2　1 challenging　2 proto-scientist　3 paid-up　4 pursuit　5 commitment
　　6 expertise　7 tribute　8 deft　9 wind up　10 intervention　11 dismay

Part 4 Reading Comprehension

1 ②

해설 첫 번째 단락은 17세기가 현대적이고 과학적인 세계관이 도래한 시기였다는 것을 뉴턴의 저서가 오늘날 현대사회에 미치고 있는 영향을 예로 들어 설명하고 있다. 두 번째 단락은 17세기의 유산이 단지 이런 유용한 이론이 아니라, 진정한 유산이 되는 것은 이런 사상에 내재된 보편성이라고 밝히고 있다. 마지막 세 번째 단락에서는 이런 최초의 과학자들이 갑자기 등장한 것이 아니라, 과학과 종교가 혼재된 17세기의 사상적 토양에서 나오게 된 것임을, 다시 뉴턴을 예로 들어 설명하고 있다. 따라서 ② (B) and (D)가 답이 된다.

2 ⑤

해설 모두 본문과 일치하는 옳은 진술이다.

3 ③

해설 이어지는 "there would be no further need for divine intervention to keep the planets in their orbits"의 내용으로 보아 "우주의 운행원리가 예측 가능하고 질서 정연하다"는 의미로 쓴 것이다.

4 ①

해설 뉴턴을 어떤 의미에서, 최초의 과학자가 아니라 마지막 주술사라고 언급하고 있는 이유는 그의 과학적인 사고가 종교적인 믿음에 근거를 두고 있기 때문이다. 뉴턴이 자신의 위대한 사상체계가 현란한 기술을 지닌 기하학자인 신(god)에게 바치는 찬사가 되길 바랐다는 앞 문장의 내용을 참조해 본다.

Part 5 Sentence Completion

1 ①

해설 주어에 해당하는 'Her manipulation of the stock market'은 수단 또는 방법의 의미로 해석이 된다. 전체 문장의 해석은 '그녀는 주식시장을 조작해서 백만장자가 되었다.'로 보면 된다. 결국 조작(manipulation)을 잘 해서 좋은 결과(millionaire)를 이끌어낸 경우가 되므로 다음과 같이 볼 수 있다.

> Her manipulation of the stock market made her a millionaire.
> 　　긍정적 원인(A)　　　→　　　긍정적 결과(B)

긍정적 원인은 긍정의 결과를 낳고, 부정의 원인은 부정의 결과를 낳는 'A = B'의 순접을 이룬다.

해석 그녀는 주식시장을 조작해서 백만장자가 되었다.

2 ②

해설 빈칸에 부정적 영향을 미치는 부사 'annoyingly'로 보아 빈칸은 부정을 전달하는 단어가 와야 한다. 이 문제는 선택지 모두가 부정적으로 묘사될 수 있는 단어로 구성되어 있기에 뒤에 이어지는 부연진술에서 근거를 찾아야 한다.

wordy **and always** repeating → redundant
⊖ = ⊖

해석 삼촌의 편지는 짜증날 정도로 불필요한 내용이 많습니다. 그것들(편지)은 장황하고 항상 이전 편지의 소식을 반복합니다.

참고

전체문장에 영향을 미치는 부사 중에는 긍정 또는 부정의 색을 분명하게 드러내는 것이 있기에 논리 완성 문제풀이의 핵심적인 역할을 한다. 부사의 색깔(긍정, 부정)이 곧 문장의 색깔이다.

예) <u>Unfortunately</u> for Gordon Brown, he inherited (the mess) started by Tony Blair, especially in Iraq.

불행히도 Gordon Brown의 경우 Tony Blair가 시작한 혼란의 상황, 특히 이라크의 상황을 이어받게 되었다.

→ 위 예문을 보면, 전체문장의 성격을 규정하는 'unfortunately'를 통해 이후 진술이 Gordon Brown에게는 좋지 않은 내용으로 적용되어야 한다. 그러므로 'the mess'와 같은 부정적 어감의 표현을 쉽게 파악할 수 있다.

예) <u>Luckily</u>, they were able to (contain) the blaze in the basement while they (evacuated) all the tenants.

다행히 지하실 밖으로 불길이 번지는 것을 잡아, 세입자들이 모두 빠져 나올 수 있었어요.

→ 전체 문장에 긍정적 영향을 미치는 'luckily'를 볼 수 있다. 이후 진술은 불길을 '잡다'와 사람들을 모두 '대피시키다'라는 긍정의 의미를 드러내는 동사와 함께 묶어 생각할 수 있다.

예) <u>Interestingly</u>, emotional tears seem to contain about 24 percent more protein than ordinary cleansing tears.

흥미로운 사실은 감정에 의한 눈물은 눈을 깨끗이 하기 위해 나오는 눈물보다 단백질을 24%쯤 더 함유한 듯하다.

→ 'interestingly'라는 표현에서 이후 진술은 일반적인 사실과는 구별되는 '관심을 유발하는' 내용으로 전개되어야 함을 알 수 있다.

3 ①

해설 부정적 결과인 poor farmhand가 결과로 제시되고 있다. 부정적 원인의 단어가 빈칸에 들어가는데 보기 항 ①을 제외하곤 모두 긍정적인 의미의 표현이다. 결국, 물주인 'laziness'는 부정의 의미를 담고 있기에 'him'에게 부정적인 영향을 미친다는 것을 알 수 있다.

His <u>laziness</u> makes him a <u>poor</u> farmhand.
게으름(부정) → 별 볼일 없는(부정)

해석 그가 게을러서 농사일을 하기에 적합하지 않다.

4 ①

해설 인과로 해석하는 물주구문으로 'His heavy dependancy on alcohol'로 인해 발생할 수 있는 결과를 생각해야 한다. 인과로 해석하는 물주구문이다.

---

heavy dependancy on alcohol → jobless

부정적 원인 → 부정적 결과

참고

물주구문에서 주어는 문장 전체의 성격을 규정한다. 즉, 이후 전개되는 진술이 긍정인지 부정인지를 결정하는 중요한 정보를 제공하기에 이에 대한 정확한 해석 연습이 필요하다.

예) A severe stomachache / prevented the representative director from attending the urgent conference to hear emergency report on the company's finance condition.

심한 복통으로 인해 대표이사는 회사의 재정 상태에 관한 긴급보고 회의에 참석할 수 없었다.

→ '심한 복통'이란 부정적인 요소로 대표이사가 빠지지 말아야 할 회의에 참석할 수 없었다는 이야기다. 즉, 인과로 해석되는 물주구문의 주어의 성격이 부정적 어감이라 이후 진술도 부정적 내용으로 전개되어야 함을 유추할 수 있다.

해석 그는 술에 너무 의존하기에 일을 가지지 못한다.

5 ①

해설 주어가 'understanding of genetics'이다. 유전학의 이해는 본문에서 긍정적으로 해석된다.

---

understanding of genetics → <u>prevent</u> many of the diseases

유전학의 이해로(긍정적 원인) 많은 질병을 예방할 수 있다(긍정적 결과)

해석 유전학의 이해로 인해 우리는 인류의 많은 질병을 예방할 수 있게 될 것이다.

6 ③

해설 If S'V', S V. 문장은 내용에 따라 5형식 물주구문으로 바꿀 수 있다.

If you carry this _____ attitude to the meeting, you will _____ any supporters you.

→ This _____ attitude will make you will _____ any supporters you

---

바꾼 문장을 살펴보면, 5형식의 make가 들어간 문장이다. 원인과 결과의 문장으로 파악할 수 있으므로 다음과 같이 파악할 수 있다.

This <u>defiant</u> attitude will make you will <u>alienate</u> any supporters you.

이런 무례한 태도(부정적 원인) ──────→ 지자를 소원하게 함(부정적 결과)

'A=B'라는 같은 개념의 단어를 고르면 된다.

[해석] 당신이 회의에서 이런 무례한 태도를 가지고 임한다면, 당신은 이 순간 얻고 있는 지지자들을 소원하게 만들 것이다.

7 ①

[해설] 부정적 의미가 들어간 주어인 toxic chemicals가 DNA에 어떤 영향을 미치는 점과 그 결과로 발생하는 부정적 내용이 분사구문인 boosting 이후에 전개되는 내용에 주목한다.

---
toxic chemicals → boosting the risk

부정적 원인 → 부정적 결과

다음 사항을 기억하자.

1) 주어가 부정 - 서술부에 부정의 의미를 형성
2) 부정의 원인은 부정의 결과를 이끌어낸다.

[해석] 이러한 독성의 화학물질이 DNA 가닥에 들어가 암의 위험과 다른 질병의 위험을 증가시킨다.

8 ①

[해설] 괄호 안의 표현에 영향을 미치는 단어는 생략된 주격관계대명사가 이끄는 'treated with contempt'이다.

---
treated with contempt(부정) → outsider(부정)

(사람들이) 경멸스럽게 대하는 → 외부인

'He was an outsider (which was) treated with contempt.'가 원래 문장이다. 보기 항의 구성을 살펴보자.

① outsider - 부정(⊖)
② erudite - 박식한의 의미로 일반적으로 중립적인 성향을 보이나, 문장완성에 주로 부정적으로 쓰이는 경우도 있으므로 참고해 둔다.
③ literate - '읽고, 쓸 수 있는'는 의미로 '문학적 소양이 있는'의 의미도 알아둔다. 일반적으로 긍정(⊕)
④ scholar - '학자'라는 의미로 수식어구 또는 문맥에 따라 긍정과 부정이 나뉠 수 있다.
→ 보기 중에서 부정적 어감을 바로 드러내는 보기는 ①밖에 없다.

[해석] 그는 경멸스럽게 대우를 받는 외부인이다.

9 ①

[해설] 괄호 안의 표현에 영향을 미치는 단어는 생략된 주격관계대명사가 이끄는 내용이다.

---
who utilized all of their dead prey → thrift people

죽은 먹잇감을 모두 이용하는 (긍정) → 검소한 사람들 (긍정)

[해석] 이들은 죽은 먹잇감을 모두 이용하는 검소한 사람들이다.

10 ③

해설 빈칸에 들어갈 단어의 성격을 규정하는 것은 목적어인 'claims'인데, 이것은 다시 관계대명사의 수식을 받고 있다. 고로, 'claims'의 성격을 먼저 규정한 후 빈칸에 들어갈 단어를 고르도록 한다.

that seemed so <u>absurd</u> to him → claims 그에게 말도 안 되어 보이는 → 주장	→	말도 안 되는 주장 (ludicrous claims)

말도 안 되는 주장을 '반박하다'의 보기 항 ③이 가장 적절하다.

해석 조지는 참고 도서관(대출은 할 수 없는 곳)에서 그에게 전혀 말이 안 되어 보이는 그들의 주장을 반박하기 위한 증거 사실을 찾는데 수 시간을 보냈다.

Unit 4 The Gleaners by Jean-François Millet

Part 2 Text Reading

Text 1

1 ⑤

해설 ① The painting "The Gleaners" by Millet primarily focuses on ~~the beauty of the landscape~~.

② Millet was ~~a prominent political figure~~ advocating for the rights of the rural working class.

③ Gleaning was a common practice ~~among all social classes~~ during Millet's time.

④ The Barbizon School mainly produced ~~paintings featuring historical and mythological subjects~~.

Text 2

2 ②

해설 The passage mentions that owning a horse was a major indicator of wealth during the time depicted in the painting. This indicates that horses were not commonly owned by the majority of people and were primarily a symbol of affluence.

3 ③

해설 The passage explains that the low skyline emphasizes the sense of recession and distance between the gleaners and the rest of the community. This suggests their marginalization and isolation from the support of the community, both symbolically and physically.

4 ③

해설 The passage describes how behind the communal workforce, there is a figure on horseback overseeing them. This indicates that the figure on horseback is depicted furthest back in the painting, symbolizing authority and wealth.

Text 3

5 ④

해설 The passage describes how the small number of sheaves gathered by the gleaners contrasts pitifully with the huge stacks gathered by the larger group. This symbolizes the unequal distribution of resources and opportunities, highlighting the plight of the women who are marginalized and have limited access to the bounty of nature compared to the larger group.

6 ②

해설 The passage describes how the flock of birds passing over, with stragglers falling behind, mimics the figures of the women down below. This suggests that like the straggling

21

birds, the women in the painting are struggling to keep up with the opportunities or resources represented by the larger group.

Text 4

7 ②

해설 The passage explains that the focus of the painting on the lives of peasants and the working classes was seen as politically threatening by the middle and upper class audience. This suggests that the painting challenged existing social hierarchies and norms, which made it threatening to those in power.

8 ⑤

해설 The passage mentions that after France's recent revolutions and turbulent history, there was a certain sensitivity among parts of society to subjects that seemed to glorify the peasant classes. This suggests that such depictions were associated with revolutionary sentiments and challenges to the established order, making them sensitive topics for certain segments of society.

Text 5

9 ②

해설 The passage explains that Millet was a religious man who looked to the working classes as examples of the continuation of Old Testament piety and spirituality. This suggests that Millet's artistic motivation was influenced by religious and spiritual themes, rather than being overtly political like Courbet's art.

10 ③

해설 The passage mentions that while the scenes Millet depicts in "The Gleaners" have vanished from France, the ideas he presented about the marginalization of the poverty-stricken remain relevant. This suggests that Millet's themes and ideas in his art continue to resonate with contemporary societal concerns.

11 ③

해설 The passage concludes with the author expressing hope that the modern middle and upper classes would react to a modern Millet in a slightly more positive way than to see it as a call to revolution. This suggests that the author hopes for a compassionate and understanding response to such artwork.

Part 3 Voca Check

1 1 hardships   2 impoverished   3 scour   4 stalk   5 license   6 desperate
7 undertake   8 identifiable   9 or lack thereof   10 be occupied with
11 champion   12 till

2 1 workforce   2 oversee   3 recession   4 hierarchy   5 demonstrate
6 marginalize   7 stack   8 sheave   9 diagonally   10 communal

3 1 homespun 2 stiffness 3 disunity 4 bounty 5 pathos 6 arduous
   7 connote 8 recommence 9 straggle 10 pass over 11 pathos
   12 a flock of 13 bring on 14 thankless 15 jar against

4 1 motif 2 turbulent 3 unveil 4 piety 5 empathize, abject 또는 poverty-stricken
   6 poverty-stricken 7 tranquility, spirituality 8 vanishing 9 innocuous
   10 unveiled 11 upsetting 12 plight 13 turbulent 14 abject

Part 4 Reading Comprehension

1 ④
   해설 ㉣ unfeasible → feasible or viable

2 ②

3 ①, ②
   해설 ① Millet, through the way he has depicted the scene has represented the class structure of a ~~urban~~ (→ rural) community.

   ② Each woman is shown at various stages of their task. The woman furthest away has just straightened up, the middle woman is picking up the grain and the nearest woman is bending down to pick up the grain.
   → 여성에 대한 묘사의 순서가 처음과 마지막이 바뀌어야 함.

   ③의 근거: One needed a licence to be allowed to do this, and only the poorest, most desperate would undertake to obtain one.

   ④의 근거: The standing woman's pose is almost torturous; she seems to have taken a pause, connoting the aching back brought on by this repetitive physical labour, but we do not see her at the point of relief, but as she returns to her work, recommencing the arduous, virtually thankless task.

   ⑤의 근거: The small sheaves that the women have gathered are contrasted diagonally with the huge stacks that the group have gathered.

4 ⑤
   해설 protruding(불쑥 튀어나온) → deleted

5 ②, ③
   해설 ② [B]를 통해서 The Gleaners를 그리는데 영감을 준 작가를 파악할 순 없다.
   ③ [C] urban이 아니라 rural이다.

   [A] 작품에서 묘사되는 주된 대상(세 여인), 행위와 사회적 위상에 대한 개괄적 설명
   [B] Barbizon School에 속한 작품의 일반적 특징, Millet의 The Gleaners의 차별적 특징
   [C] 작품 속에 드러나는 "시골 사회에 존재하는 위계질서"
   [D] 시골의 가난한 사람들의 사회적 소외를 대조적 상징물과 평행구조를 통해서 구현
   [E] 세 여성의 행위에 대한 상술. 새떼와 빛을 활용하여 pathos를 이끌어내는 방법 설명

6 ③, ⑤

해설 ③ 밀레는 자연물에 대한 사실주의적 묘사에 인간을 중심으로 그려냈다.

⑤ 영주의 거리감은 감독관을 흐리게 그리면서 더 "강화된다(strengthened)"와 같은 표현이
되어야 한다.

7 ④

해설 근거: After this turbulent recent history one can understand a certain sensitivity amongst
parts of society to subjects which seemed to glorify the peasant classes.

8 ③

해설 Meanwhile, the uppermost line of ground is occupied by peasant farmers watched
over by the foreman, ~~some of whom break the horizon, too~~.

→ none of whom break the horizon, either

9 ⑤

해설 ⓔ telling → blurry

10 ③

11 ④

해설 This expression is used not to denote imagination or high position but to illustrate the
physical limits of social mobility. It emphasizes the societal distance or gap between the
upper and lower classes rather than representing the sky as a realm of imagination or
lofty status. Therefore, the purpose of this expression is to demonstrate the constraints of
social mobility.

Part 5 Sentence Completion

1 ②

해설 'all appalled at their attempt' 부분의 내용은 '그들의 시도에 경악을 멈추지 못한'이란 그만
큼 '끔찍한 시도'라는 의미다. 정리하면 다음과 같다.

> 끔찍한(형용사) + 시도(명사) to _____**V**_____ the reputation of the chancellor

빈칸은 부정적인 단어가 와야 앞의 형용사의 성격을 적절하게 드러낸다. 또한 가정법에 담긴 역
접의 내용을 대조하는 세미콜론을 활용할 수 있다.

> their attempt to putrefy the reputation ↔ a simple, civil protest

해석 우리 모두는 수상의 명성을 더럽히려는 그들의 시도에 섬뜩했다. 정직하고 시민적인 항의가 훨씬 더 효
과적이었을 텐데.

2 ④

해설 우선 빈칸에 영향을 미치는 요소는 크게 두 가지이다.

1) take _____ : 동사 take와 자연스럽게 연결되는 목적어여야 한다. 'take measures to V'는

'~하려는 수단을 취하다'라는 뜻이다.

2) _____ + to V: to부정사의 수식을 받으므로 그 내용이 후치수식의 to부정사에 의해서 한정된다. 그러므로 다음과 같이 볼 수 있다.

> decisive measures to curb employee theft

'취하다'의 'take'와 '억제하려는' 내용과 가장 궁합이 잘 맞는 명사는 'measures'이다.

해석 그 사장은 직원들 사이의 도둑질을 없애기 위해 단호한 조치를 취했다.

3 ②

해설 빈칸에 영향을 미치는 요소는 형용사 역할의 to부정사이다.

> to provide additional information after the end of the story → epilogue
> 이야기가 끝난 후 추가적인 정보를 제공하는 (책의 부분) → 끝말

해석 작가는 에필로그를 통해 등장인물들에게 어떤 일이 일어났는지에 대한 추가적인 정보를 제공한다.

4 ④

해설 형용사 + N to V 이용

> His __(A)__ attempts to __(B)__ the reporter's questions about his inability

A와 B는 항상 같은 맥락에서 관계를 맺는다. '자신의 무능력에 대한 기자들의 질문에 _____ 하려는 그의 _____ 시도'라는 맥락에서 가장 적절한 단어를 선정하는 문제이다.

해석 도시의 예산을 맞추지 못한 그의 무능력에 대한 리포터들의 질문 공세를 회피하려는 그의 에두르는 시도는 그가 재정문제에 대한 관심을 지역 서커스의 관심으로 돌리는 것에 성공함으로 효과적이었다.

5 ②

해설 빈칸이 포함된 주어는 서술부의 내용에서 알 수 있듯이, 한 나라 사람 사고방식에도 영향을 미칠 만큼 깊숙이 스며든다는 내용과 같은 맥락의 내용이어야 한다. 고로, 북한 사람들이 외국어와 여행 사업을 연구하는 열정은 아주 크다고 볼 수 있다. 'N1 of N2 to V'를 활용한다.

> The ____ of North Koreans to study foreign languages and the tourism business

해석 북한 사람들의 외국어와 여행 사업을 연구하는 열정은, 얼마나 자본주의가 그들 사고 방식에 스며들었는지를 보여주는 지표이다.

6 ①

해설 to부정사 내 동사의 병치로 and의 용례를 활용한다. A and B는 A=B라는 점을 생각하면 접근이 쉬워진다. 악센트에 기반을 둔 차별의 기능에 관해 설명하는 부분이다.

```
accent functions to support and perpetuate unequal social structures
              A      =      B
        불평등한 사회구조를 지탱하고 영속하는 기능
```

해석 그녀의 책에서 Lisa Davis는 차별이 불평등한 사회구조를 지탱하고 영속하는 강조 기능을 하는 방식을 폭로하였다.

7 ①

해설 주어가 철학자이다. 일반적으로 철학의 어원이 love of wisdom이란 말을 알 경우 첫 번째 빈칸에 들어갈 말은 'love'와 관련된 단어임을 쉽게 파악할 수 있다. 두 번째 빈칸에 영향을 미치는 요소는 to부정사이다.

```
longing to fathom the mysteries of existence
```

외부의 신비로운 세계를 통찰하려는 "갈망/근본적 성향"이란 것을 알 수 있다. 보기 항 ①과 ③을 이끌어 낼 수 있는데, 첫 번째 빈칸의 내용에 비추어 보았을 때 보기 항 ①이 가장 적절하다.

해석 철학자들은 지혜에 대한 사랑은 인간의 천부적으로 부여받은 것이라고 생각한다. 잠재적으로 모든 인간은 존재의 신비를 간파하고자 하는 강렬한 갈망을 지니고 있다.

8 ①

해설 빈칸에 들어갈 단어는 목적에 해당하는 to부정사의 내용이다.

```
목적 : to make them more _____ of living in the city
수단 : conferred citizenship on all who practiced medicine at Rome
```

시저가 의술을 행한 모든 사람에게 시민권을 준 목적은 바로 이 도시에서 사는 것을 더 열망하게 만들게 하기 위해서라는 것을 알 수 있다.

해석 Julius Caesar는 로마에서 사는 것을 더 열망하게 만들게 하기 위해 의술을 행하는 모든 사람에게 시민권을 부여했다.

9 ②

해설 opportunity를 수식하는 형용사 용법의 to부정사구 내에 빈칸이 있다. 우선, 기회라는 단어는 긍정적 뉘앙스를 표현하기 때문에 빈칸에 들어가는 내용도 긍정적이어야 한다. 이런 의미에서 부정적인 뉘앙스를 풍기는 보기 항 ①과 ④는 제거하고 시작한다.

```
an opportunity to recapture public esteem

     대중의 존중을 다시 얻어내기 위한 (좋은) 기회
```

수식어구(A)와 피수식어구(B)의 관계는 항상 A=B이다. 즉, 수식어구가 긍정이면, 피수식어구도

일반적으로 긍정이라는 원칙을 가지고 문제풀이에 들어간다. 보기 항의 구성을 살펴보면,

① undermine 부정　　② recapture 긍정　　③ incarcerate 부정　　④ subvert 부정

보기 항에서 하나만이 긍정인 경우 그 단어가 답이 될 가능성이 높으므로, 먼저 빈칸에 대입하고 문제에 접근한다. 또한 ①과 ④는 거의 같은 개념의 단어이므로 보기 항에 들어갈 수 없다는 것을 알 수 있다.

[해석] 이번 변화는 수상이 국민의 존중을 다시 얻어내는데 좋은 기회를 제공한다.

10 ③

[해설] 부정적인 뉘앙스를 풍기는 deliberately와 빈칸을 수식하는 to부정사를 활용해 두 번째 빈칸을 먼저 채우고, 동격의 that 및 전치사 + N를 활용한다.

1) deliberately와 to부정사 활용

deliberately _____ experimental results to further their own careers

deliberately는 부정적 어감을 전달한다. 빈칸의 단어는 특정 과학자들이 이기적 욕심에 연구결과를 조작했다는 것을 이끌어 낼 수 있다.

2) 우선 recent evidence의 성격을 파악하자. 바로 뒤 따라오는 동격의 that절의 내용이 부정이므로 recent evidence도 부정이다.

Scientists' pristine reputation _____ by recent evidence

사심 없던 원래의 명성이 최근의 부정적인 증거로 '더럽혀지다'와 같은 표현이 들어가면 된다.

[해석] 사심 없는 진리 추구자로서 더럽혀지지 않은 과학자들의 명성은 몇몇 과학자들이 자신들의 경력을 향상시킬 목적으로 실험 결과를 의도적으로 조작했다는 증거에 의해 위태로워지고 있다.

Energy Requirement and Shape

Part 2 Text Reading

1 ⑤

해설 Statement II contradicts the passage, which states that populations adapted to extreme cold tend towards <u>higher</u> body mass index scores and shorter limbs, resulting in a more robust or "stubbier" body shape.

Statement III misinterprets the passage. The passage discusses how camels use their humps for heat dissipation while also storing fat for energy, but <u>it doesn't mention maximizing energy storage solely through heat dissipation</u>.

2 ④

해설 ⑧ who have adapted to live → who have adapted to living
adapt to에서 to는 전치사이다.

⑩ which → where
선행사인 region과 완전절을 가지는 점으로 보아 장소 관계부사 where이 옳다.

⑥ what we might term it̶ as → what we might term as
목적어를 포함한 관계대명사 what이다.

Part 3 Voca Check

1 1 human beings have been physically shaped by their energy requirements
2 Being warm-blooded creatures / which we achieve by controlling the ratio of our body's surface area to its volume
3 tend to have what we might describe as more "slender" bodies
4 exhibit a relatively slender body shape
5 as an evolutionary compromise between the need to dissipate heat and the need to store fat

2 1 warm-blooded   2 constant   3 internal   4 given   5 retention   6 adapt to
7 dissipation   8 limb   9 profile   10 linear   11 conceive   12 hump
13 protrude   14 coarse

1 ⑤

해설 Warm-blooded animals like humans have evolved ~~an "immune" system that is unaffected by the external environment~~.

본문에서 온혈동물이 외부 환경에 영향을 받지 않는 것이 아니라 오히려 외부 환경에 맞게 적응하고 진화해 왔다고 언급되어 있다.

2 ④

해설 This term fits the context provided in the passage, which contrasts the body types of populations adapted to living in extreme cold (like the Inuits) with those in desert regions. The passage describes how populations in colder areas tend towards higher body mass index scores and shorter limbs, resulting in a more robust or "stubbier" body shape, whereas populations in desert regions have more "linear" bodies, meaning they are relatively tall and thin.

3 ①

해설 III. Human populations in ~~warmer~~(→ cold or colder) regions have developed physical characteristics such as higher body mass index (BMI) and shorter limbs to adapt to their environment.

IV. Camels are relatively linear with ~~a large volume to surface area~~.

→ a large surface to volume ratio

4 ②

해설 낙타는 열의 방출을 높이는 표면적이 넓은 신체구조를 위해 두 개의 혹에 지방을 저장함으로 상대적으로 갸름한(linear) 신체구조를 가진다는 내용이다.

5 ④

해설 The passage discusses how different species, including humans, adapt their body shapes to maintain internal temperature regulation in varying climates. It emphasizes how body shape, particularly the surface-to-volume ratio, is influenced by the need to conserve or dissipate heat, which is crucial for survival in different environments.

1 ③

해설 첫 번째 빈칸의 내용을 먼저 파악한다.

1) to부정사의 내용에 수식을 받는다.

> _____ to expect Barnard to have <u>worked out all of the limitations</u>

자신의 한계를 모두 해결할 것이라고 기대하는 것은 불가능하거나 비현실적이라는 것을 유추할 수 있다.

2) 두 번째 빈칸은 전치사구의 수식을 받는다.

> must be <u>criticized</u> for <u>his neglect of quantitative analysis</u>

자신의 실수에 비난을 받아야 한다는 것을 알 수 있다.

3) 기본적으로 대조를 이끄는 양보는 though를 활용할 수도 있다.

<u>unrealistic</u> to expect Barnard to have worked out all of the limitations
though ↕
he must be <u>criticized</u> for his neglect of quantitative analysis.

해석 Barnard가 그의 실험의 모든 한계를 해결하리라는 기대가 비현실적이기는 하지만 그가 계량 분석에서 태만한 점은 비난받아야 한다.

2 ⑤

해설 to부정사와 양보의 although를 활용한다.

1) 첫 번째 빈칸은 to부정사의 수식을 받고 있다.

> be <u>impolitic</u> to display annoyance publicly at the sales conference

즉, 대중 앞에서 짜증을 내는 것은 무례하다는 것을 알 수 있다.

2) 대조를 이끄는 양보의 although를 활용한다.

<u>impolitic</u> to display annoyance publicly at the sales conference
although ↕
could not <u>hide</u> his irritation

해석 비록 탐은 판매 회의에서 공개적으로 짜증을 내는 것이 무례하다는 것을 알고 있었지만, 그 고객의 말도 안 되는 요구에 자신의 노여움을 감출 수가 없었다.

3 ⑤

해설 to부정사의 형용사 용법의 활용을 살펴보자.

> N + <u>to V</u>

수식어구의 내용이 피수식어구의 내용을 한정한다. 즉, 첫 번째 빈칸은 두 번째 빈칸에 들어간 to 부정사의 내용과 가장 어울리는 표현이 되어야 한다. 또한, 수식어구의 내용이 긍정이면 피수식어구도 긍정이고, 수식어구의 내용이 부정이면 피수식어구의 내용도 부정이 된다는 의미이다. 고로, N(A), V(B)라고 할 때, A = B이다. A가 긍정이면 B도 긍정, A가 부정이면 B도 부정이다.

예) a <u>good</u> deed <u>to help people with trouble</u> 곤경에 처한 사람을 돕는 선행
good = to help people with trouble
an <u>infamous</u> official <u>to bleed the people</u> 백성의 고혈을 착취하는 악한 관료
infamous = to bleed the people

본문의 내용에 적용해보자. 주어는 현 세입정책에 반대하는 후보다.

_____ ways to _____ the financing of state operations
국가 운영에 필요한 자금을 _____ 할 수 있는 _____ 대안

빈칸의 내용은 현재의 방법과는 다른 방법이므로 보기 항 ③과 ⑤가 가장 적절하며, 국가 운영에 필요한 자금을 continue한다는 표현이 보기 항 ③의 alleviate보다 더 적절하다. 고로 보기 항 ⑤ 가 답이다.

해석 현 국가 세입에 반대하는 후보는 국가 운영에 필요한 자금을 지속할 수 있는 대안을 제기할 수 있어야 한다.

4 ⑤

해설 첫 번째 빈칸이 to부정사의 수식을 받는 것을 알면, 쉽게 답에 접근할 수 있다. 우선 the sacrifice를 규정해 보자.

the <u>sacrifice</u> required in order to gain such little advantage

아주 적은 득을 위해 필요한 희생 – 즉, 그리 득이 되는 희생이 아니란 점에서 가치가 있는 희생이 아니다.

1) to부정사를 이용해 첫 번째 빈칸을 채워보자.

it would be _____ to make the sacrifice

앞에서 언급한 희생을 한다는 것은 좋지 않다고 느낄 것이다. 보기 항 ①, ②와 같은 긍정적인 뉘 앙스와 전혀 관련이 없는 보기 항 ④는 제거한다. 부정적인 뉘앙스는 보기 항 ③과 ⑤이다. 또한 두 번째 빈칸의 경우, 보기 항 ③의 encouragement는 본문의 문맥과 전혀 어울리지 않는 것을 알 수 있다.

해석 그는 따라오게 될 엄청난 혼란에 비추어 이렇게 적은 이득을 얻기 위해 요구되는 희생을 감수하는 것은 비현실적이라고 느꼈다.

5 ②

해설 대조를 이끄는 양보의 부사절과 to부정사의 부사적 용법을 활용한다.

1) to부정사의 활용을 먼저 살펴보자.

> downplayed it(the fire) to _____ his apprehensive friend

화재가 발생해 근심 가득한 친구에게 위로하기 위해 어떻게 말했을지 생각하면서 빈칸에 들어갈 단어를 생각해 본다.

2) 양보의 although를 활용할 수도 있다.

the fire also shocked him	although ↔	downplayed it to mollify his apprehensive friend.

해석 비록 불은 또한 그를 놀라게 했지만, 마이클은 그의 걱정되는 친구를 달래기 위해 그것을 대단치 않게 생각했다.

쉬어가기 **문장완성에서 자주 활용되는 전치사 'for' 정리**

전치사 'for'는 그 용례를 다루기가 벅찰 정도로 많은 뜻을 가지고 있다. 하지만 이 모든 뜻을 다 다뤄야 함은 사족일 만큼 당연한 이야기다. 그 중에서 아래 두 가지 용법은 문장완성에서 자주 활용되는 용례이므로 반드시 암기해 두도록 한다.

1) 이유 · 원인의 인과관계를 이끄는데, 'A = B'의 공식을 적용한다.

Ex 1 It is a city famed for its beauty. 아름답기로 유명한 도시이다.
     A   =   B
→ 아름답기 때문에 유명하게 된 도시라는 의미이다.

Ex 2 He was hospitalized for chest pains. 그는 가슴 통증으로 입원했다.
          A   =   B
→ 가슴 통증이 원인이 되어 입원을 하게 되었다는 말이다. 부정적 원인은 부정적 결과를 이끈다.

Ex 3 He was well liked among his friends for his good looks and good nature.
          A   =   B
그는 용모도 잘 생기고 성격도 좋았으므로 친구들이 아주 좋아했다
→ 인과의 관계를 잘 드러내고 있다.

2) (보통 all과 함께) 양보의 의미를 가진다. 'A ↔ B'의 공식을 적용한다.

Ex 1 For all that smoke pollution, Cleveland has its charms.
          A   ↔   B
저렇게 연기 공해가 심한 클리블랜드이지만, 그 나름의 매력이 있다.
→ 대조의 관계가 잘 드러난다. 'for all'의 해석에 주의한다.

Ex 2 For all the sweat and blood, the situation appeared unchanged.
          A   ↔   B
그렇게 피땀을 흘렸는데도 사정은 나아진 것이 없는 것 같았다.
→ 대조의 관계를 잘 드러내고 있다.

6 ⑤

[해설] 'N of N' ← 'N 전치사 N(V-ing)'의 형태로 수식을 받는 앞의 명사가 빈칸일 경우 뒤의 형용사 용법의 전치사구에 의미가 한정된다. 이는 'A of B'라고 할 때, 'A와 B'는 같은 속성의 단어를 연결하라는 의미로 단순화시킬 수 있다. 또한 본문에서 부연설명의 분사구문이 따라오기에 앞의 빈칸에 대한 힌트가 따라오고 있다. 다시 본문으로 와서 'N1 of N2'를 적용하여 선택지를 고르면, ②와 ⑤를 고를 수 있는데 분사구문 이후의 내용으로 보아 '방랑'의 의미를 전달하는 선택지 ⑤가 정답이다.

[해석] 나는 시골을 떠돌아다니고 구걸을 하는 방랑자의 방황적인 삶에 그리 매력을 못 느낀다.

7 ①

[해설] '_____형용사_____ N + 전치사 + V-ing(N)'을 활용한다.

Obscure longings and search for the elusive grounds of all things

---

첫 번째 빈칸이 채워지면 두 번째 빈칸의 문맥에 맞게 쉽게 고를 수 있다. 빈칸 앞뒤를 확인하고 수식관계의 적절한 공식만 적용하면 된다.

[해석] 모호한 그리움과 모든 것의 찾기 힘든 근거에 대한 추구는 19세기와 20세기 독일문학의 널리 퍼져 있는 주제이다.

8 ③

[해설] 첫 번째 빈칸은 '전치사 + 명사(V-ing)'를 활용하고, 두 번째 빈칸은 인과의 'As'를 활용한다.

1) 첫 번째 빈칸
   수식받는 빈칸의 의미는 수식하는 표현에 한정한다.

---

bitter (부정) towards his adversaries

첫 번째 빈칸은 수식하는 내용의 의미로 보아 부정의 어감을 전달하는 단어를 넣어야 한다.

2) 두 번째 빈칸
   앞의 내용을 원인으로 하여 'he'가 취할 수 있는 가장 적절한 행동을 고르면 된다.

---

resentment towards his adversaries → plotted to have their campaign funds stolen

원인(부정) → 결과(부정)

[해석] 적에 대한 그의 비통한 분노로 인해, 그는 이들이 선거공략을 계속하지 못하도록 하기 위해 선거 자금을 빼돌릴 음모를 세웠다.

9 ②

[해설] '_____N_____ 전치사 + N'을 활용한다. 형용사 역할을 하는 전치사구 및 이를 다시 수식해 주는 관계대명사의 내용이 빈칸의 의미를 한정한다.

> new substances that may help → discovery and development

위 내용으로 보아 선택지 ②가 문맥에 가장 적절한 답이다.

[해석] 제약 회사의 과학자들은 현재 류머티스성 관절염을 앓고 있는 환자의 고통을 덜어주는데 도움을 주는 새로운 물질의 발견과 개발에 힘쓰고 있다.

10 ①

[해설] 빈칸에 영향을 미치는 요소는 바로 뒤에 이어지는 전치사구이다. 즉, 'N by V-ing'의 형태로 수식하는 내용이 수식받는 내용의 의미를 한정한다.

> by putting both classical and modern works in the repertoire → versatility
> 고전과 현대 작품을 함께 작품에 소화함 → 다재다능한 뛰어난 능력

[해석] 그 발레단은 고전적 작품과 현대작품 모두를 공연목록에 넣음으로 다재다능함을 보여주었다.

Unit 6 Blood, Sweat, and Tears by Winston Churchill

Part 2 Text Reading

Text 1

1 ②

해설 In the first paragraph, Churchill emphasizes that the new Administration he is forming should be on the broadest possible basis and should include all parties, both those who supported the late Government and the parties of the Opposition. This reflects the main idea of the paragraph, which is the desire to create an inclusive government that encompasses different political parties.

2 ④

해설 The passage mentions that the three Party Leaders have agreed to serve, either in the War Cabinet or in high executive office as part of the new Administration.

Text 2

3 ⑤

해설 "In this crisis, I hope I may be pardoned if I do not address the House at any length today."

→ In this sentence, the speaker ~~is appealing to the emotions (pathos)~~ based on the crisis, explaining why the speaker won't address the House at length.

The speaker is appealing to a logical decision based on the crisis, explaining why the speaker won't address the House at length.

Text 3

4 ⑤

해설 By repeating key phrases and sentence structures, Churchill underscores the urgency and determination of the message. This parallelism serves to drive home the importance of the message and inspire a sense of unity and resolve in the audience.

5 ③

해설 In the final paragraph, Churchill employs an emotional appeal (pathos) to inspire and rally the audience. He emphasizes the importance of victory at all costs, invokes the survival of the British Empire, and speaks of moving forward toward a common goal. These emotional appeals aim to create a sense of unity and determination among the audience.

6 ⑤

해설 The context is about the determination to wage war and achieve victory, so the term "buoyancy" here signifies the speaker's positive and hopeful outlook.

1. 1 meet 2 invade 3 manufacture 4 overrun 5 newly elected 6 evident 7 oppose 8 commission 9 declare war on 10 will

2. 1 confer 2 urgency 3 represent 4 rigor 5 summons 6 submit 7 notify 8 proceeding 9 adjournment 10 summon

3. 1 undertaking 2 ordeal 3 pardon 4 approval 5 struggle 6 ceremony 7 preliminary 8 ceremony 9 grievous 10 stand

4. 1 wage 2 might 3 monstrous 4 suffer 5 cause 6 buoyancy 7 terror 8 lamentable 9 stands for 10 bravery

Part 4 Reading Comprehension

1 ②, ④

해설 ② 문단 [가]를 통해서 새 정부의 "가장 중요한, 시급한 일" 즉 연합정부가 완성이 되었다고 했지, 모든 자리가 채워졌다는 말은 본문과는 일치하지 않는다.

④ 새 정부를 위한 남은 장관 선정에 어려움 있을 거라는 내용은 없다.

2 ③, ⑤

해설 ②의 내용과 같이 Churchill이 구성하고자 하는 정부는 초당파적이다.

⑤ A War Cabinet has been formed of five Members, representing, with the Opposition Liberals, the unity of the nation.에서 볼 수 있듯이 the Liberals를 야당이라고 부르고 있다.

어휘 His Majesty = the monarch, non-partisan 초당파적

3 ①

해설 일을 처리하는 것이 "완성, 완결, 달성되다"의 수동태가 되어야 하므로 be completed가 적절하고, 그렇게 일이 다 완성되면 정부가 모든 측면에서 "온전"하게 된다는 의미이므로 be complete가 적절하다.

4 ④

해설 I considered it in the public interest to suggest that the House should be summoned to meet today. Mr. Speaker agreed, and took the necessary steps, in accordance with the powers conferred upon him by the Resolution of the House.

의장의 권한에 따른 동의와 절차를 따랐다. 신속하게 처리했다는 의미이지 절차를 없애자는 내용은 없다.

5 ①

해설 처칠이 형식적 절차를 일반적으로 중요시 여기는 사람이 아니라는 뜻이 아니라 의회 연설을 간소하게 하는 것에 대한 양해를 구하는 표현이므로 오히려 그 반대의 경우라고 보아야 한다.

6 ④

해설 (A) 문단: "전쟁 내각 구성"에 대한 요지가 명확히 드러난다.

(b) A War Cabinet has been formed of five Members, representing, with the Opposition Liberals, the ~~separation~~ of the nation.
→ unity

7 ⑤

8 ③

해설 ㉠의 의미: The phrase "extreme urgency" suggests that there was a pressing need to create the new government, while "rigor of events" indicates that the process was challenging, possibly due to the gravity of the situation or the complexity of the task. Overall, the sentence conveys the idea that forming the new administration was a difficult and urgent undertaking.

9 ③

해설 In this context, Churchill is using strong emotional language and vivid imagery to evoke an emotional response from the audience.

Part 5 Sentence Completion

1 ①

해설 거대한 양의 석유와 그로 인한 금전으로 넘쳐 나는 나라를 소개하고 있다.

> a _____ country with enormous reserves of oil and cash

빈칸을 수식하는 전치사구의 내용과 이어지는 분사구의 내용으로 보아 선택지 ①이 빈칸에 적절하다.

해석 쿠웨이트는 석유와 돈의 어마어마한 보유고를 가진 풍족한 나라로 페르시아만 최고의 항구임을 자랑한다.

2 ④

해설 수식어 전치사구의 활용과 함께 문맥에 가장 적절한 어구를 선택하는 문제로 약간 까다롭다.

> an effective ___N___ in determining whether an individual is capable of working

빈칸의 위치는 명사로 뒤의 '전치사 + V-ing'의 수식을 받기에 그 의미도 한정된다. 그러므로 '특정 개인이 일할 능력을 결정하는데 효과적인 기준'이므로 두 번째 빈칸은 'criterion'이 가장 적절하다. 영향을 미치는 요소가 아닌 것에 주의한다. 첫 번째 빈칸 앞의 내용을 보면 '퇴임을 당하는 사람'이 언급되므로 선택지 ③의 'intellectual'이라기 보단 신체적 나이를 드러내는 'physical' 또는 'chronological'이 된다. 선택지 ④가 답이다.

해석 계속해서 일할 수 있고 일할 의지가 있는 사람들을 은퇴시키는 고용주는 신체적(연대기적) 나이는 개인이 일을 할 수 있는지 없는지를 결정할 효율적인 기준이 아님을 깨달아야만 한다.

3 ③

해설 두 번째 문장은 첫 번째 문장에 이은 부연진술이다. 첫 번째 문장에서 근거를 찾아 빈칸의 단어를 추론한다. 부연진술과 형용사구의 '전치사 + N(V-ing)'이 앞의 명사를 꾸며주고 있으므로 그 의미를 한정한다.

1) 첫 번째 문장에서 심해는 'a place for nervous transient visits'에서 알 수 있듯이 아직 인간이 정복하지 못한 미지(a unknown place)의 공간임을 알 수 있다.

2) 수식어구인 전치사구가 앞의 명사의 성격을 규정한다.

> 'N 전치사 + N'

고로,

> discrepancy between one-third of the Earth's surface and two-thirds below it
> 인간이 이미 알고 있는 지식　　　　　아직 모르는 지식

두 지식 사이에는 불일치, 즉 'discrepancy'가 존재하는 것을 유추할 수 있다.

해석 해저는 불안하고, 일시적인 방문을 위한 장소를 남겨두었다. 그것은 해수면 위 지구표면의 3분의 1에 대한 인류의 지식과, 그 밑에 있는 3분의 2사이의 인류의 지식 사이에 놀라운 차이점을 이끈다.

참고 'N between A and B'에서 A와 B는 서로 역접의 관계를 갖는 경우가 많으니 기억해 둔다.

'N between A and B'라는 표현은 'A ↔ B'인 경우를 기억해야 한다.

4 ④

해설 빈칸을 수식하는 요소를 찾으면 쉽게 답이 나온다.

> standing ovation with her moving speech

긍정의 수식어구는 피수식어구의 내용이 긍정이 되도록 영향을 미친다. 고로, 보기 항 중 부정적 의미를 전달하는 단어를 제거하면 ④ 밖에 남지 않는다.

해석 올해 LPGA의 신인상을 수상한 한국 골프선수 신 지애는 영어로 발표한 감동적인 수상소감으로 기립 박수를 받았다.

5 ⑤

해설 빈칸은 before가 이끄는 전치사구의 수식을 받는다. 수식어구의 내용이 피수식어구의 내용을 한정한다.

> preliterate times before the invention of reading and writing

우리의 이야기는 읽기와 쓰기의 발명 이전에 우리의 조상들이 자신들의 문화를 입을 통해서 한 세대에서 다음 세대로 전달했던 문자 이전의 시대에서 시작된다.

6 ①

해설

1. 수식어구와 피수식어구의 관계를 이용한 접근

첫 번째 빈칸의 경우 명사의 표현을 넣는 문제인데, 전치후치 수식을 모두 받고 있다.

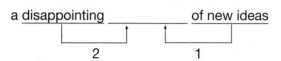

새로운 아이디어가 어떠했기에 실망스러웠는지를 생각하면 쉽게 빈칸에 들어갈 단어가 부정적 어감을 전달하는 표현임을 알 수 있다.

보기 항 ①과 ③ 둘 중 하나가 답일 가능성이 높다.

2. 순접 병렬을 이용한 접근

> a disappointing _____ of new ideas and controversial refereeing decisions
> 부정적 어감의 표현   =   부정적 어감의 표현

두 번째 빈칸의 경우 주절에 영향을 미치는 부사구의 내용에 빈칸이 들어가 있다. 주절의 내용을 먼저 파악한 후 문맥에 가장 적절한 표현을 고르면 된다.

해석 지난 번 월드컵 경기에서는 실망스럽게도 데드볼 상황과 수많은 애매한 심판 판정들에 대한 새로운 아이디어가 선보이지 않았다. 흥미로운 축구가 그토록 높은 위상을 가지는 경기에서 결승전이 팽팽하게 긴장되고 흥분되는 사건이 되어야 하는 것이 적절한 것처럼 느껴졌다.

참고

in fact는 양면성을 지닌 야누스(Janus)이다. 중요하니 두 가지 기능을 반드시 숙지한다.

in fact는 일반적으로 두 가지 기능을 가진다.

① **앞에서 진술된 내용을 더 구체적으로 기술**하는 부연기능이 있다. 'A in fact B'는 'A = 또는≦ B'이다.

    예) I used to live in Korea; **in fact**, not far from where you're going.
        전 예전에 한국에 살았어요. 사실은 당신이 가려고 하는 곳에서 멀지 않은 곳입니다.
    예) It was cold. **In fact**, it was freezing.
        날씨가 추웠어. 사실 얼굴이 얼 정도로 추웠어.
    예) Zadie Smith's first novel, White Teeth, was a tremendous success; **in fact**, it won three widely acclaimed literary awards.
        제이디 스미스의 첫 소설 《하얀 이빨》은 대단한 성공작이었으며, 실제로 이 작품은 널리 인정받는 세 개의 문학상을 받은 바 있다.
    예) He takes dope; **in fact** he's high on dope now.
        그는 마약을 복용한다. 사실 지금도 마약에 취해 있다.

② <u>앞에서 진술된 내용과 반대의 내용을 기술</u>하는 부연강조의 기능이 있다. 'A in fact B'는 'A ↔ B' 이다.

예) I thought the work would be difficult. **In actual fact**, it's very easy.
나는 그 일이 힘들 거라고 생각했어. 실제로는 아주 쉬워.

예) This $10 note looks genuine but it is, **in fact**, a fake.
이 10달러 지폐는 진짜처럼 보이지만, 사실 가짜다.

예) I thought the talk would be boring but **in fact** it was very interesting.
나는 회담이 지루할 것이라고 생각했지만, 사실 아주 흥미로웠다.

예) People speak of him as if he was something special. **In fact**, he was an ordinary person.
사람들은 마치 그가 특별한 사람인냥 말한다. 사실 그는 평범한 사람이었다.

---

7 ④

해설 주어가 종교적 순수성을 강조하는 'the puritans'이다. 극장을 폐쇄할 정도로 어떤 내용의 연극이 행해졌을지 생각한다. 전체적으로 분사구문인 종속절이 원인이 되어, 주절의 결과가 발생하게 된 내용이다. 종속부사절만을 따로 떼어 아래와 같이 파악해 보면,

Disturbed by the salacious nature of the plays

마음이 어지럽혀지다(부정) ← 연극의 외설적 성격으로(부정)

부정적 원인이 부정적 결과를 가져온다는 단순하면서도 자명한 원리를 활용하면 쉽게 접근이 가능하다.

해석 공연된 연극의 외설스런 성격에 마음이 어지러워진 청교도들은 1642년에 이 극장을 닫았다.

8 ③

해설 1) 빈칸이 들어간 표현에서 'gossip columnist'의 성격을 먼저 규정하면,

the gossip columnist who seemed out to ruin his reputation

→ 부정적 대상임

2) 빈칸은 'of' 이하의 전치사구에 직접적으로 수식을 받고 있다.

the _____ criticism of the gossip columnist

부정적 대상의 비판의 성격은 당연히 <u>부정적 단어</u>이다.

주어인 '그 주인공'이 자신의 명성을 파괴하려고 하는 사람들의 어떤 비난에 화가 났을지 생각한다.

해석 그 연기자는 자신의 명성을 해치려고 밖에 있는 것처럼 보이는 가십 칼럼리스트의 독설적인 비평에 화가 났다.

9 ③

해설 빈칸의 주어가 'charge'라는 점과 'for'가 이끄는 전치사구에 수식을 받는 점을 파악한다.

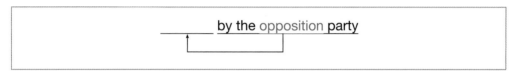

증거의 부족으로 기소가 어떻게 될지 생각해 보면 답이 쉽게 나온다.

해석 비록 그가 유죄라는 것에 이의가 거의 없지만, 그 고소는 증명할 증인의 부재로 인한 증거의 부족으로 무효가 되었다.

10 ①

해설 빈칸이 전치사구에 의해 수식을 받는 점을 파악할 경우 쉽게 접근이 가능한 문제이다.

```
_____ by the opposition party
        ↑_____|
```

즉, 반대당에 의해서 여당이 제기한 의안은 기본적으로 '방해를 받는'이란 부정적인 단어가 들어가야 한다.

해석 그 법안을 통과시키려는 노력은 야당에 의해 좌절되었지만 여당은 현재 교착상태에 빠진 개혁안들을 통과시키기 위해 진력할 태세이다. 여당은 국가보안법 폐지를 전담할 신설기구 설립을 계획하고 있다.

Part 2 Text Reading

1 ③

해설 This situation reflects the proverb "Don't count your chickens before they hatch," which warns <u>against assuming a positive outcome before it has been achieved, as the animal in the passage experiences both joy and suffering on its journey to freedom.</u>

Part 3 Voca Check

1
1 constraints, imposed
2 met, complacent
3 beyond, leaving
4 spectrum

2
1 Irreversibility, irreversible, confines, revert, ignorance
2 challenging, sustenance, unpredictability
3 remaining, previous, transformative

Part 4 Reading Comprehension

1 ④

해설 놀면서 우연히 문을 연 것이 아니라, 자다 깨면서 문이 열려 있다는 것을 발견한다.

2 ③

해설 The individual's needs are met ~~with much effort~~ (→ effortlessly) - food, water, and rest are readily available.

3 ①

해설 케이지 내에서 주인공(수컷동물)은 모든 필요가 충족되는 상황에서 만족하면서 살았다.

4 comfortable / the invisible hand(= the invisible hand's will) / free
5 Freedom has its price.

Part 5 Sentence Completion

1 ③

해설 빈칸은 'with'가 이끄는 전치사구의 수식을 받고 있다.

> besmirch my reputation with her vicious gossip
>
> 그녀의 사악한 말로 나의 명성을 더럽히다

수식어구가 부정적인 의미를 담고 있기에, 피수식어구도 부정적인 단어가 된다.

해석 나의 과거 죽마고우는 그의 악한 입담으로 나의 명성에 오점을 남기려 했다.

2 ②

해설 빈칸의 자리는 동사이다. 동사에 영향을 미치는 요소는 본문에서 주어인 'His musical ability'와 전치사구인 'by his other accomplishments'이다. 그의 음악적 능력이 다른 업적에 의해서 빛을 발하지 못했다는 내용으로 전개되어야 한다.

> obscured by his other accomplishments
>
> 무색하게 되다 ← 그의 다른 업적으로 인해

해석 그의 음악적 재능은 그의 다른 성취에 의해서 무색하게 되었다.

3 ②

해설 다음 두 단계를 거쳐 풀이한다.

1) 첫 번째 빈칸은 역접을 이끄는 'It is surprising, but'을 활용한다.

> unruly people ↔ serene
>
> 즉, 'unruly'와 대조적인 단어가 첫 번째 빈칸이다.

2) When에 걸리는 내용은 'serene'을 적절히 수식하는 부사구가 되어야 한다.

> unruly people become (serene) if they treated with (compassion) by their peers

해석 제멋대로인 사람들도 때로 동료, 친구 그리고 이웃에 의해서 애정으로 다뤄질 때 침착하게 된다.

4 ②

해설 '전치사 + 명사'가 부사구로 동사를 수식하며 내용을 한정한다.

> ___V___ + 전치사 + V-ing(N)
>
> be overwhelmed by (considerable) numbers
>
> 압도당하다 ←──────── 엄청난 수에

해석 군인들은 한동안 저항했지만, 결국 엄청난 수에 압도당했다.

5 ③

해설 주어가 경찰이라는 점과 빈칸에 직접적인 영향을 미치는 요소는 부사구(for further

questioning)이다.

> The police _____ the suspected murderer for further questioning

계속적인 심문을 위해서 경찰이 취하는 태도는 무엇인지 생각한다.

해석 경찰은 더 심문을 하기 위해 살인 용의자를 구금했다.

6 ④

해설 'with'에 걸리는 부정적인 뉘앙스의 전치사구가 'threatened'를 수식하고 있다. 부정의 수식 어가 되어야 부정적인 의미를 전달하는 피수식어가 된다는 점을 활용한다. 보기 ①과 ②는 제거하고 시작한다.

> threatened with extinction

또한 본문은 일반 진술과 구체적 진술로 나눠져 있다.

A great many animals and plants are threatened with extinction (일반 진술)
Dolphins and whales, gorillas and wild elephants (구체적 진술) = endangered animals

해석 수없이 많은 동식물이 멸종의 위협을 받고 있다. 돌고래와 고래, 고릴라 그리고 야생 코끼리는 현재 멸 종 위기의 동물로 구별된다.

7 ④

해설 첫 번째 빈칸은 전치사구 내에 위치하면서 frustrated를 수식하고 있다.

1) 전치사구 활용

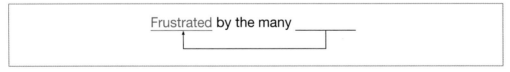

> Frustrated by the many _____

부정적인 단어를 수식하고 있기에 부정적인 단어가 빈칸에 들어간다. 보기 항을 보면 ①은 긍정 적인 단어이기에 빈칸에 들어갈 수 없다.

2) 인과의 분사구문을 활용한다. 주어는 과학자이다.

> Frustrated by many complications → reluctantly terminated his experiment.
> 부정적인 원인 → 부정적인 결과

reluctantly는 '마지못해'로 해석한다. 여러 가지 복잡한 일로 인해 좌절하여 마지못해 자신의 연 구를 그만둔다는 내용으로 전개되고 있다.

해석 많은 혼란 때문에 좌절해서, 그 과학자는 마지못해 실험을 그만두었다.

8 ④

해설 전체 문장에 영향을 주는 부사 역할의 전치사구를 활용한다. 주어는 식당이다.

> By buying <u>directly</u> from fishing boats → keeps its lobster menu <u>affordable</u>
> 긍정의 원인 → 긍정의 결과

고기잡이 어부에게서 직접 고기를 구입한 결과에 해당하는 내용이 답이 된다. 보기 항 구성을 보면,

① shabby   부정
② effortless   긍정(쉽게라는 의미에서)
③ expensive   부정
④ affordable   긍정

보기 항 ①과 ③은 먼저 소거하고 나머지 두 보기 항 중 문맥에 가장 적절한 것을 고른다.

해석 낚시 배에서 직접 구매함으로써 그 레스토랑은 바닷가재 요리를 싼 가격으로 유지한다.

9 ②

해설 빈칸은 to부정사 내에 위치한다.

> One way (to show our _____ to our mentors)
> 우리의 스승에게 _____를 보이는 방법

위 표현을 볼 경우 스승에게 보이는 것이 무엇인지 생각해 보면 쉽게 답에 접근할 수 있다. 보기 항 ②가 가장 적절한 것을 알 수 있다. 보기 항 ①은 유사한 단어일 뿐이며, 보기 항 ④는 정답과 반의어 관계이다.

해석 스승님들께 감사를 표하는 한 가지 방법은 우리가 이루어 낸 성과에 의해서이다.

10 ③

해설 though에 걸리는 내용과 주절에 걸리는 내용이 서로 양보의 대조가 되어야 함을 파악해야 한다. 우선 두 번째 빈칸의 내용을 먼저 파악할 수 있다.

1) 수식어구와 피수식어구의 관계를 활용하여 접근한다. 두 번째 빈칸은 바로 뒤에 이어지는 전치사구의 수식을 받고 있다.

> must be <u>criticized</u> for his neglect of quantitative analysis
>
> 계량분석을 무시한 점은 비판을 받아야 한다는 내용이 온다는 것을 알 수 있다.

2) 양보의 though로 보아 주절의 내용이 부정적으로 전개되기에, though에 걸리는 내용은 이와 대조적 관계를 이루어야 한다.

> be <u>unrealistic</u> to expect Barnard to have <u>worked out all of the limitations</u>

해석 Barnard가 그의 실험의 모든 한계를 해결하리라는 기대가 비현실적이기는 하지만 그가 계량 분석에서 무시한 점은 비난받아야 한다.

The Matrix Is The Real World

Part 2 Text Reading

Text 2

1 ①

해설 III. The film seems to encourage viewers to consider the Matrix as a legitimate reality, conforming to (→ challenging) the traditional binary distinction between reality and illusion.

2 ①

해설 forefront의 사전적 의미: (the ~) 최전부, 최전선; (흥미·여론·활동 따위의) 중심; 가장 중요한 위치[지위]

Text 3

3 ③

해설 II. Plato uses the allegory of the cave to illustrate the concept of enlightened (→ unenlightened) human nature.

4 ③

해설 Ⓐ onto which Ⓑ to adjust → adjusting Ⓒ being deemed Ⓓ where Ⓔ watching
Ⓕ to which → about which

Text 4

5 ③

해설 III. There are different levels of reality, with the shadows representing a higher level of reality compared to the mere objects.

→ There are different levels of reality, with the objects representing a higher level of reality compared to the mere shadows.

Text 5

6 ②

해설 allusion 암시, 변죽울림, 빗댐; 언급 (= reference)
An allusion is a reference to something, often a literary or historical work, person, or event. In this context, the statement made by the punk is an allusion to Cartesian doubts about one's existence, as it echoes the philosophical concept famously expressed by René Descartes: "Cogito, ergo sum" ("I think, therefore I am").

7 ①

해설 Rene Descartes' "Meditations on First Philosophy" chart Descartes' philosophical journey from doubting the existence of the external world to finally arriving at his conclusion that God, the external world, and minds do indeed exist.

8 ②

(해설) Descartes argues that <u>if we can feel as if we are awake during sleep</u>, it is quite possible that we could always be in a sleep state and are merely imagining (가)_____, like those in the Matrix.

밑줄 친 내용에서 알 수 있듯이, 자는 동안 "깨어있다"고 느끼는 것이므로 "의식의 상태"를 상상할 수 있다는 맥락에서 consciousness가 (가)에 적절하다.

(나)의 경우 "this evil genius"이 놓은 덫에 걸려 the illusions and dreams를 믿게 되는 것이므로 그 덫의 용도는 나의 "credulity"를 이끌어내려는 것임을 파악할 수 있다.

Text 7

9 ②

Ⓑ for → against

(해설) 근거: This line not only calls into question how we experience 'reality' and 'existence' but also the value we attach to it. For Cypher, the Matrix and its blissful ignorance are more valuable than the 'real world.'

10 ②

(해설) The correct inference from the passage is that Cypher, a character in the Matrix, values the illusion of the Matrix over the reality of the 'real world.' He expresses this preference for ignorance and the bliss of the Matrix in the passage when he says, "Ignorance is bliss." The passage discusses how Cypher is willing to betray Zion and return to the Matrix, even with his memory wiped, because he finds the Matrix more valuable than the 'real world.' This reflects his preference for the illusion of the Matrix.

Text 8

11 ①

(해설) Ⓐ the Matrix to be but shadows and like shadows on a cave wall, the Matrix can bear ~~consequences~~(→no consequences) to the real world.

The <u>Platonic</u> Morpheus이므로 동굴의 그림자와 같이 매트릭스는 실제 현실에 어떠한 여파도 미치지 못한다는 내용이 나와야 한다. 그런 의미에서 Neo가 매트릭스를 나왔을 때 코피를 흘리고 있는 상황에 당황함을 표현하면서 Morpheus에게 "I thought it wasn't real."이라고 말하는 것을 파악할 수 있다. 해당 문제의 경우 The <u>Platonic</u> Morpheus와 Morpheus를 구별하면서 내용을 파악하는 것이 중요하다.

Part 3 Voca Check

1　1 cast　2 perception　3 mere　4 reflection　5 hypothesize　6 meditation
7 orchestrate　8 deceitful　9 devoid

2　1 skepticism　2 forefront　3 embodiment　4 reflect　5 adjust to
6 double-life　7 alias　8 deem, apocalyptic　9 plunge　10 supreme

3 1 cascade 2 transcendence 3 resurrect 4 chart 5 abet 6 akin
7 realization 8 manipulate 9 enlightened 10 transcendence

4 1 retrieve 2 allusion 3 engineer 4 ponder 5 devise 6 malicious
7 reference 8 ponder

5 1 sentinel 2 credulity 3 endorse 4 paragon 5 hack 6 ontology
7 representation 8 projection 9 wipe

6 1 amalgam 2 sentiment 3 inkling 4 gaze 5 goop 6 consequences
7 inhibit 8 linger 9 suppress 10 apocalyptic

Part 4 Reading Comprehension

1 ⑤

해설 ⑤의 문장의 마지막 단어인 sense를 reason으로 바꾸어야 한다. 감각적 경험은 실체의 부분만 인식하거나 허상에 대한 인식일 뿐이다.

2 ④

해설 동굴에 갇혀 사는 사람들은 그림자가 실체라고 인식한다. 더 reality가 가까운 숫자에 대한 인식 자체가 없다.

3 ④

해설 artist가 만들어내는 대상이 바로 shadow이다. shadow는 실체의 모방이자 열등한 존재이므로 이를 가장 잘 설명한 것은 ④이다.

4 ②

해설 근거: * For Plato, the shadows on the wall are not reality but rather mere reflections of more real objects.

* In the cave, the empirical world of our senses/images, the shadows on the wall are the least real things there are. More real than the shadows are the objects that cast them — the men, statues, and animals passing in front of the fire.

5 ②

해설 Platonic idea에 해당하는 내용을 찾으면 된다. 보기 ②의 내용은 the Matrix(cave)는 그림자일 뿐이며, 어떠한 실체도 가지지 않는다고 했으므로 the anti-Platonic possibility의 반론에 해당하는 내용이다.

6 ③

해설 "우리는 인식되기 위해서 투영물의 세계(영화)로 다시 되돌아 가려는 투영물(actor)을 본다"란 의미는 "존재는 인식되는 것"이란 의미다. 즉, 존재하기 위해선 먼저 인식되어야 한다는 말이므로 인식이 존재를 선행한다는 ③이 정답이다.

7 ④

해설 근거: Through analyzing Descartes' later meditations, the work of anti-Platonic philosopher Stanley Cavell, and the motivations of the character Cypher in the film, one may argue that the Matrix is indeed reality unto itself and retains the same value as the "real world."

8 ②

(해설) ⓒ The shadows reflected on the wall were ~~not anything but real objects.~~

not anything but = nothing but = only

ⓔ Prisoners freed ~~would soon realize~~ that what they thought were real were nothing but the shadows.

근거: Socrates then explains the various reactions of the prisoners when they are released — their trouble adjusting physically and mentally to their new reality.

ⓜ Plato's setting up of prisoners getting free is to represent ~~one's innate ability to change and willingness to accept new truths.~~ ← 오히려 반대 내용이 맞음.

9 ⓒ

(해설) anti-Platonic → Platonic

근거: the Matrix, and all the humans in it are akin to the prisoners watching shadows on the cave wall.

10 ②

(해설) The division of the line is between what is visible and what is intelligible, with the visible portion ~~being equal to~~ the intelligible portion.

→적어도 그림에 제시된 것으로 보아 visible과 intelligible은 동일한 비율이 아님.

11 ②

(해설) ⓒmetaphysical → empirical

12 ③

(해설) 근거: Descartes' philosophical journey from doubting the existence of the external world 에 해당하는 부분의 예시에 해당한다.

13 ④

(해설) 본문에서 inkling의 "의심의 낌새"라는 의미로 쓰이고 있으므로 a slight suspicion 정도가 적절하다.

14 ②, ③, ④

(해설) ①근거: Among these things to be doubted is the existence of one's own mind.

⑤근거: Neo's skepticism proves true after he takes the red pill and discovers his old world was a simulation devised by malicious artificial intelligence known as sentinels.

15 ②

(해설) 문맥상 "반대하다"의 의미로 argues against와 같은 표현이 들어가야 한다. tune을 활용하자 면 is epistemologically out of tune with가 적절하다.

16 ②

(해설) Option ② aligns with the idea presented in the passage that reality is tied to our perception of it and the value we attach to it. George Berkeley's philosophy, "To be is to be perceived," suggests that reality exists as it is perceived by the mind. Therefore, reality is dependent on our perception of it, and the value we assign to reality is also influenced by our perception.

17 ②

해설 ② acceptance → resistance

②의 문장에서 콜론(:)은 순접부연의 기능으로 앞의 내용과 같은 맥락의 내용이어야 한다. 그리고 전치사 to와 말뭉치가 되는 표현에 주의해서 접근한다.

a positive skepticism that takes pleasure in the unstable nature of things and in our inability to reduce them to specific, humanly defined functions: this type of skepticism celebrates the [acceptance / resistance] of things to our attempts at conceptualizing i.e., using them.

a positive skepticism의 특징은 밑줄 내용에서 보듯이 사물의 불완전한 본질과 이것들(불완전한 사물)을 구체적이고 인간적으로 정의되는 기능으로 표현하지 못하는 점이다. 이런 특징을 가진 a positive skepticism은 이러한 사물을 개념화하려는 우리의 시도를 "저항/거부" 하려는 속성이 있음을 파악할 수 있다.

Part 5 Sentence Completion

1 ①

해설 수식어구의 내용에 따라 피수식어구의 내용이 한정된다.

_____ for a period of time before becoming active again

활동하기 전 단계인 휴면상태를 나타내는 단어가 빈칸의 표현이다. 보기 항의 단어를 볼 경우 유사하게 보이는 단어를 두어 혼동을 유발하고 있다.

해석 이런 구근들은 겨울철 땅속에서 다시 활동을 하기 전 일정 기간 휴면 상태로 남아 있다.

2 ①

해설 글 전체의 맥락에서 접근하면, rather를 기점으로 앞뒤 내용이 대조되는 점을 활용할 수 있겠지만, rather 문장 내 수식관계를 바탕으로 접근이 가능하다.

the obstetrician to listen to the infant heartbeat with a _____

산부인과 의사가 아이의 박동을 들을 때 사용하는 도구는 stethoscope이다. 논리정보장치를 활용하기 보단, 문맥상 가장 적절한 표현을 고르는 어휘문제라 볼 수 있다.

해석 오늘날 거의 모든 산모들이 등을 바닥에 대고 누운 상태로 아기를 분만하는데, 이는 반드시 산모의 편의를 위해서라기보다는 산부인과 의사가 청진기로 아기의 심장고동 소리를 보다 듣기 쉽게 하기 위해서이다.

무생물 구문은 말 그대로 주어가 사람이 아니라 물건이라는 뜻이다. 여기서 물건이란 의지를 가지고 주체적으로 행동하지 못하는 대상을 모두 지칭한다. 예를 들어, 'His carelessness caused him a lot of trouble'과 같은 문장에서 'carelessness'는 물주구문의 주어가 된다. 물주구문에서 주부는 일반적으로 부사로 해석하는데, 앞에서 잠시 언급했듯이 부사는 긍정과 부정의 성격을 드러내기에 이를 잘 활용하면 문제접근이 용이해진다. 아래의 예문을 통해 확인해보자.

Ex 1 This failure of the family to provide the fundamental satisfactions which in fact it is capable of yielding is one of the most deep-seated causes of the (discontent) which is prevalent in our age.
가정에서 생산해 낼 수 있는(제공할 수 있는) 가장 기본적인 만족을 제공해 주는 기능을 가정이 수행하지 못하는 것은 우리 시대에 만연해 있는 가장 뿌리 깊은 불만족의 원인 중의 하나이다.

→ 주어가 'failure'이다. 이로 인해 발생하는 결과는 부정적인 어감을 전달하는 표현이 되어야 함을 유추할 수 있다.

Ex 2 The application of the new machinery to agriculture and of scientific methods to crop production greatly (diminishes) the number of man that otherwise would be required.
새로운 기계를 농업에 적용하고 새로운 과학 방법을 곡식 생산에 적용하는 것은 그렇지 않더라면 필요하게 될 인부의 수를 크게 줄여줄 것이다.

→ 'new machinery'의 적용은 일반적으로 긍정적 결과를 예상하고 실천하는 행위이므로 이후 긍정적 내용이 자연스럽게 이어져야 한다.

Ex 3 Excessive messaging can cause (pain) in the shoulders and the thumb and fingers.
과도하게 문자를 보내면 어깨, 엄지, 손가락에 고통을 일으킬 수 있다.

→ 부정적 어감의 'excessive'는 부정적 결과를 가져온다.

Ex 4 Carelessness in responding to a notice will do (nothing) to help you win the role.
통지에 주의를 기울이지 않는 것은 네가 그 역할을 따내는데 전혀 아무 도움이 되질 않는다(통지에 주의를 기울이지 않으면 그 역할을 따내지 못한다).

→ 부정적 원인(A)은 부정적 결과(B)를 낳는다(A = B).

Ex 5 Prison life with its endless privations and restrictions makes one (rebellious).
끊임없는 박탈과 제약이 존재하는 감옥 생활은 사람을 반항적으로 만든다.

→ 부정적 원인(A)은 부정적 결과(B)를 낳는다(A = B).

Ex 6 (Illness) prevented him from going to school.
그는 아파서 학교에 가지 못했다.

→ 병에 걸린 부정적인 원인으로 학교에 가지 못한 결과가 발생했다.

Ex 7 Lately reckless driving **has brought many people to** (an early grave).
최근 무분별한 운전으로 많은 이들이 일찍 무덤으로 갔다(죽었다).

→ 부정적 원인으로 작용하는 무분별한 운전으로 많은 이가 죽게 되었다는 부정적 결과가 발생했다.

3 ②

(해설)

> The _____ speech, given on the spur of the moment

'the spur of the moment'의 내용을 제일 잘 반영하는 단어는 선택지 ②이다.

대조의 특징을 드러내는 A와 B를 연결한다. 역접의 'A as ~ as B'를 활용한다.

> carefully planned ↔ impromptu

(해석) 즉흥적인 연설은 순간적인 충동을 고려해 볼 때 조심스럽게 계획된 연설만큼이나 매스컴의 관심을 얻었다.

4 ②

(해설) 빈칸에 들어갈 단어에 영향을 미치는 요소는 'created'에 걸리는 과거분사이다.

> The environmental _____ created in economically poor countries

또한 A includes B는 A=B라는 점을 활용한다.

> The environmental havoc = destruction of forests and other habitats

(해석) 경제적으로 빈곤한 나라에서 발생한 환경적 파괴는, 산림과 다른 거주지의 황폐화와, 침식 그리고 종의 멸종을 포함한다.

5 ③

(해설) 빈칸을 수식하는 요소는 'telling' 이후의 현재분사에 걸리는 내용이다.

> a short autobiographical paragraph telling who you are and what you have done

(해석) 당신은 당신이 누구인지, 그리고 지난 2년 동안 당신이 무엇을 했는지에 대해 글로 나타내는 짧은 자서전을 잘 쓸 수 있을 것이다.

6 ③

현재분사의 수식을 받는 곳이 바로 빈칸이다. 수식어구의 내용은 피수식어구의 내용을 한정한다는 단순하지만 효과적인 방법을 활용한다.

an _____ meaning seemingly foolish **but in fact** extremely cunning

수식어구의 내용을 보면, 역접의 but in fact로 연결되어 있는데 겉으론 바보스럽게 보이지만 사실 극히 교묘하다는 모순적 상황을 드러낸다. 고로 보기 항 ③이 정답이다.

그 의도된 형태대로 사용될 때, '여우처럼 아주 빈틈없는'이란 표현은 겉보기에는 어리석어 보이지만 사실은 너무나도 교활하다는 것을 의미하는 모순어법이다. 만약 당신이 누군가를 '여우처럼 아주 빈틈없는'이라고 표현했다면 그 사람은 교활하고 지혜가 남보다 뛰어남을 의미한다.

7 ⑤

How could로 시작하는 구문은 일반적으로 하나의 속성에 대조되는 성격을 드러낸다. 예를 들자면, '어떻게 그가 그럴 수 있는가?'라고 했을 때 평소의 그리고 보기 힘든 전혀 다른 특정 행위를 했다는 의미가 내포되어 있다.

첫 번째 빈칸을 먼저 파악하도록 한다.

1) 수식어구는 피수식어구의 의미를 한정한다.

certain _____ meanings specified in a dictionary

2) A and B에서 A와 B는 인과의 관계를 형성한다.

create obscurity → actually to prevent thought from being communicable
부정적 원인   부정적 결과

전체적으로 해석을 통해서 접근하기 보단 주어진 빈칸 주위에 위치하는 논리정보장치를 활용하면 다소 쉽게 답을 이끌어 낼 수 있다.

단어가 개별적으로 쓰일 때면 (그 의미가) 사전에 명시된 대로의 정확한 의미로 한정되지만, 집단으로 결합할 경우에는 어떻게 모호해지면서 사고의 전달을 방해하게 될까?

8 ①

빈칸에 영향을 미치는 요소는 '주어'와 후치 수식을 하는 '전치사 + 명사'의 형용사구이다.

1) be동사 활용

proficiency **is** a _____
proficiency = 지원자의 능력/조건

2) '____N____ + 전치사 + 명사' 활용

_____ for joining this advanced course

즉, 1)과 2)를 동시에 만족하는 '수업을 듣는데 필요한 능력/조건'이란 단어는 보기 항 ①이다.

해석 영어를 어느 정도 능숙하게 할 수 있는 능력은 이 고급 과정을 듣는데 필수조건이다.

9 ①

해설 'A be indicative(representative) of B'는 'A = B'임을 활용한다.

Such <u>arrant hypocrisy</u> = a thoroughly <u>opportunistic</u> approach

그러한 악명 높은 위선은 (부정) = (관직 출마를 위한) 철저한 기회주의적 접근 (부정)

보기 항에서 부정의 의미를 담고 있는 선택지가 한 개가 아니다. 이럴 경우, 단순히 부정적 어휘가 들어간다는 정보만으로 답을 구할 수 없으므로 문맥에 맞는 적절한 어휘 선택이 필요하다.

해석 그렇게 터무니없는 위선은 철저하게 관직 출마를 위한 기회주의적 접근을 나타내는 표시이다.

10 ②

해설 A remain B는 'A = B'임을 활용한다.

<u>Burning</u> of refuse and garbage at open dumps = a major <u>cause</u> of air pollution

부정적 결과 = 부정적 원인

해석 폐기물과 쓰레기를 공터 쓰레기 더미에서 태우는 것은 여러 우리 도시가 안고 있는 공해의 주된 원인이다.

Unit 9

The Story of An Hour by Kate Chopin

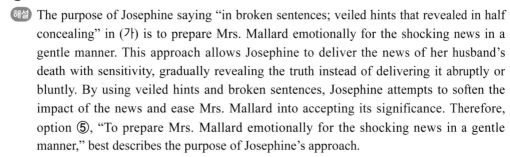

Part 2 Text Reading

Text 1

1 ⑤

해설 The purpose of Josephine saying "in broken sentences; veiled hints that revealed in half concealing" in (가) is to prepare Mrs. Mallard emotionally for the shocking news in a gentle manner. This approach allows Josephine to deliver the news of her husband's death with sensitivity, gradually revealing the truth instead of delivering it abruptly or bluntly. By using veiled hints and broken sentences, Josephine attempts to soften the impact of the news and ease Mrs. Mallard into accepting its significance. Therefore, option ⑤, "To prepare Mrs. Mallard emotionally for the shocking news in a gentle manner," best describes the purpose of Josephine's approach.

2 ⑤

해설 From the phrase "She did not hear the story as many women have heard the same, with a paralyzed inability to accept its significance" in (나), it can be inferred that she reacted to the story differently than most women, masquerading a lack of emotional restraint. This suggests that while many women might typically react with shock, disbelief, or an inability to accept the significance of such news, Mrs. Mallard's reaction was different. She did not exhibit the typical paralyzed inability to accept the significance of the story; instead, she reacted with sudden, wild abandonment, weeping in her sister's arms, therefore "masquerading a lack of emotional restraint."

Text 2

3 ①

해설 The passage describes a scene where the surroundings are coming to life with spring, rain, and the sounds of nature and human activity. These elements collectively symbolize the idea of renewal and freshness associated with the arrival of spring, making ① the most appropriate choice.

4 ⑤

해설 inner weakness → inner strength

The highlighted choice that doesn't quite fit the context is "inner weakness" in option ⑤. The description of the protagonist's face and lines suggests "repression" and "a certain strength," which don't necessarily align with the notion of "inner weakness." Instead, it implies resilience or fortitude in the face of challenges or emotional suppression.

Text 3

5 ③

해설 The passage suggests that Mrs. Mallard is ~~more than ready to~~ acknowledge her feelings as joy because of the recent death of her husband.

근거: She did not stop to ask if it were or were not a monstrous joy that held her.

Text 4

6 ③

해설 The phrase "A kind intention or a cruel intention made the act seem no less a crime" suggests that the protagonist recognizes that even actions done with good intentions can be perceived as morally wrong. This reflects her complex perspective on love and the circumstances surrounding her husband's death, emphasizing the moral ambiguity of the situation.

7 ③

해설 The phrase "Free! Body and soul free!" reflects the protagonist's emotional state as jubilant, given the newfound sense of freedom and self-assertion she experiences after her husband's death.

Text 5

8 ④

해설 ④ enduring → fleeting

The phrase "enduring" in option ④ is out of place in the context provided. The protagonist's realization of her newfound freedom is not necessarily portrayed as enduring; rather, it is cut short by her sudden death upon seeing her husband alive. The focus is more on the suddenness and intensity of the emotional rollercoaster she experiences, rather than the duration of her freedom.

Part 3 Voca Check

1 1 stifle 2 haunt 3 hasten 4 elusive 5 dull 6 strive 7 tumultuous
   8 roomy 9 bespeak 10 possessed 11 conceal 12 exhausted
   13 forestall

2 1 slender 2 implored 3 feverish 4 run riot 5 procession 6 keen
   7 composedly 8 descended 9 elixir 10 persistent 11 unwittingly
   12 piercing 13 importunity 14 monstrous 15 travel-stained

Part 4 Reading Comprehension

1 ③

해설 The statement from the excerpt that most strongly supports the idea of a woman feeling burdened by her marriage and looking forward to living independently of her husband is ©: "There would be no one to live for during those coming years; she would live for herself. There would be no powerful will bending hers in that blind persistence with which men and women believe they have a right to impose a private will upon a fellow-creature." This statement directly speaks to the protagonist's realization that with her husband's death, she is free from the societal expectations and pressures of marriage, allowing her to live for herself and not be subjected to the will of another person.

즉, 남편으로부터 독립을 의미하는 문장을 찾으면 된다.

2 ④

(해설) The reaction from 정우 (④) is the most awkward. It misinterprets the meaning of "the joy that kills" and makes an unfounded assumption about Mrs. Mallard's feelings towards her husband. The phrase "the joy that kills" doesn't necessarily imply dislike towards her husband; rather, it suggests that the sudden surge of joy followed by the despair of realizing her newfound freedom led to her death.

3 ③

(해설) Based on the description provided, option ③ seems to be the most fitting. Mrs. Mallard's physical weakness, as described in the passage, likely encourages those around her to stifle her emotions and overprotect her due to societal norms and expectations of the time. This aligns with the historical background mentioned, where women were expected to be passive and delicate, and such expectations could lead to overprotection and emotional stifling.

4 ④

(해설) The most awkward analysis among the options provided is ㉣: "That Louise will not regret seeing her husband's dead body emphasizes the fact that she held a grudge against him." This interpretation seems unsupported by the text. The fact that Louise doesn't regret seeing her husband's dead body doesn't necessarily imply that she held a grudge against him. It's more likely an expression of her newfound sense of freedom rather than animosity towards her husband.

Part 5 Sentence Completion

1 ④

(해설) 빈칸이 들어간 문장은 주어와 보어로 구성된 'A is B' 즉, 'A = B'이다.

> the prosecution's attempts to <u>frighten</u> the old lady = a terrible example of <u>intimidation</u>

빈칸은 A의 성격을 가장 잘 드러내는 단어를 B에 넣으면 된다. A의 성격은 본문의 to부정사의 내용('to frighten the old lady')이다.

(해석) 검사는 나이든 증인을 계속 끈질기게 심문하는 것을 멈추라고 그 판사는 명령하면서, 나이든 여인을 공포로 몰아넣으려는 검사의 시도는 끔찍한 협박의 대표적 예이며, 이러한 행위는 법원에서 허용되지 말아야 한다고 선포했다.

2 ④

> 해설   A is not unlike B(A = B)를 사용한다. 선택지 ②와 ④를 혼동할 수 있지만, 'sojourn'의 경우 우리말의 '인생의 여정'과 같은 장기간의 여행을 말하는 것이고, 배를 타고 미지의 세계를 탐험한다는 단어는 'voyage'가 적절하다.

> Moving about in an unfamiliar environment = a voyage into the unknown
> 'is not unlike'는 'A = B'의 'be'동사이다.

> 해석   익숙하지 않은 환경에서 돌아다니는 것은 그것이 국내건 외국이건 종종 미지의 개척되지 않은, 그러니까 이해할 수 없는 곳으로 여행을 떠나는 것과 마찬가지다.

3 ③

> 해설   'To be A is to be B. (A = B)'를 활용한다.
>
> 첫 번째 빈칸은 'restrained'의 동의어를 찾는 것이고, 두 번째 빈칸은 첫 번째 빈칸을 더 구체적으로 표현하는 부사이다.

> To be ＿＿＿＿ is to be ＿＿＿＿ restrained.
> 1) A(형용사)   =   restrained(형용사)
> 2)   부사(morally)

즉, 자제라는 단어인 'restrained'가 'continent'보다 더 큰 개념이다.

> 해석   금욕하는 것은 도덕적으로 자기를 절제하는 것이다.

4 ①

> 해설   'red-handed'는 '현행범의'란 뜻이다. 조건부사절을 활용하여 특정 표현의 정의를 다루는 문장이다. 조건부사절의 'be'동사적 활용은 다음과 같다.
>
> Being caught red-handed means that someone is caught while he/she is in the act of doing something wrong. ← 'A means B' 곧, 'A = B'이다.

> Being caught red-handed = caught while he/she is in the act of doing something wrong
> 현행범 = 잘못된 짓을 하다 걸림

> 해석   만약 어떤 사람이 현장에서 검거되면, 그는 잘못된 행위를 하다 걸린 것을 말한다.

5 ①

> 해설

> Getting rich quickly = go into the jackpot
> 갑작스레 부자가 됨 = 개천에서 용나다

jackpot은 일반적으로 "hit the jackpot"으로 자주 활용되어, "(갑작스레, 한 번에) 대성공하다"의 의미를 가진다. "go into the jackpot"은 자주 사용되는 표현은 아니지만 문제에서 사용된 quickly 의 문맥으로 보아 ①이 적절하다. go from rags to riches의 영영풀이는 다음과 같다.

to <u>start</u> your life very poor and <u>then later in life</u> become very rich.

해석 어떤 사람이 갑자기 부자가 된 경우, 우리는 이 사람이 개천에서 용났다고 말한다.

6 ④

해설 'A is B' 공식 중에서 'A는 B의 속성'을 드러내는 응용문제이다. 같은 개념의 단어가 두 빈칸 에 들어간다는 점만을 고려해도 쉽게 답을 구할 수 있다.

> Trepidation <u>is the mark of</u> coward
> 겁에 질려 떠는 것은   =   겁쟁이의 특징

해석 겁에 질려 떠는 것은 겁쟁이의 특징이다.

7 ①

해설 인과를 이용해 문맥에 가장 적절한 단어를 선정할 수 있지만, 'A is B'를 활용한다.

> leprosy = such an <u>unsightly</u> disease
> A = B (외적으로 보기 흉한)

해석 나병은 보기에 아주 흉한 병이기에, 사람들은 그 환자들을 회피한다.

8 ②

해설 'A be not apt to B'는 'A is not B'로 응용이 가능하므로 결국 'A ↔ B'가 된다.

> taciturn people ↔ apt to engage in small talk
> 과묵한 사람   잡담을 잘 하는 경향

해석 말수가 적은 사람은 잡담을 하지 않는 경향이 있다.

참고

주어의 성향을 드러내는 동사가 활용된 문장은 'A = B'로 단순화시킨다.

> A tent to B(v) = A is apt to B(v) = A is inclined to B(v)

B는 모두 A의 성향을 드러내는 단어이다.

예) An <u>affected</u> person tends to <u>show off</u> his or her wealth.
    젠체하는 사람은 자신의 부를 자랑하는 경향이 있다.

9 ④

해설 'A means B'는 결국 'A=B'를 고르라는 말이다.

felony = a serious case of lawbreaking

중범죄 = 심각한 법을 어긴 사례

해석 중범죄는 심각한 범법행위를 의미한다.

10 ③

해설 'A is B'를 활용한다. 주격관계대명사는 기본적으로 명사절인데, 이는 '형용사 + 명사'로 바꿀 수 있다. 아래의 표현을 살펴보자.

예) A person **who works hard** → a **diligent** person

열심히 일하는 사람 → 부지런한 사람

본문에 이를 적용할 경우, 결국 군복무의 의무를 저버리는 사람은 어떤 사람인지 물어보는 문제이다.

해석 군복무에서 도주하는 사람은 탈영자이다.

MAGNUS 리딩 에이 원 프리미엄 독해 시리즈: 문학/비문학편

특목고(외고/국제고), 자사고 대비 문학·비문학 고급 영문 독해 수험서

www.bansok.co.kr 값 23,000원

13740

9 788971 729915

ISBN 978-89-7172-991-5